In Our Own Best Interest

In Our Own Best Interest

How Defending Human Rights Benefits Us All

William F. Schulz

Executive Director,
Amnesty International USA

Foreword by Mary Robinson

BEACON PRESS • BOSTON

Beacon Press
25 Beacon Street, Boston, Massachusetts 02108-2892
www.beacon.org

Beacon Press books
are published under the auspices of
the Unitarian Universalist Association of Congregations.

06 05 04 03 02   8 7 6 5 4 3 2

This book is printed on recycled acid-free paper that meets the uncoated
paper ANSI/NISO specifications for permanence as revised in 1992.

Text design by Boskydell Studio
Composition by Wilsted & Taylor Publishing Services

Library of Congress Cataloging-in-Publication Data
Schulz, William F.
In our own best interest : how defending human rights benefits us all /
William F. Schulz
p. cm.
ISBN 0-8070-0226-7 (cloth)
ISBN 0-8070-0227-5 (pbk.)
1. Human rights.   I. Title
JC571   .S3852 2001
323—dc21
2001000392

FOR BETH

Contents

Foreword • ix
Preface to the Paperback Edition • xiii
Preface to the First Edition • xxi
Introduction • 1

1
"Like the Home-Born among You"
The Moral Underpinnings of the Struggle for Human Rights
17

2
"When the Birds No Longer Hide"
The Role of Human Rights in Promoting Democracy and Peace
38

3
The Bottom Line
Why Human Rights Are Good for Business
66

4
Forest and Ice
Human Rights and the World around Us
105

5
Only a Plane Ride Away
Public Health and Human Rights
120

6
Saving Money while Saving Lives
The Economic Rewards of Defending Human Rights
135

7
No Innocent Place
Human Rights Violations in the Sweet Land of Liberty
147

8
David Trimble's Tears
What We Can Do to Promote Human Rights
177

Appendix • 198
Notes • 203
Acknowledgments • 225
Index • 228

Foreword

More than fifty years ago a group of men and women from diverse cultures, traditions, and faiths came together in Paris to offer humanity an extraordinary vision of how the world could be. In 1948 they adopted the Universal Declaration of Human Rights, which half a century later continues to address directly what is necessary for a life of dignity for every human being.

The Universal Declaration is not just another international document. It is the primary proclamation of the international community's commitment to human rights as "a common standard of achievement for all peoples and all nations." Its message is one of hope, equality, liberation, and empowerment. It is a message to all who are committed to freedom, justice, and peace in the world.

This message must be heard again and again in our time. The devastating experiences of millions of victims of human rights violations continue to demonstrate how far the world still is from realizing the ideals which guided the General Assembly in 1948. Still today intimidation and even the brutal murder of human rights activists in many countries have taken place. These are painful reminders of the unrelenting challenges we face at the threshold of a new century.

One of the great privileges of my work as United Nations High Commissioner for Human Rights has been the opportunity to meet and observe at close hand some of the most admirable heroes and heroines our world contains, human rights champions whose lives are sometimes at risk but whose spirits never flag, whose futures are often uncertain but whose sense of hope remains firm and true. A few such people become known to the general public; the vast majority of them toil without international recognition. But what they all have in common is a willingness to work for human rights values, even at the expense of their own comfort. For forty years Amnesty International and many other human rights organizations have offered such defenders their protection, assistance, and acclaim.

If human rights are to become truly embedded in the way the world conducts its business, however, the work of these individual human rights advocates must be supplemented by a legal regimen that makes explicit the universal obligations human rights entail; by international institutions designed to monitor and enforce that regimen; and by individual governments which make human rights a priority in their own policy making.

How seriously the United States government takes human rights will depend at least in part on how seriously they are taken by American citizens. The place of the United States in the history of human rights is well known. I think of the inclusion of the Bill of Rights in the United States Constitution, which has proved to be a model for many other nations, and I think of the key part played by Eleanor Roosevelt in the drawing up of the Universal Declaration of Human Rights. Today the question is whether the United States will build on that history of support or instead adopt a posture of what William F. Schulz calls in this book, as others too have labeled it, American "exceptionalism," the notion that the same rules that apply to other countries need not apply to the United States (or, as Schulz quotes one professor as putting it, "International institutions are not good in themselves but good only insofar as they contribute to furthering the well-being of the American nation"). The world needs desperately for the United States to opt for the former choice, and once again the American people will play a significant part in determining whether it does.

To convince Americans that the evenhanded enforcement of human rights norms is not only consistent with the highest American values but good for the United States, to say nothing of the rest of the world, is a formidable task but an essential one. That is the task this book undertakes. Whether it is successful will help determine whether we live in a humane world or a brutal one, a just world or a world in which parents may not want to raise children.

Seamus Heaney ends his poem "From the Republic of Conscience" with a telling reminder to all human rights defenders: "and no ambassador would ever be relieved." A culture of human rights is growing throughout the world. Governments have taken many important steps to place human rights at the top of international and national agendas. Civil society—countless organizations working in their own countries and internationally to advance the cause of dignity and freedom, especially for those who are most vulnerable and disadvantaged, and in need of our support—is expanding its vital contribution. And the United Nations family has made important progress in integrating human rights throughout the work of the entire system, thus enhancing our ability to assist all partners in our common goals of peace, development, and democracy.

All human rights for all—this should be our common call to action. I am convinced that by combining our action and determination, by building partnerships between governments and civil society, international organizations, and the media, religious, and academic communities, we will succeed in realizing the vision of the future which the Universal Declaration first called for half a century ago.

MARY ROBINSON,
United Nations High Commissioner
for Human Rights

Preface to the Paperback Edition

When I was writing this book in 1999–2000, I considered including a chapter on the relationship between human rights and terrorism. Ultimately I was dissuaded by the fact that, while other countries had been victims of random attacks against civilians for political purposes, the United States had been relatively immune from such carnage, certainly on its own territory. It is true of course that Americans had been the victims of the 1993 World Trade Center bombing and had been among those killed and wounded in the 1998 assaults on U.S. embassies in Kenya and Tanzania. The number was so relatively few, however, that I thought that my American readers, at whom the book was principally aimed, would find the subject of only esoteric interest. In that respect I was dead wrong and inexcusably shortsighted.

The events of September 11, 2001, touched all of us at Amnesty International USA very personally. Our offices in New York City are only about forty blocks north of where the World Trade Center stood. Many of our staff saw the planes hit the towers firsthand. Of far more importance is that two of our staff lost close relatives in the explosions. The wife of a member of our Investment Committee was killed in the plane that hit the Pentagon. As an organization that for forty years has fought impunity for those who commit crimes like this—what Mary Robinson, who wrote the foreword for this book, quickly labeled a "crime against humanity"*—Amnesty International is ineradicably committed to seeing that those responsible be brought to justice. Anyone who

*"UN chief: Attacks on US 'Crime Against Humanity,'" Associated Press, September 25, 2001.

would seek to excuse these acts as just recourse for a misguided U.S. foreign policy is worse than reprehensible. There is no excuse for mass murder. Ever. Under any circumstances.

The question foremost in the minds of most of us, however, is not only how can those who did these ignoble deeds be punished but also how can we prevent future attacks of this kind, both in the United States and around the world. The answer of course has a security dimension to it and a financial and a geopolitical dimension, but it also is profoundly linked to human rights. Indeed, September 11 tragically exemplifies the thesis of this book: that Americans' interests are intimately bound up with those of the rest of the world and, specifically, that we ignore human rights violations at peril to our very lives.

Take the fertile soil out of which those who flew the planes on September 11 apparently grew, namely, Egypt and Saudi Arabia. Both are rife with corruption. (Said the well-connected Saudi ambassador to the United States, Prince Bandar, "If you tell me that building this whole country . . . we misused or got corrupted with fifty billion, I'll tell you, 'Yes . . . So what? We did not invent corruption. . . .' ")*

Both display massive differentials in wealth. Both are renowned for the brutality with which they treat their residents and citizens. And neither of them provides nonviolent, democratic, human rights–respecting means through which their people can express frustrations and change their governments.

Egypt, for one, has operated under emergency rule since President Mubarak took power in 1981. Having crushed most of its radical Islamist opposition by the mid-1990s, the government took out after democracy advocates such as Professor Saad Ibrahim, who had no sympathy for the Islamists but who had criticized the government for election irregularities. Ibrahim was sentenced to seven years in prison and his Ibn Khaldun Center for Development Studies closed down. Opposition political candidates and their supporters are regularly arrested prior to elections.†

In Saudi Arabia the repression is even worse. No dissent is allowed whatsoever. No political parties. No public criticism of the ruling royal

*Seymour M. Hersh, "King's Ransom," *The New Yorker*, October 22, 2001.
†Human Rights Watch, "Egypt: Human Rights Background," October 2001.

family. Religious minorities are regularly persecuted. Article 39 of the Constitution bans anything that may give rise to "mischief and discord," and the government enforces that ban with capricious arrests, long-term detention without charge, torture, and executions.*

Egypt and Saudi Arabia are awash in young people. More than 55 percent of the people are under twenty-five years of age in Egypt; in Saudi Arabia the number is 60 percent. Unemployment among such young people is high in both countries. Where do they turn for meaning and direction, absent nonviolent channels through which to make their needs and voices heard? Far too often the answer has been the religious extremists.† Much has been made of the fact that the nineteen plane hijackers were educated and relatively well-off economically but they too were susceptible to the hate-filled message of an Osama bin Laden.

Part of that message has been that the United States props up "Muslim tyrants" like Mubarak and the Saudi royal family, whether to maintain control in the Middle East or protect its oil interests—a charge that finds receptive ears throughout the region. As Bernard Lewis, one of the foremost experts on Islam, put it: "Middle Easterners increasingly complain that the United States judges them by different and lower standards than it does Europeans and Americans. . . . They assert that Western spokesmen repeatedly overlook or even defend actions or support rulers that they would not tolerate in their own countries."‡ How much easier it would be to refute this charge and, in the process, win sympathy on the so-called "Arab street," if the United States had made the pursuit of human rights in places like Egypt and Saudi Arabia a more virile and visible part of its foreign policy.

Unwilling to create space in their own countries for institutions of civil society, the Saudi chieftains ceded much education and culture building to the radical Islamists. By financing thousands of extremist schools not just in Saudi Arabia but in places like Pakistan, our erstwhile Saudi allies guaranteed that tens of thousands of Muslim young

---

*Amnesty International, "Saudi Arabia: A Secret State of Suffering," March 2000, and Amnesty International, "Saudi Arabia: A Justice System Without Justice," May 2000.
†"Despair Beneath the Arab World's Rage," *New York Times,* October 14, 2001.
‡Bernard Lewis, "The Revolt of Islam," *The New Yorker,* November 19, 2001, p. 56.

people would be implanted with hostility toward the West.* If, after September 11, anyone can doubt the importance of promoting what I call in this book "democratic communities of rights" as one means through which to make the world a safer place, they have willfully chosen to remain blind. Even a prominent member of the Saudi royal family has recently come around to this view, at least partially. A few weeks after September 11, Prince Walid ibn Talal called for limited democracy in the Kingdom. "If people speak more freely . . . you can really . . . make them part of the process," he said. "We should not take this matter for granted, the loyalty of our people."†

But what about the Israeli-Palestinian dispute? Isn't the demise of Israel at the heart al Qaeda's vicious agenda? Though there is considerable question as to whether bin Laden actually gives a hoot for the plight of the Palestinians, in whom he has over the years shown little interest, it is certainly true that anti-Israeli rhetoric is a sure guarantor of a sympathetic hearing in most of the Arab world. Part of the reason for that is because that world, thanks to the denial of the rights to free speech and a free press, lacks a diversity of voices. Again, Bernard Lewis: "Resentment of Israel is the only grievance that can be freely and safely expressed in those Muslim countries where the media are either wholly owned or strictly overseen by the government. Indeed, Israel serves as a useful stand-in for complaints about the economic privation and political repression under which most Muslims live, and as a way of deflecting the resulting anger."‡

Yet it has to be added immediately that Israel has made it infinitely more difficult for itself by manifesting a profoundly checkered human rights record of its own, including the practices of assassination and torture and the killing of civilians. Israel's right to exist within secure borders ought to go without saying. Random attacks on civilian targets, such as Israel has experienced for years, are reprehensible and have been systematically condemned by Amnesty International and other human rights groups. The problem is that retaliation by Israel that in itself violates human rights makes it far harder for moderate Arab

---

*Saad Mehio, "How Islam and Politics Mixed," *New York Times,* December 2, 2001.
†"Saudi Prince Proposes Speedy Elections," *International Herald Tribune,* November 29, 2001.
‡Lewis, "Revolt of Islam," p. 56.

voices to call successfully for a nonviolent resolution of the Middle East conflict. And when the United States tolerates, if not encourages, Israeli violations, we appear to confirm that we have different standards for our friends than we do for others.

Unfortunately such a double standard is not new in U.S. foreign policy. Between 1980 and 1991, the United States supplied $3 billion worth of military and other assistance, via Pakistan, to Afghan rebel forces, including precursors of the Taliban, because those forces, while guilty of massive human rights violations themselves, were fighting the Communist government in Afghanistan. In fact, many of the caves in Afghanistan in which bin Laden and al Qaeda forces hid themselves were originally rebel strongholds, outfitted and upgraded in the mid to late 1980s by U.S. dollars. Soviet Army reports at the time referred to these caves as "the last word in NATO engineering."*

How much easier the U.S. military's task might have been today had the U.S. government in the past exercised more discretion in supplying assistance to foreign military units guilty of human rights violations, as it is now required to do.

But even when the Taliban came to power, we seemed not to have entirely learned the lesson that those who are guilty of massive human rights abuses—in this case, largely against women, sexual minorities, and political or religious opponents—are capable of great mischief. Initially greeted in 1996 with some appreciation by the United States for bringing apparent stability to Afghanistan, the Taliban were soon denounced by the Clinton administration for their excesses. But the administration never took definitive steps to challenge Taliban power, such as putting pressure on the only three countries that maintained diplomatic relations with Kabul—Pakistan, Saudi Arabia, and the United Arab Emirates, all ostensible U.S. allies—to cut their ties. One can only suspect that the reason for our relative forbearance was that we perceived the Taliban to be a threat only to their own citizens. But, as I make clear in this book, women and gay and lesbian people are often the "canaries in the mineshaft," their persecution a harbinger of still greater crimes to come. Had we taken that persecution more seriously in this case and made life tougher for the Taliban from the begin-

*"Bin Laden Is Reported Spotted in a Fortified Camp in Eastern Afghanistan," *New York Times*, November 25, 2001.

ning, who knows whether al Qaeda would have found such a receptive home in Afghanistan? At the very least efforts to offer women relief from their oppression would have encouraged the economic development (and thereby the political stability) of that tattered land, for, as Harvard's David S. Landes says in his definitive work, *The Wealth and Poverty of Nations,* "The best clue to a nation's growth and development potential is the status and role of women."*

But if all this may be dismissed as twenty-twenty hindsight, what the United States *has* claimed to recognize in the course of this latest war is that the defeat of "worldwide terrorism" will not come solely through military means. Just as important is how the war effort is perceived, especially on the proverbial "moderate Arab street" in countries like Jordan and Pakistan and Indonesia. That is presumably why the United States sought, whether successfully or not is hard at this point to tell, to minimize civilian casualties in the Afghan campaign; to discourage its Northern Alliance allies from committing war crimes once they had the military advantage; and to provide road access for the supply of relief aid to refugees and the internally displaced. All these goals reflect the tacit recognition that world opinion counts and that respect for human rights plays a major role in the shaping of it.

In other respects, however, the United States has been far more insensitive to the impact human rights claims on world opinion and hence on the ultimate goal of building a safer world. This war is, after all, being fought in the name of preserving "American values," and high among those values is respect for the rule of law. If the United States re-adopts a policy of assassinating its political opponents (and this outside of a military context); if it detains thousands of U.S. residents without charge; if it tortures those detainees to extract information from them, as sources in the FBI have suggested may be necessary, or deports them to countries that routinely torture suspects; if it insists on trying those accused of terrorist crimes before military tribunals instead of in civilian courts and then sentencing them to death; if, in short, it sacrifices its fundamental commitment to human rights, the result will not just be some moral quagmire or the loss of a precious heritage, important as those are. The result will be a compromise with

---

*Quoted in Nicholas D. Kristof, "The Veiled Resource," *New York Times,* December 11, 2001.

the very thing in whose name this struggle is presumably being waged. And the result of *that* will be the alienation of tens of thousands of people who otherwise would look on this country with admiration and favor. The reaction of Cheikh Melainine ould Belal, a Mauritanian taken into custody shortly after September 11 and held for forty days before being released without criminal charge, is typical: "I used to like the United States," he said, "but now I don't understand it. I was going to learn English but now I don't ever want to speak it again."*

Perhaps we can fight the war against terror successfully without the sympathy or help of a Cheikh ould Belal, but we cannot fight it without the cooperation of our European allies, one of which, Spain, has already indicated that it would not extradite eight suspected terrorists to the United States without assurances that they would be tried before civilian courts. Nor can we fight it if evidence uncovered in a military trial is ruled inadmissible on constitutional grounds in later civilian trials. Nor can we fight it with the kind of notoriously inaccurate information that is produced by interrogations using torture. Nor can we fight it if the world at large believes that, despite our years of rhetorical support for human rights in other countries, we are prepared to compromise them the moment our own lives are threatened here at home.

All of which simply reinforces the principal conviction of this book: that respect for human rights both in the United States and abroad has implications for our welfare far beyond the maintenance of our ethical integrity. Ignoring the fates of human rights victims anywhere almost invariably makes the world—*our* world—a more dangerous place. If we learned nothing else from the horrific events of September 11, perhaps we learned that.

During the last U.S. presidential campaign, Condoleeza Rice, now the National Security Adviser, wrote this remarkable sentence: "Foreign policy in a Republican administration . . . will . . . proceed from the firm ground of the national interest, not from the interests of an illusory international community."† An *illusory* international community? I was struck dumb by that sentence when I first read it almost two years ago and I have thought of it frequently since September 11 as Dr.

---

*"Wide-ranging Federal Sweep Changes Attitudes of Immigrants About US," *New York Times,* December 5, 2001.
†Condoleeza Rice, "Life After the Cold War," *Foreign Affairs,* January/February, 2000.

Rice and President Bush have worked arduously to build a coalition of common interests out of what they apparently regarded previously as little more than an illusion. I can only presume that they, like many others of us, were taught a tough, sad lesson by the events of last September. I can only hope that they now have at least one very good reason to understand that our interests and those of the rest of the world are inextricably linked. If they have any further doubt about that, they will find within the pages of this book several dozen more.

Preface to the First Edition

It was only her mother. Surely it would be safe to see her mother. If it had been her father or her brother—no way. But her mother was coming and would bring the papers, and she would sign the papers and it would all be over. Well, not *all* over. This was Pakistan and for women it was never all over in Pakistan, but it would be better. After all, Hina would be there, and if her mother tried to scold or intimidate her, Hina would step in; Hina would take care of her.

Such were Samia Sarwar's thoughts as she waited for her mother to arrive at the lawyer's office. At least those were the thoughts Hina would later speculate had filled Samia's twenty-six-year-old head as she waited for her ordeal to end. Married at sixteen to her first cousin, Samia had borne a son shortly afterward but from the beginning she had found her husband vulgar, dirty, alcoholic, and violent. She had tried to leave him many times, and each time her parents had refused to take her back. For women in Pakistan, even those from relatively wealthy families like Samia's (her father was a prominent businessman, her mother a doctor), if the young woman's family will not take her back, there are very few other places to go. When Samia was pregnant with her second child, though, her husband had kicked her down the stairs and her parents finally relented. They took her back. That was five years ago.

In those five years Samia's life had improved. True, she and her parents still fought and she still had no real life of her own, but she had met another man. Finally she had a bit of hope for her son's future and for hers. She would get a divorce from her husband and become this new man's wife—a better man, a gentle one, no alcoholic. But when

Samia raised the subject of divorce, her parents became enraged. Separation, yes, but divorce? No, it would be a disgrace. Remember, her husband was Samia's first cousin, part of the family. She could live apart from him, could live with them, but she could never divorce, and she certainly could never be with another man. It was unthinkable.

So Samia ran away. Far from where her parents lived in Peshawar, she ran to the city of Lahore. She fled to the women's shelter there about which she had heard so much. Everybody had heard so much: the women's shelter and the famous woman lawyer, the most famous woman lawyer in Pakistan perhaps and certainly the most controversial, the woman lawyer who had stood up for women throughout Pakistan and who would now stand up for Samia. She would take care of Samia, would tell her what to do. Samia Sarwar ran away and she ran to Hina Jilani.

Hina Jilani is a confident, serious person, almost stern. Wrapped in her sari, its colors muted, her hair pulled back, she conveys firmness, determination, even before she speaks. Her presence invokes gravitas, a gravitas that has its roots steeped deep in personal history. "My father," Hina has said, "was a politician, but he was the kind of politician who stays in prison most of his life." Not for corruption—Malik Ghulam Jilani was anything but corrupt—but for being a rebel, for challenging Pakistan's military government when it took over in 1959. "My father," Hina recalls, "was elected to Parliament in opposition to the government, but he was more a human rights activist than a politician—he could never maintain party discipline—and so he was constantly criticizing everybody but especially the government, and they were constantly putting him in prison for it." Prison was not the worst of it. In 1965, the president of Pakistan, General Mohammad Ayub Khan, arranged for Malik to be assassinated. Hina was home the day that a journalist came to interview her father. "Poor fellow," Hina said years later. "They mistook him for my father and, just as he rang the doorbell, they mowed him down. I was very young and it was my first exposure to violence."

It was not easy growing up with a father frequently under lock and key and often under threat, but the experience proved valuable. For one thing it instilled in Hina a vibrant social conscience and immense sympathy for those who suffer. For another it made her unafraid . . . of prison and the state. Best of all, it introduced her to the law. From age fourteen, Hina and her sister, Asma, filed petitions before the courts on behalf of their father, arguing for his release. It never occurred to Hina then that she herself would one day be a lawyer, much less a famous one. But later, after college, after she had given up linguistics and the wish to teach it, after the law had taken hold of her, she realized that the seed of her newfound passion had been planted long before in those visits to the prisons and the courts on behalf of her beloved and immensely stubborn father.

When Hina Jilani finished law school at Punjab University in Lahore, however, she was faced with the fact that opportunities for female lawyers in Pakistan were acutely limited. But Hina was not one to be discouraged. Giving up her criminal practice at an established firm, she and Asma (who had also gone into law) and two other female attorneys formed the country's first all-female law firm. Not surprisingly, many of those who came to the firm for help were also women— women, for instance, who, having been raped by men, were charged with having sexual relationships outside of marriage. The maximum punishment for this crime was death by stoning. Pakistan then was a society in which the degradation of women was not just a matter of social practice; it was written into law. Under the laws of evidence, for example, a financial document could be attested to either by two men or one man and two women.

So Hina and her colleagues set out to change the laws and to better the condition of Pakistani women. She vehemently argued cases before the courts and, somewhat to her surprise, the courts occasionally listened. But gradually Hina came to realize that, although she might win sporadic victories in court, the real battle was in society at large, in the dictates of religious extremism, and in the prevailing attitudes toward women in the family. She realized too that the struggle for women's rights was part of the larger struggle for democracy that had so preoccupied her father. With that recognition Hina and her colleagues formed the Women's Action Forum, and in 1983 thousands of Pakistani women took to the streets to demonstrate for both personal and political freedom. They were met with beatings, house arrest, and imprisonment. Twice Hina was confined to jail, and on a regular basis she was subjected to government surveillance. But the inspiration of her father never failed her. "You have to keep knocking," he had said, "or your opponents will go to sleep." Hina kept on knocking, both as a leader of growing numbers of women who were now demanding equal justice and as a lawyer arguing in court for women's rights.

Gradually the situation for women in Pakistan changed. The assumption that the laws of the state had to be grounded in Islamic teaching came under fire. After all, there were seventy-two different sects of Islam in Pakistan. Whose interpretation of Islamic law was the right one? In 1989, Hina won a landmark case in which women gained equal admission to medical college—a privilege previously allocated largely to men. But what changed little, if at all, were the social attitudes toward women among many Pakistani families. So-called honor killings, in which women were executed by their relatives for allegedly violating sexual mores or defying the authority of their fathers or husbands, were all too common. So common in fact that in 1999, Hina and her allies established a women's shelter in Lahore. In less than a year fourteen hundred women came to the shelter for protection from their families. One of those women was Samia Sarwar.

"I've left my house," she told Hina, "and they will never forgive me. They will kill me." So Hina put Samia in the shelter and agreed to take her case, to help her file for divorce. "I was surprised that a timid woman like Samia had resolved to take on the enmity of her family," Hina observed. "She seemed well educated, but I had the impression that she lacked confidence."

Two or three days later Samia's parents arrived in Lahore and asked to see her, but every time Samia was told that her parents were nearby, she would turn pale, start to tremble, and insist that she would never consent to meet them. "They will kill me," she said, "the minute they see me." The standoff continued for several days, the parents pleading, Samia refusing, until finally her parents sent word that they had reconsidered, that they would agree to the divorce and that her mother would bring the papers.

Samia Sarwar sat in Hina's office on April 6, 1999, waiting for her mother, for the papers, for her freedom. "It will be all right," Hina thought as she waited with Samia. "It is just the mother and, after all, the mother is a doctor." But when Samia's mother arrived and walked into the office, she was not alone. "Who is that man?" Hina demanded of Samia's mother, who clutched a stranger's arm. "He is my helper; I cannot walk," she offered. In the next instant the stranger unloaded a pistol into Samia's head.

"What I can never overcome," Hina said later, after one of the bullets had whizzed past her own head; after Samia's mother had calmly turned around and walked out of the office; after Hina's law colleague had been taken hostage; after the assassin himself had been killed by a guard in the office; after Samia's mother and family members had all made their escape; after her father, informed that "the job was done," had seemed content; after the police had been bribed to look the other way; after the Pakistani Parliament had defeated a resolution condemning the killing, one legislator saying, "What sort of human rights are being claimed by these girls in jeans?"; after several religious organizations had issued fatwas against Hina, promising to pay rewards to anyone who killed her; after Samia's family, absurdly, had filed a lawsuit against Hina for allegedly abducting and murdering their daughter; after Hina had herself been appointed United Nations Representative for Human Rights Defenders. "What I can never overcome is that this woman had come to us for protection and we had failed to provide it. Is there no safe place for women in this country? Even in a law office before dozens of witnesses?"[1]

Samia Sarwar's story is made atypical only by the venue in which she was killed. No sensitive American, reading of this tragic turn of events, could remain unmoved. A few may even be outraged. It is a terrible shame. Things like that should not happen. We share a common humanity with this young woman, and in some measure we are touched by her tale. But what does Samia's fate and that of the many women like her around the world—not only in Pakistan but throughout Asia, Africa, parts of Europe, and the Americas—really have to do with us? How might it affect our lives, living as we do so far away? How might it have an impact on U.S. interests?

That question is at the heart of this book: Is supporting human rights both around the world and at home in the United States a mere moral luxury? Or is it, in ways we rarely see and our own leaders often fail to understand, integral to the pursuit of Americans' own best future? I argue that the latter is the case, that Samia's demise and Hina's struggle and the adversities of thousands of others like them around the world have a profound impact on Americans—politically, economically, environmentally, and in dozens of other ways. I argue that caring about the fate of our "neighbors" is far more than a matter of conscience. It is in truth a matter of survival—our own survival. Because our welfare is bound up in theirs, and when their dreams die, our health and security die with them.

Introduction

"But what does all of this have to do with a person in East Tennessee?"

The question from the talk show host on Knoxville's National Public Radio station was not a hostile one. I had been talking about Burma (Myanmar) and Bosnia, China and Chiapas, refugee camps in Congo, and police brutality in New York City, and now the interviewer was simply trying to bring it all home to his listeners. "I mean, I'm sure we all agree that these kinds of human rights violations are morally repugnant," he said, "But if I'm barely scratching out a living in East Tennessee, worried about having enough money to get my kids a decent education or to make the payments on a bigger house, what difference do all these abuses taking place so far away make to me?"

It was an excellent question, and in the hundreds of interviews I had given for Amnesty International over the years, it was one I had never been asked before. Nor was it a question that we in the human rights movement often ask ourselves. We have assumed that if we describe the suffering dramatically enough, good people will respond and want to stop it. And of course many good people have. But not enough, by any means. Not enough, for example, to make human rights the kind of issue to which politicians pay regular attention. Not like the attention given to issues of pollution or abortion or prayer in schools, issues that readily command widespread public debate.

Why was that? Was it one of the consequences of the end of the Cold War? Were Americans just too self-satisfied to care about the plight of others? Did these problems just seem too intractable? Or was there really very little connection between what was happening "out there" and how most of us in the United States live?

That Knoxville interviewer had posed a question for which anyone in the business of changing the world had better be ready. "OK, but what does this have to do with me?" For the most part this is not a question that human rights campaigners are well prepared to answer.

I was five years old in 1955 when Rosa Parks refused to move from the front of that Montgomery bus; thirteen when Dr. Martin Luther King Jr. led the March on Washington; and eighteen when the Tet Offensive broke the will of the United States to carry on the Vietnam War. The civil rights and anti–Vietnam War movements were, before all else, moral crusades. Those who supported them from the very beginning did so because they thought it the right thing to do. The practical benefits were of secondary importance. But before these two great moral movements would grow to their maximum strength, capturing the sympathy of hundreds of thousands across the country, they had to add to their moral authority a host of pragmatic reasons for Americans to support them.

In the case of the civil rights movement, those black Americans who might at first have viewed Dr. King and his colleagues with skepticism were soon convinced that this was a crusade worth fighting for. They were convinced not only by Dr. King's rhetoric and courage but also by the practical changes the movement proposed to make in people's lives—*their* lives and those of their children. White sympathizers also responded to the moral message of equal rights, but they recognized as well that the United States could no longer remain a divided society without doing untold damage to itself. Those people too recalcitrant to see this reality early on were jolted into awareness when several U.S. cities went up in flames in the 1960s.

Similarly, public opinion about the Vietnam War gradually shifted for both ethical and practical reasons. The infamous photograph of a South Vietnamese general executing a terrified man with a point-blank shot to the head as well as the image of a nude, screaming child fleeing a village on which U.S. troops had dropped napalm had an enormous impact on Americans' sense of themselves as a virtuous people. But such moral outrage had to be coupled with growing numbers of U.S. boys returning home in body bags and a deeply divided society before mainstream opinion finally turned against the war.

Since these crusades of the 1960s and 1970s, nearly every movement for social change in the United States, whether right wing or left, has combined a moral, religious, or aesthetic dimension with a pragmatic rationale in its campaign to win public approval. Those who advocate prayer in public schools, for example, do so both to glorify their God and also because they believe that prayer in schools will improve children's morals and perhaps prevent another Columbine High shooting. Some people support the environmental movement simply because they love the pristine beauty of the rain forest, but others complement that love with concern about global warming and the desire to shield their families from polluted air and hidden toxins. In much the same fashion, citizens support women's causes, gun control, or restrictions on pornography because these causes embody a moral vision that is important to them, but also because they want adequate access to reproductive health care, a drop in the crime rate, or to protect their children from sexually explicit material.

Nearly every movement to change the world frames the benefits of what it offers in both visionary and practical terms. Almost every one. Except, more often than not, the human rights movement.

Almost four thousand years ago a Babylonian king named Hammurabi issued a set of laws to his people. Among other things, Hammurabi's Codes established fair wages, offered protection of property, and required charges to be proven at trial. The Codes, while often harsh in their punishments, provided standards by which Babylonians could order their lives and treat one another. The Codes said nothing, however, about how Babylonians were to treat their archenemies, the Assyrians. Presumably Babylonians could convict Assyrians of crimes without trial or steal their property as avidly as they liked. Furthermore, the Assyrians certainly never acquiesced in Hammurabi's Codes.

Over the centuries human beings have devised (or in the case of such figures as Moses and Mohammed, "received") different sets of standards by which to measure our obligations to one another. The Romans were probably the first to establish the concept of citizens' rights, but the modern American notion of rights derives from such seminal documents as the Magna Carta (1215), the English Bill of Rights (1689), the U.S. Bill of Rights (1791), and the French Declaration of the Rights of Man and the Citizen (1789). The problem with all of these statements of rights, however, eloquent as they are, is that they applied to only one set of people, to only the English or to the Americans (and, given the "inconvenient" presence of women and slaves, not even to all English or American people). Moreover, even when these statements attempted to articulate rights that held for all of humanity, as the French Declaration did, only one group—in that case, the "representatives of the French people, organized in National Assembly"—had adopted them.

Remarkable as it seems, it took almost four thousand years from the days of Hammurabi for the world to agree on a statement of rights that nearly everybody active on the international scene at the time acknowledged applied to everybody else—even to one's enemies!—simply because everybody is a human being. It took a world body (the United Nations), horrific carnage (the Holocaust of World War II), and an extraordinary woman (Eleanor Roosevelt) to carry it off, but in 1948 the United Nations passed the Universal Declaration of Human Rights. A Mexican diplomat once said of Mrs. Roosevelt, who served as chair of the U.N. Human Rights Commission that drafted the Universal Declaration, "Never before have I seen naivete and cunning so graciously blended." And indeed, it took large doses of both of these qualities for her to finally get the document adopted.

Once it was adopted, however, the world had a formal itemization of rights—thirty articles of them, in fact—that anybody could claim, from Hammurabi's rights to wages, property, and a fair trial to the rights to marry freely, to join trade unions, to receive an education, to speak an opinion, and to not be tortured. The mere articulation of such rights and their near universal acclamation was a formidable achievement.

But then came the need to enforce these rights, which of course was a problem. The only ones who had the power to enforce human rights, either directly or through the United Nations itself, were the very powers—nation-states—that might be guilty of violating them. It may not be true, as Yeats had it, that "there is no longer a virtuous nation and the best of us live by candlelight." Unfortunately, however, a 1997 Reuters story datelined Mok Kampul, Cambodia, captures all too vividly the degree of seriousness with which many governments take human rights. Describing the death by torture of political dissident Thong Sophal, the Reuters item said: "His eyes had been gouged out, his head smashed in, the skin had been stripped from his lower legs and all his fingers and one ear had been cut off." And then the news service added sardonically, "Police said they suspected Thong Sophal had killed himself."

If governments, then, could not be trusted to implement the Universal Declaration, despite having voted for it, what other power might be brought to bear? The first candidate was moral suasion, what human rights champion Aryeh Neier has called "the mobilization of shame." After all, the creation of the Universal Declaration had been prompted in no small part by the experience of the Holocaust. Moral argument appealed to human emotion, to a sense of decency and fair play. It depended on evoking feelings of revulsion at the harsher forms human rights violations sometimes take and resonated with the familiar invocation, "Never again!"

By telling the stories of individuals and their suffering—people like playwright Vaclav Havel of the former Czechoslovakia or journalist Jacobo Timmerman of Argentina—human rights workers managed to put compelling human faces on larger political dramas. This was a particularly effective approach in the Cold War years. Although non-Communist governments were responsible for profound human rights violations in places like South Africa, Greece, or Chile, the dynamics of East-West tension meant that the epithet "human rights hero" would become peculiarly attached in the popular mind to brave Soviet dissidents like Andrei Sakharov and Anatoly Sharansky. Thanks to such authors as Aleksandr Solzhenitsyn and Varlam Shalamov, the gulag came to supplement the Nazi concentration camps as an exemplary locus of the hell into which human rights victims might be cast. Moral rhetoric quickly became the favorite lexicon of the human rights struggle in consonance with Camus' observation that "there is no evil that cannot be surmounted by scorn."

But the Universal Declaration had been born not just out of the Holocaust. The Nuremberg and Tokyo trials could make an equal claim to its parentage. So the second candidate to serve as counterweight to the perfidious fickleness of governments when it came to enforcing human rights was law. Although the Universal Declaration had not initially been intended to have the force of law (and, indeed, the U.S. State Department was so concerned that it not that the department carefully labeled the declaration a "hortatory statement of aspirations"), the Universal Declaration gradually assumed that status.

Over the years national constitutions took the strictures of the declaration as guidelines for their own descriptions of rights. Legally binding treaties, covenants, conventions, and protocols,[1] most of them derived in good measure from the Universal Declaration, were built up. The declaration eventually took on the character of what is called "customary law," and to violate somebody's human rights became not just a matter of doing something wrong but a matter of doing something illegal. Legal rhetoric became the second favorite lexicon of the human rights movement. Despite Canadian jurist Louise Arbour's observation that "international law is the aristocrat of law, practiced by people in limousines being polite,"[2] in recent years the International War Crimes Tribunals for the former Yugoslavia and Rwanda have tried hard to turn principles into prison time for human rights criminals.

These two forms of discourse—the moral and the legal—have remained for more than fifty years the principal argots in which human rights have been discussed. This is because they reflect two of the most invaluable resources we can bring to bear in the struggle to end human agony—appeal to conscience and resort to court. Without them, the human rights movement would find itself bereft of both passion and precision. As a clergyperson myself, I would never disparage the former, sympathetic as I am to the observation that "if you laid end to end all the people who fall asleep in church, they would be a lot more comfortable." As one who first joined the American Civil Liberties Union at age sixteen, the son of a law professor who served up case talk with the carrots each night at the dinner table, I would be loath to belittle the latter.

It is not that we who care about human rights are wrong to speak in the tongues of ethics and law. Not at all. It is just that they alone are not enough. Not enough to win a major audience. Moral arguments may appeal to a relatively small segment of a community for a very long time or they may appeal to a fairly large segment of a community for a rather short time, but they are unlikely, by themselves, to hold a large number of people's attention forever. If the "CNN effect" has been credited with forcing American politicians to "do something" to stop the mayhem voters see on their televisions at night, "compassion fatigue" has been equally as popular an explanation for the apparent limits to people's interest in foreign catastrophes. After all, human rights crimes are messy; severed limbs and piles of corpses do not make for pleasant breakfast viewing. Appeals to morality reach in a consistent fashion only that portion of the public for whom morality bests convenience in its long-term understanding of the world.

And whichever part of the populace is not turned off by the persistence of the brutality will be put to sleep by the legalisms. There may be more lawyers per capita in the United States today than ever before, and there may even be more of them than is good for us ("Father, forgive me!"). But those members of the public who are fascinated by the intricacies of law (and particularly of international law) will never fill a football stadium.

What we need to make the human rights "sale"—to build a broader constituency for human rights, to convince larger numbers of people that human rights matter—is a third form of rhetoric, a third set of arguments, a third understanding of suffering's significance. What we need are compelling practical reasons why respect for human rights is in the best interests of the United States. If ethical issues are to hold people's attention over an extended period of time and if legal issues are to be of consequence to someone other than jurists, they must be framed, to the extent possible, in the language of realpolitik. If the American public is to care about human rights crimes committed against their fellow citizens in the United States, they must understand how those crimes endanger their own interests. If large numbers of Americans are ever to care about human rights violations around the world, they must be able to see the implications of those violations for their own lives here at home.

I am not suggesting that Americans are callous, self-absorbed narcissists. In fact we are some of the most generous people in the world. For example, Americans gave over $190 billion to charities in 1999.[3] I am simply suggesting that the human rights movement try, as it can, to complement moral vision with pragmatic punch. I am simply suggesting that, like every other movement for social change, we be ready to answer the question "But what does all of this have to do with me?"

Americans may not be tightfisted when it comes to philanthropy, but it is rumored that we have grown indifferent to the sweep of events beyond our borders. Of that $190 billion in charitable giving in 1999, only $2.7 billion went to organizations that deal with international affairs. When asked whether what happens in western Europe or Asia has any personal relevance, Americans reject the notion by substantial margins. Even in the case of Mexico, 55 percent say that events there have no impact on them.[4] Such apparent indifference is reflected in the diminishing coverage U.S. news outlets give to international affairs. The time devoted to foreign news on network television, for example, has declined from 45 percent in the 1970s to 13.5 percent in 1995.[5] International coverage in newsmagazines has similarly evaporated.

Furthermore, when asked by the Chicago Council on Foreign Relations to describe what the United States should take as its most important foreign policy goals, Americans appear preoccupied with domestic needs. Although preventing the spread of nuclear weapons is named as the most important foreign policy goal (82 percent), the next two most critical objectives are considered "stopping the flow of illegal drugs into the United States" (81 percent) and "protecting the jobs of American workers" (80 percent). "Promoting and defending human rights in other countries" scores low on the list (39 percent, down from 58 percent in 1990).[6] (Perhaps I may take some comfort in the fact that when asked to name the greatest invention of all time, 11 percent of Americans picked the television game show *Wheel of Fortune*.)

When we look more closely at Americans' opinions about the country's role in the world, however, the results are more encouraging. Two-thirds say, as they have for more than two decades, that the United States should take an active part in world affairs rather than try to isolate itself. Almost as many Americans believe that the United States should take part in United Nations peacekeeping operations in troubled parts of the world. When asked for a rationale for this tilt toward globalism, the public displays a fairly sophisticated grasp of the interconnection between morality and pragmatism. Although 66 percent say that "when innocent civilians are suffering or are being killed," the United States should contribute troops to a U.N. effort "whether or not it serves the national interest" (a highly moralistic position),[7] even more (78 percent) agree that "if we allow things like genocide or the mass killings of civilians to go unaddressed, it is more apt to spread and create more instability in the world so that eventually our interests would be affected" (a far more strategic insight). More telling still are the number (79 percent) who concur with the observation that "because the world is so interconnected today, the United States should participate in U.N. efforts to maintain peace, protect human rights, and promote economic development. Such efforts serve U.S. interests because they help create a more stable world that is more conducive to trade and other U.S. interests."[8]

Legend has it that there is a beetle in the Sahara Desert which, when it runs out of water, finds a sandy incline, begins to climb it, tumbles to the bottom when the sand gives way, and endlessly repeats the process, like Sisyphus, until it produces a bead of sweat on its own abdomen. At that point the beetle stops climbing and slurps from its belly.[9] Americans know that their country cannot hope to emulate such self-sufficiency, both because it would not be right and because it would not work. They also know that more often than not, the right thing to do is not only *not* at odds with U.S. interests but that a good deal of the time the two go hand in hand.

Reinforcing that connection—for the public at large and also for those who shape public opinion—is critical to spreading the human rights message. Doug Clifton, the executive editor of the *Miami Herald,* may not have been happy that his July 1995 e-mail message to his newspaper staff appeared in *Harper's* magazine under the heading "Bosnia: One Big Yawn." But he need not have been too distraught, for he is far from alone in his sentiment: "If anyone has an idea on what to do with the Bosnia story," he wrote near the height of the killings in that country, "I welcome it." He went on to admit:

> I'm embarrassed to say I long ago stopped reading this story of enormous human tragedy and significant global consequence. Why is that? Some of it is my personal failure. I'm callous, parochial, and maybe even stupid. But more of it may be my—our—professional failure.
>
> We dutifully report each day's events, every one a bit more horrible than the last, and pretty soon all begin to look and sound alike. . . .
>
> Yes, I care about man's inhumanity to man, but I care more about whether this latest event brings the world or the U.S. closer to the brink. A reader—even a high-minded, liberal-thinking one with a worldview—wants to know, "What does this mean to me?"[10]

Clifton's admission, I suspect, made not a few human rights activists queasy. We come to this work out of a sense of conscience and are often impatient with those who fail to share our urgency. But the truth is that we have few people to blame but ourselves. By emphasizing the field's legal and policy dimensions, we have lent the impression that human rights are the business of specialists. By relying on national media and high-level contacts to influence decision-makers, we have, with a few exceptions, paid little attention to grassroots organizing.

In this last respect we have been richly rewarded. Counting the number of people who join environmental organizations as indicative of how many Americans care deeply about environmental issues, there are more than two million active supporters of environmentalism in the United States. Similarly, the women's movement can claim more than a million affiliates. The NAACP alone has five hundred thousand members. But human rights organizations focused on international issues would be hard-pressed to muster four hundred thousand, and most of those belong to one group, Amnesty International. What is the consequence of such pitiful numbers? Perhaps journalist and author David Rieff put it best in his provocative article "The Precarious Triumph of Human Rights." He noted that "today's human rights workers wield great clout in Washington on an issue to which the public is not paying much attention." Rieff went on to say:

> But when risks are involved—and members of Congress are getting countervailing pressure from their districts—the weaknesses of the insider approach become apparent. The Rwandan genocide of 1994 was the most tragic case in point. Anthony Lake, then the national security adviser, reportedly told a [human rights] representative who had quietly come to lobby him for United States action that he would be unsuccessful in pressing for an intervention unless a great deal of popular protest began to occur. But the human rights movement was in no position to mobilize it. It could merely publish more reports, issue appeals and dispatch more wrenching videotapes to the media.[11]

Of course Tony Lake should not have needed "popular protests" to stop genocide; the Rwandan massacre is the most shameful foreign policy matter of Bill Clinton's presidency. But the fact that the human rights movement couldn't generate popular pressure to stop it is an indictment of the movement as well.

There are many ways to mobilize action. One of the best methods in the short term is to put moral claims front and center. That is no doubt what should have happened in the case of Rwanda. To have made claims of self-interest in the face of mass slaughter might well have been perceived to be intellectually tenuous or to have rung ethically false. But in the long run, the way to build a widespread demand for any social agenda, the way to reach the millions of people who are not now and never will be "activists," the way to prepare public opinion to respond to genocide when it occurs is to couple moral pleas with cogent practicality. Do that and we take a critical step toward gathering a constituency. But to do that we must be willing to entertain Doug Clifton's question: What does this mean to me?

One of the striking features of the Chicago Council on Foreign Relations poll cited earlier regarding what Americans believe to be our most important foreign policy goals is that at least two of the top three goals—"stopping the flow of illegal drugs into the United States" and "protecting the jobs of American workers"—are linked to combating human rights abuses. That is also true of some of the other goals Americans rank highly, such as "controlling and reducing illegal immigration," "improving the global environment," and "reducing our trade deficit." Yet "promoting and defending human rights in other countries" ranks relatively low on the list. Obviously, despite the public's affirmation that morality and national interest are related, there is a "disconnect" when we get down to hard cases. The average American is fuzzy about just how human rights violations affect the world around them.

In that respect Americans are in distinguished company.

One of the highlights of my professional career was being attacked on the editorial page of the *Washington Post* by Senator Jesse Helms. As one who had grown up lionizing the great Senate liberals of my childhood—the Humphreys, the Churches, the Clarks, and the Kennedys —this was the evidence I needed to count myself a junior member of that pantheon. Senator Helms was unhappy that I had written a letter to Secretary of State Madeleine Albright criticizing her for suggesting that the decision of whether General Augusto Pinochet of Chile should be extradited to Spain to stand trial should be left to the Chilean people.[12]

Pleased as I was by Senator Helms's opprobrium, my view of his politics had shifted slightly since I had become the head of Amnesty International USA in 1994. Although I still disagreed with him about 95 percent of the time, on a few human rights issues (not surprisingly, those involving such Communist countries as China and Cuba) Senator Helms could be a staunch ally. I had even testified before his Committee on Foreign Relations regarding China's sale of the organs of executed prisoners. On the issue of economic sanctions against human rights violators, Senator Helms turned out to favor, well, shall we say, a "liberal" use of them.[13]

What a "liberal" or "conservative" view of human rights issues might be is sometimes hard to fathom. Is it "liberal" or "conservative" to want to stop torture? Is it "liberal" or "conservative" to oppose human rights violations overseas that result in greater numbers of immigrants coming to this country? Is it "liberal" or "conservative" to believe that those who commit human rights crimes around the world should be punished for them? Is it "liberal" or "conservative" to speak against religious persecution or female genital mutilation? Is it "liberal" or "conservative" not to want to waste taxpayers' dollars settling liability claims against brutal cops? Is it "liberal" or "conservative" to think U.S. arms should not be used to commit human rights abuses?

Because the terms "liberal" and "conservative" are rarely helpful when it comes to matters of foreign policy, analysts have sometimes divided foreign policy makers into the categories "realist" or "moralist." Henry Kissinger is often considered the quintessential "realist" who made decisions about international relations not on the basis of the world as we might like it to be but on the basis of the world as it is in all its shoddy, backstabbing, dangerous complexity. Jimmy Carter is regarded as the epitome of a moralist, who as president tried to base U.S. relations with other countries on principles of justice, mutuality, and human rights. But neoconservatives like Robert Kagan and William Kristol, the latter Dan Quayle's former chief of staff, also champion using U.S. power to advance moral concerns.

In part because aspects of Carter's presidency, including his foreign policy, are often popularly considered to have been unsuccessful, human rights over the past two decades have come to be associated with weakness and self-indulgence. To the extent that subsequent presidents have employed human rights concerns in foreign policy at all, it has often been in the fashion of an amateur cook with a favorite spice used either to disguise a bad recipe or to make a new one taste more familiar (Recall, for example, Central American policies, Bush's war in the Persian Gulf, and Clinton's tough stance in Haiti—all pursued for hard-edged political and economic reasons but all presented to the public pungent with the whiff of rights). However it may appear, "realism" has largely dominated foreign policy thinking, and "realists" tend to have little truck with human rights.

Here, for example, is Alan Tonelson, a fellow at the Economic Strategy Institute in Washington, D.C.: "During the Cold War a plausible case could be made for denying an ideologically hostile rival superpower targets of opportunity by fostering democratic practices abroad. But in the absence of such a rival, the state of human rights around the world does not have, and never has had, any demonstrable effect on U.S. national security."[14] Here is the grandpappy of "realism," diplomat George Kennan: "I would like to see our government gradually withdraw from its public advocacy of democracy and human rights. . . . I don't think any such questions should enter into our diplomatic relations with other countries. If others [private parties] want to advocate changes in their conditions, fine—no objection. But not the State Department or the White House. They have more important things to do."[15]

"Realists" regard the pursuit of rights as an unnecessary, sometimes even a dangerous extravagance, often at odds with our national interest. What they seem rarely to garner is that in far more cases than they will allow, defending human rights is a prerequisite to *protecting* that interest. What we require is not less realism but a more expansive, sophisticated, comprehensive form of it—a "new realism" for an interconnected age.

I do not want to claim too much here. I am not suggesting that every human rights crime is a matter of national consequence. In many instances only moral qualms can provide the motivation to stop abuses. Nor am I pretending that human rights are always the most important policy consideration or that morality and national interest are joined at the hip. But neither are they the strange bedfellows the "realists" would make out. By emphasizing morality to the exclusion of pragmatism, we human rights advocates have allowed ourselves to be dismissed as idealists or ideologues, as either too mushy-headed in our thinking to be taken seriously or too rigid in our priorities to be trusted with power.

At least for the foreseeable future, respect for human rights will remain largely a matter of voluntary compliance by governments or armed opposition groups. It will remain largely a matter of *raison d'état*, of perceived self-interest. If we are unwilling to make our case at least in part in those terms, we concede the argument before it is even joined. More important, however, by failing to engage "realists" on at least a portion of their own ground, the human rights community has too often for the past twenty years ceded U.S. foreign policy to those in government and business who care the least about human rights. The problem with that is both stark and simple: it has allowed the tyrants of the world to get away with murder.

Fortunately the connection between human rights and national interest is becoming more clear to an ever-expanding circle of observers. As *The Economist*, that bastion of respect for capitalist values, editorialized not too long ago:

> Morality is not the only reason for putting human rights on the West's foreign-policy agenda. Self-interest also plays a part. Political freedom tends to go hand in hand with economic freedom, which in turn tends to bring international trade and prosperity. And governments that treat their own people with tolerance and respect tend to treat their neighbours in the same way. Dictatorships unleashed the First and Second World Wars, and most wars before and since.[16]

Even Prince Talal bin Abdelaziz of Saudi Arabia, half-brother of King Fahd, has noted that "political reforms are coming as part of globalization and we must prepare ourselves for this new development from all aspects. . . . Globalization is currently based on democracy, human rights and market economics."[17]

Whether it be war and peace, international trade, economic growth, the security of jobs, the state of our environment, the public health, the interdiction of drugs, or a host of other topics, there is a connection between Americans' own interests and international human rights. If we are talking about human rights violations committed in the United States, the connection is even more direct, not just for those residents who may themselves be the victims of human rights abuses but for every American. It is this book's burden to make those connections clear.

Three caveats, however, before we begin. First, despite the criticism I level at traditional "realists," this book is not designed for the foreign policy mandarin. I am honored to be a member of the Council on Foreign Relations and I hope this work will be taken seriously, but I propound here no grand new theory of international relations nor offer revelations about human rights that are unavailable to the avid reader of high-quality newspapers. Rather, this book is intended to reframe the debate about human rights for the intelligent layperson who wants to understand the role human rights play in the life of the United States and its people. It is designed to take the human rights debate out of the hands of the "experts" (on both sides) and make it accessible to the average American. After all, their interests are *really* at stake here, and it is they who will pay the highest price for American indifference. I am convinced that such people's opinions can have as great an effect on the course of our future as can the most erudite scholar's.

Second, the human rights I treat herein are the traditional civil and political ones, like the right to vote, to express opinions without fear of retaliation, to demand a fair trial, to be free from torture. I am not sympathetic to the profusion of "rights" being claimed under the oddest of banners ("This is like the state telling me I have no rights," protested the owner of a South Carolina video poker parlor when the state shut down such games. "It's pretty close to being communist."[18]), but I fully affirm social and economic rights. With the exception of labor rights, however, I do not for the most part deal with them in this book. Although Americans have reached close to a consensus about support for civil and political rights, we have, much to our shame, been far more lax to recognize social and economic rights. If I offer a critique of "realism," it must be in the context of civil and political rights because most "realists" choke on the very notion of any other kind. The best I can do is to name my own and this book's limitations and to invite someone else to write the book that will obviate them.

Third, I need to be clear that I am not speaking in this book on behalf of Amnesty International but only for myself. Amnesty takes no position on many of the issues I address or policies I espouse in these pages.

"But what does all of this have to do with a person in East Tennessee?" the reporter had asked. I had but a moment to think and about thirty seconds to respond.

"Well, if that person's child is in the military and might be stationed in Haiti or Bosnia, it certainly has a lot to do with him or her," I answered. "Or if the person holds a job that might be lost because U.S. companies are attracted by lower wages in countries that abuse labor rights, it has a lot to do with him or her. Or if the person is concerned about drugs and learns that U.S. arms to fight the Colombian drug wars have been diverted to kill innocent people, he or she might want to give a thought to human rights. If you've ever made an investment in an international stock or if you're in a pension plan that does, you better believe human rights have something to do with you."

I do not know if my answer satisfied either the reporter or my hypothetical listener in East Tennessee, but when I got off the air, I decided the question deserved a more thorough reply. This book contains all that I didn't get to say in those thirty seconds.

And the first thing I didn't get to say is what human rights are anyway and why, from the perspective of morality alone, other people's suffering matters.

I

"Like the Home-Born among You"

....

The Moral Underpinnings of the Struggle for Human Rights

Be knit together in this work . . . delight in each other,
mourn together, labor and suffer together.
—JOHN WINTHROP, Puritan governor
of the Massachusetts Bay Colony

IKE SO MANY high school classes across the United States, this one in Houston appeared bored to the point of desperation. The introduction of a guest speaker who was going to talk about human rights had hardly lifted the students out of their torpor. Throughout my years as a human rights activist, I have spoken before the United Nations, to street toughs in Northern Ireland, to militia members in Liberia, to twenty-five thousand quizzical Japanese who never did figure out who I was, and to Andy Rooney at a cocktail party, but high school kids are often my toughest audience. Interestingly enough, however, the conversation almost always follows a familiar pattern, as did this one in Houston. Here, in condensed form, is how it went:

"I'm here today to talk with you about your rights," I began. "But first let's try to figure out if you have any and, if you do, why. Do any of you believe you have such a thing as 'rights'?"

There were general nods of agreement.

"Well, if you do, what are some of these rights?"

Desultory replies of "free speech," "freedom of worship," "right to a trial." And then: "Freedom to watch as much television as I want." Low chuckles.

"Let's take the right to a fair trial," I said, ignoring the comic. "If somebody tries to tell you that you don't have that right, on what basis would you argue that you do?"

A little more interest now at the specter of somebody trying to deny rights. "It's the law." "It's in the Constitution."

"Yes," I started, "but what if somebody says, 'I think your Constitution is wrong.' How do we convince him or her that the *idea* of a fair trial is a good one, a correct one? Before you answer that, tell me this: Do only Americans have the right to a fair trial or to free speech?"

"No," most of the kids replied. "Everybody does."

"OK, but since our Constitution only applies to Americans, on what basis would we argue with somebody who says either 'Your Constitution is just plain wrong' or 'Well, OK, maybe your Constitution is right for you but not for me and my people. We don't believe in all those rights you allow your people to have'?"

At this point the more alert students were starting to turn some of these questions over in their minds.

"I'd say, 'It's because God gave us those rights,'" somebody interjected.

"But what if the person we're talking to doesn't believe in God, or what if he or she is of a different religion than we are and says, 'Well, my God didn't give me those rights'? What do we say then?"

"We could say that human beings just deserve those rights," a smart kid retorted. "Rights are what make us human. Chairs and tables don't have rights. Rights are just the right thing to do. It's just the moral thing."

"But what if somebody tells us that he or she thinks what makes us human is obeying the wishes of our leaders, even if the leaders deny us our rights. What if somebody tells us he or she thinks it is perfectly moral to torture a person or throw someone in jail without a trial. How do we refute that?"

After we had gone round and round on these questions for a few minutes, a girl in the back tried to settle the matter: "Well, OK," she said. "Maybe we can't argue others into believing our way for sure. But what we *can* do is to say to them, 'Look, this is just the best way to live. Do you really want to live in a world without any rights? We think this way works best, and we think you should try it too.'"

"And as a matter of fact," I added, "we can say even a little more than that. We can say not only 'We think this way will work best.' We can also say, 'And almost every government in the world says that it agrees.'" It usually takes about thirty minutes to get to this point, as it did in this classroom talk, but where this conversation had led us was to the Universal Declaration of Human Rights. What is particularly intriguing about these conversations—and I have participated in at least fifty of them—is that in the process of getting there, we almost always touch on all three of the major grounds on which human beings have tried over hundreds of centuries to establish the inviolability of rights—God, natural law, and pragmatism. Those high school students in Houston are political philosophers just as surely as Augustine, Locke, and Dewey were. Their sentence structures are just a bit less convoluted.

It would be wonderful if we could prove to the world's satisfaction that God had imbued human beings with a set of rights, and even better if we could show that those rights happened to coincide with those articulated in the Universal Declaration. Christians believe of course that human beings derive their dignity from the fact that they are children of God. God has often been cited, most notably in the U.S. political tradition in the Declaration of Independence, as the source of rights ("We hold these truths to be self-evident, that all men . . . are endowed by their Creator with certain unalienable rights"). Some Christian thinkers have even argued that no one has a "right" to talk about human rights unless he or she believes that rights derive from God.

But it does not take a sophisticated thinker to realize that given the diversity of religious opinion in the world, God's injunctions are not going to provide satisfactory grounds for defending the notion of rights beyond a certain circle of believers. Even within singular religious traditions, there is often widespread disagreement about how God wants human beings to order their lives here on Earth. My favorite example of such a difference of opinion within the Christian tradition concerns the school of devotees in the Early Church called the Montanists, who believed that only by eating a steady diet of radishes could a person be saved. Had the Montanists' view prevailed, today's Christians would take vegetables with their communion wine rather than bread! Every other religious tradition has been rent by similar divisions, to say nothing of the fact that millions would claim to have no use for religion at all.

It was exactly because of this recognition—that to base a justification of rights on an appeal to deity or religion was bound to result in endless disputes and to alienate those for whom such talk is foreign— that those who composed the Universal Declaration firmly rejected placing any reference to God in the document.[1]

But if God is not the direct source of rights, perhaps she or he has seen to it that human beings are put together in such a way as to deserve rights based simply on our nature. Or perhaps we can leave God out of this entirely and claim that because human beings possess some special quality that distinguishes us from other animate beings and certainly from all insentient things ("rationality" has been the most popular candidate), we deserve to be treated with dignity and respect. Whichever it be, Thomas Jefferson covered all of his bases in the Declaration of Independence when he claimed that the colonists were entitled to act as they did based on both "the laws of nature and of Nature's God." The second major argument in defense of rights has been that those rights are derived from our humanness, from natural law. It is a theory as old as the Stoics that evolved through Augustine to Grotius, Hobbes, and Locke, but it has rarely been put as concisely as it was by that student in Houston: "Rights are what make us human. Chairs and tables don't have rights. . . . It's just the moral thing."

Moral thing or not, the doctrine of natural rights, along with its co-adjutant hypothesis—the social contract, by which human beings allegedly commit to create a livable world together—gradually came apart. The decline of natural law theory is far too complex to describe here, but suffice it to say that it began with David Hume's contention that even if Reason were our defining trait as humans, that in itself implies no obligations with regard to how we treat one another. To the extent that some social contract might have been struck in a primitive era and be maintained today, it was due to a combination of self-interest and habit. The idea that natural law provided an objective measure of human value eroded steadily as the doctrine, originally conceived to protect the weak from tyranny, became the rallying cry of the bourgeoisie (in the name of the "right to property") against the disenfranchised. That natural law could all too easily be cited in defense of the status quo to maintain male hegemony, to say nothing of human dominion over animals and the Earth, and that the twentieth century has witnessed far more irrationality than sweet reason has not helped the doctrine's cause in contemporary times.

Quite apart from its social history, however, what makes an appeal to the "laws of nature" a problematic basis for defending human rights is not too different from why God fails the test. It is simply impossible to discern, to the satisfaction of a fractious world, what counts as ethical imperatives derived from observation of human nature. After all, whose "nature" provides the standard? "What is man," Isak Dinesen asked, "but an ingenious machine for turning red wine into urine?" Is that the measure?

Nonetheless, although they recognized that an appeal to natural law provided a perch at the edge of a quagmire, the creators of the Universal Declaration allowed a form of natural law language to be incorporated into the declaration's first "Whereas" ("Whereas recognition of the *inherent* dignity and of the equal and *inalienable rights* of all members of the human family is the foundation of freedom, justice and peace in the world") and first Article ("All human beings are *born* free and equal in dignity and rights").[2] They very quickly followed the first "Whereas" with three more, however, the first appealing to conscience and the next two to self-interest. Although natural law language is obviously an attractive idiom in which to frame human rights, it remains—unless it be understood poetically rather than philosophically—a controversial ground on which to build a structure of rights.

But it is not the philosophy contained within the Universal Declaration, such as it may be, that is the most important thing about the document. Most important is the very existence of the document itself and the fact that nations all over the world recognize its claims as valid. For there is a third broad way to justify human rights, which although it does not provide them the status or "security" of God's endorsement or Nature's sanction, does ground human rights in the experience of the human community. That third way goes by many names— pragmatism, communitarianism, and postmodernism are but three of them. But whatever the label, it makes its appeal to that which is recognizable throughout the world: the consequences of cruelty and the signs of suffering.

The only hotel still open in 1997 in Monrovia, the capital of Liberia, following the 1990–96 civil war, had a stunning view of the ocean from its front porch. Monrovia had been all but destroyed by the fighting, but this hotel had survived (its Lebanese owner, I was told, would rush out waving dollar bills at any soldiers who approached it with impure intentions), and its front porch had become the city's center of intrigue. The afternoon I arrived on a human rights mission, the porch resembled nothing as much as the setting of a Graham Greene novel.

In one corner sat two mercenaries, their rifles propped against the railing, enjoying their beers and swaggering loudly. In another corner a couple in tie-dyed T-shirts and Birkenstocks chatted about their next destination, the smoke from their hash mixing lazily with the humidity. In still a third corner a middle-aged man hunched over his table, a jeweler's magnifying glass clenched in his eye examining mineral specimens, their apparent value signaled by the frequency with which he glanced warily over his shoulder. But it was the occupant of the fourth corner that made the scene complete: a beautiful parrot, chained by his left foot to the perch, that repeated the same refrain at ten- to twelve-second intervals: "Welcome to Liberia. Fuck you! Welcome to Liberia. Fuck you!"

If the hotel's porch was straight out of a novel, the city's prison could have been lifted from Bosch's depiction of Hell. Sixty-four prisoners, most still awaiting trial, usually on charges of theft, occupied six or eight filthy cells. Dried vomit and feces caked floors, walls, and the one mattress provided per cell. Scabies and gangrene were rampant among the prisoners. It was one youngster, about sixteen, who stands out in my memory. His body was covered with red dots. He gave no sign of having been beaten or tortured in the conventional fashion, and he readily admitted that the Nigerian peacekeeping forces had caught him stealing a radio. But how to account for the dots? When the Nigerians had taken him into custody, it seems they were not content just to turn him over to the local authorities or to toss him in prison. Rather, they had decided to have some fun: they had forced the young man to lie down for more than an hour in a pit of red ants. Even a week later the bites were driving him mad.

I hear stories of mistreatment like this all the time. Sometimes the perpetrators' ingenuity takes my breath away. Before they were largely defeated by the Taliban, the Mujahedeen in Afghanistan had devised a simple but terrifying form of punishment: they had strapped their prisoners to dead bodies and left them "coupled" for days on end, after which the prisoners were forced to eat what they were told was human flesh. When the Taliban came to power, they at least equaled the ferocity of the Mujahedeen, chopping off the thumbs of women seen in public wearing nail polish and executing gay men by ordering battle tanks to topple concrete walls onto them, crushing them to death in front of a crowd of spectators.[3] Or consider the practice of some units of the U.S.-trained Salvadoran military during the decade of war in the 1980s there. Not only did one of the battalions reportedly harden its men by having them slit the throats of their prisoners, but other soldiers took part in what was called "dewombing" in which a pregnant woman was killed, her fetus ripped from her womb and tossed into the air, to be caught by the soldiers on bayonets.[4]

Whenever I hear stories like this, I am, as I think most people would be, both heart stricken for the victims and repulsed by the cruelty. Why do I have those reactions?

I am stricken at heart because I have the imagination to know at least in proximate form what the experience, the pain, must have felt like. I am stricken at heart because on some level I identify with the victims; I know what it is to bleed. Although I have never been bitten by a horde of red ants or had a thumb amputated or been crushed by a wall, I have enough acquaintance with human suffering, either my own or that of those I love, that my memory of that acquaintance stokes my recognition.

In a magnificent essay called "The Moral Necessity of Metaphor," the novelist Cynthia Ozick quotes a biblical passage from Leviticus: "The stranger that sojourneth with you shall be unto you as the home-born among you and you shall love him as yourself; because you were strangers in the land of Egypt." She goes on to say that it is exactly because we remember when we too were strangers in the land of Egypt and can apply it metaphorically to others that:

> Doctors can imagine what it is to be their patients. Those who have no pain can imagine those who suffer. Those at the center can imagine what it is to be outside. The strong can imagine what it is to be weak. Illuminated lives can imagine the dark. . . . We strangers can imagine the familiar hearts of strangers.[5]

Robert Frost once observed that poems begin with a lump in the throat, and I think human rights do too. A third way to justify human rights, far better than by appeals to God or Nature, is to point to the capacity to identify with others, the capacity for human empathy or solidarity. This is a capacity of such richness and complexity that something like it, at least concerning mothers and children, is required for the propagation of the species. Children in our own culture as young as one have been known to evidence it, and some ethologists even believe it can be identified in animals.[6] It is a phenomenon so widespread, if not universal, that we can hardly imagine a society existing without it.

I use the verb "point to" advisedly, however, because in fact I don't need to prove that compassion is found everywhere to draw on it as a resource for rights. I am not trying to replace "reason" with "empathy" as a universal human trait or the defining basis for a new form of natural law. I only need to show that it exists somewhere, anywhere, to prove that it is within the spectrum of responses of which human beings are capable and in which we can therefore choose to indulge.

But how can empathy, solidarity, or fellow feeling (what used to be called "fraternity"), the recognition of our common humanity and fate, be the grounds for human rights when we are confronted on a daily basis with overwhelming evidence of its exact opposite, of human cruelty? What about the incontrovertible fact that torturers often simply deny the very humanity of their victims, deny that their victims even belong to the human species, and liken them to brutes or animals? In Shakespeare's *The Merchant of Venice*, Shylock cries out, "I am a Jew. Hath not a Jew eyes? Hath not a Jew hands, organs, dimensions, senses, affections, passions? Fed with the same food, hurt with the same weapons, subject to the same diseases, healed by the same means? If you prick us, do we not bleed? If you tickle us, do we not laugh? If you poison us, do we not die?"[7] What do we say to the killer who responds to Shylock, "Yes, a Jew has eyes but so does a pig"?

The answer is twofold. First, the existence of cruelty does not necessarily vitiate the power of empathy, conceived of as the capacity to identify with what another suffers. In some ways it can even confirm it. For how could those Nigerian soldiers have known that throwing the Liberian prisoner into an ant pile would inflict pain if they themselves lacked the capacity to imagine such suffering, were they the victims? It is not that all torturers are incapable of understanding suffering. In a sense some understand it all too well. This is one of the reasons it is not helpful to label the purveyors of torment "monsters," "demons," "animals," or "sickos." It is exactly because most of them are, in Nietzsche's phrase, "human, all too human" that their actions are in some measure recognizable to us. Most torturers are not pathological in the clinical sense; they are, unfortunately, in many cases quite common or, in political philosopher Hannah Arendt's famous word, "banal" human beings.

Earlier I said that when I heard of cases of cruelty, I responded with revulsion. But it is not the kind of revulsion I might feel at a science fiction character's violence or at a lion attacking a human child. It is a revulsion grounded in part in recognition. Recognition not that I am capable of inflicting exactly that kind of pain, I trust, but recognition that the capacity to inflict suffering, like the capacity to feel compassion, is a familiar one.

When I was a child, I made friends with a gentle little dog across the street from my home. Every day after school the dog Amy and I would play together. One of our favorite games was a dancing game in which I would take her forepaws in my hands and we would dance around the yard. I noticed though that after a minute or two of dancing, Amy's hind legs would get sore and she would pull away. The first few times I sensed her discomfort, I let go of her paws immediately and we went on to another game. But one day, when I felt Amy pull away, I decided to hold on. Finally, after three or four minutes, when she yelped in agony, I let her go. But the next day I repeated my demonic act. It was fascinating to feel this little creature so entirely under my control.

Naturally the longer I kept this up, the less eager Amy was to see me until finally she cowered and whimpered at my approach. I was lucky that she was such a gentle dog, for she would have had every right to have bitten me and, when I realized what I had done, I was deeply frightened of myself and ashamed. Whatever could have taken hold of me that I would hurt something so tame and innocent that I had thought I loved? I tried to make amends to Amy but our relationship was never again the same. Years later I came to understand much better why I had acted as I had, but this incident taught me at any early age how easy it is for every one of us to acquaint ourselves with cruelty.

Studies of how torturers are trained reveal that they often are intentionally subjected to extreme forms of physical and verbal abuse by their trainers, designed not just to induce pliability but to stimulate anger and stress so profound that it readily trumps any feelings of compassion that may have been present before the training began.[8] It takes much more than this of course to make a torturer, but the point is that, though cruelty is pervasive in this world, that fact does not nullify the importance of empathy; it merely reinforces the need to buttress it, to encourage whatever impulses in me finally led me to let poor Amy go.

This is exactly why the world has created rules or norms, in the form of human rights, to "institutionalize" empathy, if you will—rules with which to respond to he who would claim that a Jew is no different from a pig. This is the second part of the answer to the challenge of cruelty: that far from invalidating the claims and imperatives of memory and metaphor, our human capacity to wreak havoc, to ignore the angels of our inspiration, leads directly to the need for some agreement among us as to how best to order our common lives, especially in relationship to strangers and the weak.

That the international community has formally agreed on a set of norms (the Universal Declaration and other human rights instruments) by which all nations are expected to abide in their treatment of strangers (nonkin), the weak, and the oppressed, a set of standards designed to counter cruelty and organize society for the common good, is a remarkable achievement. What the Universal Declaration supplies all of us are rights in the form of norms to which every person can appeal, rights that the international community has derived from the human capacity to identify with others' plights (what the second "Whereas" refers to as "conscience") and that are designed to depict the best way we know of at the moment to counter cruelty and build a decent society. In this sense rights constitute a set of promises that those with power make in recognition of their obligations to order our collective lives in a way consistent with what we regard as humane.

Such a concept of rights does not lend them the kind of irrefragable authority that God's will or Nature's command might. Theoretically the Universal Declaration could be rescinded or amended. Human concepts of rights *do* change and there is no reason to believe that today's notions and norms will be identical to those of the twenty-second century any more than our norms are identical to those of the nineteenth. This concept of rights does have its advantages, however. For one thing its authority devolves in part from the fact that it reflects values that all member states of the United Nations have at least implicitly agreed to share. This is very helpful in responding to those who would criticize the notion of universal human rights because they claim that the rights itemized in the Universal Declaration grew out of a Western Enlightenment tradition and therefore have no bearing on non-Western practices.[9] To hold us accountable to your standards, such critics say, is like calling the ancient Aztecs to account for human sacrifice when, according to their beliefs, it was necessary to make the sun rise every day.

The response is simple. The Universal Declaration does not pretend to reflect cosmic values ascertainable by some process uninfluenced by culture. Of course it emerged out of an Enlightenment tradition. But all values have some cultural source and their origin is no measure of their validity. The Universal Declaration provides a set of norms affirmed by as wide an assortment of nations and cultures as we are ever likely to find designed to describe how best to organize certain aspects of society *today.* If one rejects these norms, that puts a leader or a country at odds with the vast majority of the members of the international community. The question to ask about rights is not, Are they true? The question is, Do they work? Do they work to spread empathy, combat cruelty, and protect the weak from their oppressors? The experience of the international human rights community is that these do.

So the young woman in the Houston classroom was not far off the mark. "We can say, 'Look, this is just the best way to live. Do you really want to live in a world without rights? We think this way works best and we think you should try it too.'"

In the last analysis, of course, the human rights movement welcomes all comers to the struggle, no matter what they think the source of rights is. No matter what your philosophy of rights, the issue soon becomes why we should pay them any heed. Granted that it may be the moral thing to do, why should Americans care about morality? How, in other words, do we convince people to be good?

Immanuel Kant left his hometown of Königsberg only once in his lifetime, and yet despite this dearth of experience, he claimed to have constructed a philosophy that proved the reality of God, freedom, and immortality, among many other things. Kant didn't need wide acquaintance with the world to do it, though, because the fundamentals of his philosophy made no appeals to experience or empiricism.

I studied all of Kant's major works in graduate school and at one time could have (barely) passed a test on them, but something about

Kant always bothered me. At first I thought it was that I identified, as I surely did, with the renowned French phenomenologist Maurice Merleau-Ponty, who is alleged to have remarked that he had read Kant's *Critique of Pure Reason* seven times and every time he understood it less. This is in marked contrast to Thomas Aquinas, who, when asked what was the greatest grace he had ever received, replied, "To have never read a book I didn't understand." But it was not only Kant's complexity that baffled me. It was his conviction that an act, even one that on the surface looks like what we would call a moral act, loses its claim to be a fulfillment of moral duty if it is motivated by anything other than fidelity to moral principle itself. To be moral, in other words, an act must be understood to constitute an end in itself and not be undertaken for some ulterior motive, like popularity or self-gain.

Now the reason this baffled me was pretty simple. I had always thought of myself as a reasonably moral person, the experience with Amy the dog aside, but as I examined my acts, I could not find a single one in which, upon the most honest reflection, my motives had not been mixed. One late-winter day I was puzzling about this on my way home from a philosophy class when I saw an elderly woman walking perhaps thirty yards in front of me slip on the wicked Chicago ice. She was having trouble getting up, so I quickened my pace to help her. I could have crossed to the other side of the street; I could have pretended not to see her; I really didn't want to have to interrupt my plans and make sure that she got to a hospital if she were badly hurt. But nonetheless I ran to her and helped her up. I felt sorry for her; I felt compassion, empathy, mercy. Here, then, I thought to myself: a truly moral act from which I had nothing to gain and perhaps even something to lose (time or, what's worse, as more than one Good Samaritan has discovered, a lawsuit).

A truly moral Kantian act. But of course, upon reflection, it was no such thing. Had I ignored the old lady, I would have suffered immense guilt pangs. Or what if someone was watching from a window and saw me avoid responding? Furthermore, my going to her rescue made me feel good about myself. After all, I surely did not want to live in a world (or a neighborhood) in which human beings went around leaving old ladies sprawled on the ice. The sidewalks would quickly become impassable that way.

Maybe Kant established this impossible standard because he had rarely left Königsberg. Or maybe citizens of Königsberg were just a lot more pure of heart than the rest of us (although I doubt it, because anti-Semitism was rampant in Kant's day). My experience is that acts of morality are never undertaken solely out of principle (although having the principles in the first place is surely important). What's more, that does not diminish their value or significance.

Now of what relevance is this discourse to human rights? First, to the extent to which we want to appeal to morality in support of human rights, we need to find ways (like witnessing a fragile old lady's fall) to evoke those feelings of compassion in others. Second, practicing morality may in and of itself bring rewards. And third, it does not hurt, it does not diminish the value of our moral response, if we appeal as well to other, less apparently "pure" motives to make our case.

In thousands of instances the violation of somebody's human rights will have no impact whatsoever on the interests of other people far away. The fact that a Liberian youngster was bitten all over his body by red ants makes no practical difference that I can see to the life of the prototypical family of four in Peoria. That is why we must rely in many instances on the influence of morality and the power of law to treat human rights abuses. The question before us is, In those instances in which morality is all we've got, how *do* we convince people to care? The answer is that we show them the pain and tell them a story.

Joseph Kony is a child abductor. Were he committing his crimes in the United States, he would no doubt have been sentenced to multiple life terms. But Kony abducts children in Uganda to carry on his quasi-mystical quest to unseat the Ugandan government in the name of the Lord's Resistance Army. Girls as young as eleven have been stolen from their homes and schools and forced into servitude or sexual slavery by Kony and his soldiers. Boys of similar age are kidnapped and brutalized in a campaign to turn them into child soldiers. One fifteen-year-old told of being forced to kill a companion named Oyet who had tried to organize an escape:

> At 2:00 A.M. they clapped their hands, which meant we had to get up. They placed a mat on the floor with three lamps and brought in Oyet. The commander told us that Oyet would be hit three times and then "sent home" [in other words, he would be killed]. Then the com-

mander picked one boy. This boy made a small noise because he did not want [to kill Oyet]. The commander got angry and called for a [machete]. His escorts started beating the boy until he was spitting up blood. . . . Then the commander chose another boy. He was given an ax and Oyet was told to lie down. The boy was told to hit Oyet once. Then he was told to hand the ax to another boy who hit Oyet a second time. And then I was given the ax as the third person. I hit Oyet a third time. I know that it is my blow that sent him home.[10]

It would be hard to argue that the abduction and enslavement of children on the remote Uganda-Sudan border has any direct impact on Americans (although it might conceivably have a future impact if those children should turn into international terrorists). To the extent to which stability in Uganda is important to Americans, the Lord's Resistance Army poses little threat to the Ugandan government. Yet when we hear of children being forced to become sex slaves or butchers, it turns our stomachs.

The best that we human rights advocates can do in situations like this is to paint a picture, show a photograph, share the testimony, and trust in Americans' sense of morality. The philosopher Richard Rorty has argued exactly this point:

It [is not] the moral educator's task [he says] to answer the question "Why should I be moral?" but rather to answer the much more frequently posed question, "Why should I care about a stranger, a person who is no kin to me, a person whose habits I find disgusting?" The traditional answer to the latter question is "Because kinship and custom are morally irrelevant . . . to the obligations imposed by the recognition of membership in the same species." This has never been very convincing. . . . A better sort of answer is the sort of long, sad, sentimental story which begins "Because this is what it is like to be in her situation—to be far from home, among strangers" or . . . "Because her mother would grieve for her." Such stories, repeated and varied over the centuries, have induced us, the rich, safe, powerful people, to tolerate, and even to cherish, powerless people—people whose appearance or habits or beliefs at first seemed an insult to our moral identity.[11]

Amnesty International and other human rights organizations have successfully used this tack to put human faces on human rights crimes. This is what prompted the Dutch writer Abel Herzberg, a survivor of the Bergen-Belsen concentration camp, to observe that the Nazis did not kill six million Jews; rather, first they killed one Jew, then another, then another . . . six million times. This truth inspired Joseph Stalin's well-known aphorism to the effect that the deaths of millions are a statistic while the death of one is a tragedy. This reality also persuades *60 Minutes* producer Don Hewitt that any topic that the program tackles must be put in the form of an individual's story. And it is this insight that disposes me to offer the stories of individuals who are emblematic of the issues I explore in the following chapters.

How the international community or the United States should react when it is touched by suffering, how it should try to effect a cure—well, I treat that complicated question in the final chapter. That we often remain beyond the reach of touch, either out of fear or fatigue, ignorance or boredom—is also very true. Not all of us can respond the way novelist Milan Kundera describes one passerby as doing in pre–Velvet Revolution Czechoslovakia: "Right in the middle of Prague, Wenceslaus Square, there's this guy throwing up. And this other guy comes along, takes a look at him, shakes his head, and says, 'I know just what you mean.'" But that once the story reaches our hearts, we generally feel under obligation to respond—*that* has something to do with our history and our image of ourselves as a people.

"Realists" regularly disparage basing policy on moral qualms but even the dean of the "realists," political scientist Hans Morgenthau, acknowledged that a nation is a moral as well as a physical entity and that the perpetuation of the nation's existence at the expense of its ideals is a tragedy no good strategist, no matter how hard-hearted, would want to advocate.[12] The founders of the United States knew that a country that sacrificed its ideals, that ignored its moral obligations, that abandoned what was referred to, in that day far more than in this, as Virtue, put itself at grave risk. The Revolutionary leader Samuel Adams spoke for many others when he placed morality at the heart of the American enterprise by saying, "We may look up to Armies for our Defence, but Virtue is our best Security. It is not possible that any State should long remain free, where Virtue is not supremely honored."[13] We can certainly argue about how to implement our moral obligations but that a moral vision, applicable to all humankind, has been endemic to the American experiment from the beginning is beyond dispute. The same is true today of a country like Israel, founded on a moral vision, and is the reason Israeli human rights violations weaken more than the country's security; they weaken its moral authority as well.

To ignore a moral vision, then, is to jeopardize more than other people's rights: it is to betray ourselves. It is to step into a sea of hypocrisy. It is to count our ideals as so much rubbish and our hearts as nothing but flesh. As the British Foreign Secretary Robin Cook put it, "Part of the national interest is being confident and proud of your values."[14] Nations rarely if ever act contrary to what they perceive, often incorrectly, to be in their national interests. The reasons to include morality in the calculation are not just out of loyalty to Kantian moral principle. In many ways they are the same reasons I rushed all those years ago to lift the old lady off the ice. To conform rhetoric to reality, action to image. To reassure ourselves that we are the kind of people we think and say we are. To avoid guilt, not only because it is an unpleasant sensation but also because it is a dangerous basis on which to make public policy. ("Realists" are hardly realistic when they underestimate the lengths to which people will go to avoid feeling guilty.) And to model the kind of behavior in the world that we want to see exhibited by others. As the only superpower at the moment, this last reason is far more than a trivial consideration for the United States. By contributing to international peacekeeping operations in Bosnia and Kosovo, for example, the United States has encouraged other countries (e.g., Australia in East Timor) to share responsibility for such undertakings elsewhere.

Contrary to what the "realists" have claimed, to include morality in our strategic decision-making is far more than a luxury. As Joseph S. Nye Jr., the dean of the Kennedy School of Government, has said: "A democratic definition of the national interest does not accept the distinction between a morality-based and an interest-based foreign policy. Moral values are simply intangible interests. Leaders and experts may point out the costs of indulging these values. But if an informed public disagrees, experts cannot deny the legitimacy of public opinion."[15]

A year or more ago John Bolton of the American Enterprise Institute and I appeared at a debate on human rights before a group of midlevel civil servants in Charlottesville, Virginia. Bolton argued the typical "realist" position that the national interests of the United States are rarely served by making human rights a priority in our foreign policy. I made the case, as I do in this book, that those interests are served far more frequently than we have recognized or allowed. I had not, however, had time to make the plea for morality that I lay out in this chapter.

Our audience was hardly a radical one and perhaps not even a progressive one, but when the question and answer period began, I sensed a certain frisson in the air toward both Bolton and me. Finally one gentleman raised his hand. "Frankly," he said, "both of you disgust me. Of course we have to be very cautious about sending our young people into danger. No, we don't want to be the world's police force. But you, Mr. Bolton, seem to think that we Americans can just sit still for thousands of people being slaughtered and not even *try* to do anything about it. Most of us couldn't live with ourselves if we took your attitude. And you, Dr. Schulz, should be ashamed of yourself. You're a human rights advocate and, although all of those good things you say about our national interest being served by human rights may be true, you've forgotten to tell us our moral duty as well. And if you don't do it, who will?" There was thunderous applause.

Bolton did not seem fazed by the incident, but I was both suitably chastised and delighted. Had this been a group of college students, I would not have been surprised by the reaction, but this was a group of bureaucrats. I remembered reading sometime in the middle of the Kosovo War of a comment by a retired postal worker in Kalispell, Montana, who put his opinion of the war quite straightforwardly when he said, "They [NATO] can't just let this guy [Milosovic] go around murdering people." I then resolved never to fail to say first, when arguing for human rights, that the most fundamental reason to support them is because every single one of us knows that if you are cut, you feel pain just as surely as I do. We respond on a human level to the agony in a young woman's face when she is threatened with genital mutilation or the dry terror in a young boy's mouth when, forced prematurely to abandon childhood for "military service," he is beaten within an inch of his life. These people are *real*. To fail to recognize that and to want to help them is to suffer above all else from a failure of imagination—a

failure to recognize that within the heart of every stranger lurks a reflection one's own.

So morality comes first, be it for principled or self-serving reasons.
But when morality is not enough—well, then, there is always the law.

In June 1862, following a hard-fought Civil War battle in Virginia, one
of Confederate general Stonewall Jackson's officers remarked to the
general that the Yankees had behaved with unusual valor and it seemed
a shame to take the lives of such brave foes. But Jackson was adamant:
"No," he said, "shoot them all. I do not wish them to be brave." Jackson
was a deeply religious man but, as one observer put it, he "found every
bit as much comfort in slaughter as he did in prayer."[16]

Because morality alone so often fails us and compassion can be a
short-lived phenomenon; because the victims of human rights violations are not always themselves such sympathetic characters; because,
as the theologian Reinhold Niebuhr reminded us so long ago, individuals may well succeed in acting morally but groups and nations are
captives of politics and power;[17] because human rights norms, to be
universally applicable, must be interpreted and applied equitably and
judiciously, or else we will never escape the charge that they are mere
devices of ethnocentrism—for these and other reasons the world has,
since Stonewall Jackson's time, elaborated a constellation of laws designed to outlaw humanitarian crimes and human rights violations.

From the first war crimes trial in 1474[18] to the first Geneva Convention in 1864 to the Nuremberg and Tokyo trials after World War II to
the covenants and conventions adopted under the auspices of the
United Nations to the statutes that guide such regional bodies as the
European Court of Human Rights to the War Crimes Tribunals for
Rwanda and the former Yugoslavia to Spain's indictment of General
Pinochet in 1998, which established at the very least that former heads
of state do not enjoy diplomatic immunity from prosecution for atrocities, international human rights law has developed a complex framework within which to assert that human rights principles apply to everybody, even trumping the sovereignty of the state.

That moral standards have been translated into legal code is enormously helpful—not only because it can be the instrument of justice
when states cooperate, but also because it guards against the kind of
corruption of heart that Stephen Spender discovered so disconcert-

ingly in himself. "When I saw photographs of children murdered by the Fascists [in Spain]," he wrote in *The God That Failed,*

> I felt furious pity. When the supporters of Franco talked of Red atrocities, I merely felt indignant that people could tell such lies. In the first case I saw corpses, in the second only words. . . . I gradually acquired a certain horror of the way in which my own mind worked. . . . It was clear to me that unless I cared about every murdered child impartially, I did not really care about children being murdered at all.[19]

But there are serious limits to the enforceability of international law or even recognition of its jurisdiction. It is not just that butchers ignore it at will or that there is in most instances no equivalent of the police, county sheriff, or U.S. marshal to see that judgments are executed. U.S. courts have, until recently, been notoriously reticent to allow a litigant to invoke international law in an American courtroom. The U.S. government has used its veto at the United Nations to block implementation of rulings of the World Court of which it disapproved, such as the court's finding it illegal for the United States to have mined the harbor at Managua, Nicaragua. The U.S. Congress has delayed ratification of human rights treaties for decades (it took forty years before the United States ratified the Convention Against Genocide); ratified them with reservations, insisting that provisions it didn't like do not apply to the United States; or failed to ratify them at all. Every country except the United States and Somalia, for example, has adopted the Convention on the Rights of the Child, but we have resisted its ratification because it would outlaw the execution of juvenile offenders. But then, as a spokesperson for my "friend" Senator Helms once said, "There's only one court that matters here. That's the U.S. Supreme Court. There's only one law that applies. That's the U.S. Constitution."[20]

The failure to honor international legal bodies and instruments often has a deleterious effect on U.S. interests. It is awfully hard, for example, to convince the Chinese to adopt the International Covenant on Civil and Political Rights without reservations when the United States so readily invokes exceptions to treaties it signs—but obviously the effectiveness of international human rights law is in large measure a political question, not only a legal one. If advocates of international human rights law are unable to muster popular support for ratifying treaties or recognizing jurisdiction; if the public and hence the politicians they elect do not see the disadvantages of holding the United States aloof from a global framework of law, then human rights standards remain little more than preachments on parchment.

It is understandable why human rights activists, lawyers or otherwise, resist making the case for human rights in terms of national interest— because we want to say that human rights norms apply at all times under every circumstance, not just when they are convenient or serve our own purposes. We want to say that human rights should be respected because they are both morally and legally justified. And of course they should be. Sometimes, as I have said, enforcing human rights standards may have nothing to do with our political or economic interests, and in some rare cases it may even contradict them. But if we fail to make the case that respecting human rights frequently serves us well and certainly far more often than the so-called "realists" would countenance, we risk never expanding the base of those who will support the cause.

By trusting solely in morality and often unenforceable law to make the grade, we risk relegating human rights, in the eyes of its detractors, to the realm of rhetoric, if not phantasm. We need to recognize that our sanctity will not be tarnished by a little toughness. We need to be unafraid to say to Americans, both to the public and to policy makers, that human rights are not only moral imperatives or legal commitments. We need to be unafraid to say, "Support human rights! They're good for us!"

Because in some cases the risks of ignoring human rights violations are enormous. Advancing human rights is by no means the only consideration policy makers must take into account when setting the course of our country. Preventing nuclear war must always take precedence, for one. Economic interests, terrorism, the distribution of resources, the state of the environment—all of these compete for attention. But all of these issues also turn out to have a human rights dimension in ways far more complex than the "realists" customarily credit. It is time to restore the balance, time for both the human rights community and its critics to adopt a "new realism."

On the wall of a dance studio in Arizona hangs a plaque containing words from the Zuni Indians: "We dance for pleasure . . . and the good of the city." I do not claim that adding our own interests to the reasons we should support human rights will *in and of itself* make the human rights cause a more popular one. I simply contend that we who care about our brothers' and sisters' rights should not be hesitant to acknowledge that we do so for many reasons, not the least of which is the good of the city.

2

"When the Birds No Longer Hide"

....

The Role of Human Rights in
Promoting Democracy and Peace

> Without democracy, you have no understanding of
> what is happening down below.
>
> —Mao Tse-Tung, Chairman
> of the People's Republic of China

THE FIVE-YEAR-OLD HAD VISITED her father every week in prison, and each time she had brought him a crayon drawing but each time the guards had confiscated it. "No pictures of people!" they shouted the first time, so then the little girl brought a picture of the family dog. "No pictures of animals!" the guards commanded, so the third time the child brought a picture of birds. But still no luck: "We said no animals—birds are animals." Finally the girl brought a picture of a forest and the guard let her through. The father, who was in prison for criticizing the regime, was overjoyed. "What a beautiful picture!" he exclaimed. "The trees, the branches, the leaves . . . and what are these round circles in the trees. Fruit?" "Shh," whispered the little girl fearfully. "Those are the eyes of the birds. They're hiding."[1]

This true story comes from the days of right-wing repression in Uruguay in the 1960s and 1970s, but it could just as well have been Argentina or Chile under the dictators, or South Africa under apartheid, or Cambodia under the Khmer Rouge, or Eastern Europe under the Communists, or Burma (Myanmar), Cuba, China, or Syria today.

More than twenty years ago when I first visited a police state, I remember waking up in Cold War Prague and thinking to myself, "I've got to be careful today what I say." It was an entirely new experience for one who had been raised in a democracy, albeit one that no doubt had tapped my phone during the Nixon years. My concern was not for myself but for my hosts. I knew full well not to implicate them in any way. I knew the government was listening. So trained were Czechs of that day to exercise caution that it was not until my host and I were on a West German train steaming toward Munich that we even broached the subject of politics. Even then in a private train compartment, my friend was wary. He spoke in hushed tones, almost in code. He glanced around warily although we two were the only ones there. What was so remarkable about this performance was that he was *defending* the Czech government!

That is one of the things repression does to people: it makes them *think* in unnatural ways. In Argentina under the dictatorial generals it was not illegal to wear a beard, but everyone was required to carry an ID card and beards were not permitted in ID photographs. In Uruguay the government was so fearful of Communists that a young pianist was forbidden from performing in public Ravel's "Concerto for Left Hand Alone." Of course, these are not the worst things that happen when human rights are abused. The worst things are the beatings, the killings, the torture, the disappearances. But unfair trials, intimidation of the press, harassment of political opponents, surveillance of dissidents, the outlawing of unions, and mistreatment of women—it all adds up to terror.

Occasionally, though, the truth breaks through. The novelist Milan Kundera begins *The Book of Laughter and Forgetting* by describing the day in February 1948, when the Czech Communist leader Klement Gottwald stood on a balcony to proclaim a new era in Czech history. It was a cold day and Gottwald's colleague, a man named Clementis who was standing beside him, took off his fur cap and placed it on Gottwald's head. The photograph of that historic event was distributed throughout Czechoslovakia and printed in schoolbooks. But four years later Comrade Clementis was convicted of treason and hanged. His image was airbrushed out of that picture. After that, Gottwald appeared to stand on the balcony alone. No more sign of Clementis. Except that his fur hat remains on the top of Gottwald's head.[2]

When the tanks rolled into Tiananmen Square in 1989, they made deep ruts in the pavement. The Chinese subsequently tried to smooth them out. Today, I'm told, when you approach the Square, if you listen carefully, you can still hear the *ta-bump ta-bump* beneath your tire tracks.

Occasionally the truth breaks through. But rarely by its own light alone. Somebody almost always has to help it along.

When Americans think of the great international human rights heroes of our day, we think primarily of those who have championed democracy: Nelson Mandela in South Africa, Vaclav Havel in the Czech Republic, the late Andrei Sakharov in the former Soviet Union. Among the things these brave souls had in common was a willingness to "speak truth to power," even at the risk of their own welfare.

Those who plead the case for freedom in the face of tyranny tend to be outspoken and stubborn—whether it be Aung San Suu Kyi, the leader of the opposition in Burma (Myanmar), who has been either under house arrest or subject to continual harassment since 1989 because the ruling generals find her so threatening; or Wei Jingsheng, the "Father of Chinese Democracy," finally released into exile to the United States in 1997 after seventeen years in prison for claiming that in addition to the four arenas Deng Xiaoping wanted to modernize (agriculture, defense, science, and technology), a fifth area was deserving of upgrade: namely, democracy. Suu chose not to return to England in 1998 to see her husband, Michael Aris, a fellow at Oxford, even though she knew he was dying, because she also knew the generals would never let her back into the country to continue to lead her people's struggle. And Wei sat in a prison cell year after year even though the authorities would love to have sent him out of the country years earlier. (I once asked Wei if he had ever received any of the thousands of letters Amnesty International supporters and others had sent him in prison over the years. He replied, "Not one. But I knew people were writing because my sister told me and because a guard once slipped up and said, 'Old Wei, you're getting a lot of mail lately,' and whenever the letters came, my treatment would improve, and when they slowed, I would be mistreated once again.")

One of the reasons these votaries of democracy are so obstinate is because they know that they are fighting for something considerably more far-reaching than democracy in the term's limited or formal sense, changes far more sweeping than just "free elections." They are fighting for the kind of society—popularly dubbed "civil society"—that makes free elections meaningful. They are fighting for the kind of nation in which differences are not dismissed but are trumped by recognition of a common humanity. ("I was born among human beings," a Hutu woman said following the Rwandan massacre in 1994 that killed up to one million people, most of them Tutsi. "I am a human being. I have loved. I was loved. And I lived peacefully with the Tutsi people.") In short, these human rights heroes are fighting not just for democracy but for that community of rights on which true democracy is predicated. As Suu herself put it, "Democracy [is] not merely . . . a form of government but . . . an integrated social and ideological system based on respect for the individual. . . . In other words . . . the basic human rights which would guarantee a tranquil, dignified existence free from want and fear."[3]

Such a community cannot be built on civil and political rights alone. A free press means little to a society teeming with illiteracy. The right not to be tortured is all well and good unless one is dying of hunger anyway. But similarly social and economic goods, as I argue in more detail in chapter 3, are in some significant measure dependent on civil and political freedoms. Literacy is of limited use if one's choice of literature is radically circumscribed and, as Cambridge University's Nobel Prize–winning economist Amartya Sen has demonstrated, there has never been a famine in a "functioning multiparty democracy." Indeed, Sen argues that "political freedoms (in the form of free speech and elections) help to promote economic security."[4]

What makes a "free election" meaningful, however, is not just that more than one candidate is permitted to run for office. What matters also is that the opposition be unintimidated and the media unbowed. What matters is that the courts and arbiters be independent; that voluntary associations of all stripes be allowed to flourish. What matters is that minority rights be respected and the mores of civil society be in place. A democracy is not the equivalent of a society that respects human rights. Human rights crimes flourish in many democracies, not least the United States, and more than one "democracy" has held a contested election on a playing field starkly tilted to favor one party or another or to frighten a segment of the population into acquiescence.

Charles Taylor is no doubt the only graduate of Bentley College in Waltham, Massachusetts, who is responsible for the slaughter of tens of thousands of people. The most notorious warlord in Liberia's six-year civil war (1990–96), Taylor employed child soldiers to whom he gave such nicknames as General Fuck Me Quick and Babykiller to carry out his military commands. Enriched by diamonds and gold looted from Liberia's mining areas and having eliminated many of his chief rivals, Taylor went "legitimate" in 1996 by running for president against eight or ten other candidates. He won a simple majority on the first ballot, having made it clear that, if he were *not* elected, he would take over the government by force. ("He killed my ma, he killed my pa, but I'm going to vote for him anyway" was one of his campaign slogans.[5]) The Liberian electorate made the rational decision to avoid further bloodshed even at the cost of having a murderous thug as their president. Both Liberians and I had good reason to think him a thug—Liberians because they had watched him operate for more than a decade, and I because he had threatened my life.

The circumstances of the threat were a telling mark of Taylor's commitment to democracy. I was in Liberia leading an Amnesty International research mission a few months before the election and was asked by a local newspaper opposed to Taylor's election if those who had committed human rights crimes should be allowed to run for president. I replied that Amnesty took no position on who should be allowed to run for political office but in general believed that anyone who had committed a crime should be swiftly brought to justice. The next day the newspaper displayed a banner headline, "War Criminals May Not Run for President" and attributed it to "Dr. Schulz of Amnesty International." Knowing that such a distorted news story would make our task in Liberia almost impossible, I went to the newspaper office, explained Amnesty's position again, and asked for a correction. "No problem," the editor assured me politely. But in the next day's paper appeared an even larger headline, " 'YOU WILL BE BOOKED!' " attributed again of course to me.

When my two Amnesty colleagues met a day or two later with the Taylor camp, my flight having long been scheduled to leave before the day of the meeting, Taylor's aide-de-camp, Milly Buchanan, had a message for me from the candidate: "Tell Dr. Schulz of Amnesty International that we are very concerned for his health. Tell him that we are concerned that *he* will be booked by a bullet if he should ever return to Liberia. And tell him to keep an eye on his back . . . even in New York." When I heard of this threat, I was both bemused and chastened. Bemused that Taylor felt so insecure as to need to bandy about threats of assassination against someone who surely had limited influence in Liberia but chastened to think that although I would probably not be spending my next vacation there, at least I could leave the country when I wanted. But that admittedly manipulative editor and other Taylor opponents had to live with such intimidation every day of their lives.

Democracy depends, then, not just on competition but on a commitment to play by the rules and allow everyone else to do likewise. This includes, not incidentally, allowing one's opponents to live free of fear for their lives. That is why Natasa Kandic, for example, is as much a "democracy" advocate as anyone else, even though in her country, Yugoslavia, unlike in Burma (Myanmar) or China, contested elections were permitted, even under Slobodan Milosovic, and some media dared to criticize the ruling regime.

Natasa walks with a limp and smokes incessantly. A Serb born in a village not far from Belgrade, she is now in her fifties and her eyes reflect an unexpungeable sorrow. She has, after all, seen too much. In 1971, as a sociology student in Belgrade, she led student strikes protesting the treatment of workers under Tito's regime. A few years later she helped establish the first Free University in Yugoslavia, a university not under the control of the authorities, where politics and economics could be debated without restraint. More than once the state security forces investigated her, especially after she wrote a book in 1980 deploring the loss of autonomy for the Yugoslavian province of Kosovo, a place sacred to Serbs for both religious and historical reasons although they made up fewer than 10 percent of its population.

It was not until after Milosovic came to power in 1987, however, that Natasa Kandic began to engage in systematic political action. Milosovic's dream of spreading a greater Serbia throughout the Balkans at the expense of Croats, Bosniacs, Albanians, and others and the war mobilization that his dream required were anathema to her. Perhaps it was because her father had been a war resister who had spent four years in prison during the Second World War, or perhaps it was because her husband, a noted film director, had concluded that there was no future in Yugoslavia and had left the country and his wife as well, or perhaps it was a native distrust of bullies. For whatever reason, in 1991 Natasa began organizing.

At first she organized little more than candlelight processionals. Then columns in the opposition daily, speaking out against the mobilization. Then larger demonstrations demanding a referendum to determine if the Serb people really wanted war. And then in May 1992 more than 150,000 people in the streets protested the shelling of Sarajevo. That year Natasa decided to do more than merely march. That year she founded the Humanitarian Law Center in Belgrade.

Over the next few years as the war in Bosnia grew worse, Natasa and the Law Center began to document the atrocities—the rapes, the beatings, the massacres—and report what they found to the International War Crimes Tribunal for the former Yugoslavia. Repeatedly she visited the victims and their families, gathering information that would eventually contribute to dozens of indictments, including that against Milosovic himself.

In 1999 when the Kosovo crisis came to a head, when NATO ordered its first air strikes, when the mass expulsions of Albanians began, there was only one place for Natasa Kandic to go. More than twenty times during the war this small Serbian woman, using any excuse she could think of, crossed Serb checkpoints into Kosovo from Belgrade, meeting with the survivors and gathering facts. During the bombardment she was the only human rights observer (other than the Kosovars themselves) inside that battered land.

Only once did the Serb guards become suspicious. On May 23, 1999, Natasa's car and driver were stopped near the border. They were found to be carrying an Albanian with them. For eight hours the Serb police interrogated her, accusing her of being a spy. Finally, to win her release, Natasa summoned immense bravado. That very day, she knew, the War Crimes Tribunal had announced the indictment of Milosovic, an indictment her own research had helped to bring about. "You have heard about the president?" she asked the guards. They acknowledged that they had. "And how would it look that the very day the president is indicted for human rights crimes, you arrest a human rights activist?" The logic, such as it was, prevailed and the guards let her go. "In this case," Natasa told me months later, "the truth [behind the indictment] really did set me free."[6]

Whether it be tracking the trials and treatment of Albanians in Serbian prisons or providing legal aid to Serb victims of police abuse, Natasa and the thirty-three employees of the Law Center struggle to provide the kind of protections from threat and arbitrary punishment without which a democracy cannot flourish. Elections or no, Milosovic managed for many years to remain in power by using the Serbian police and military to beat protestors, close down newspapers, terrorize minority ethnic groups, and in general short circuit all the elements of a civil society on which genuine democracy depends.[7] Natasa Kandic insisted that democracy in Yugoslavia could never be more than a shell game if it was not practiced in a context of respect for human rights, and her conviction turned out to be remarkably prescient. For when Milosovic finally fell in October 2000, he fell because the people—sick to death of the denial of their human rights, including the right to a clean and fair election—took to the streets and reclaimed their country.

Kandic, Wei, Suu, Sakharov, Havel, Mandela, and hundreds of others have earned America's respect for their determined pursuit of democracy and its attendant framework of rights. They also deserve our gratitude, for their sacrifices portend not only greater freedom for their own countries but more peace, justice, and stability for the world at large—and that cannot help but be good for the United States. This is obvious in a case like that of Natasa Kandic. Had her commitment to human rights in Kosovo been shared more broadly in Yugoslavia, NATO is unlikely to have undertaken its bombing there. But in a far more generic sense, human rights and a more peaceful world go hand in hand.

The philosopher Immanuel Kant may have taught that a moral act loses its moral potency when it is undertaken for pragmatic ends, but when it came to explaining why "republican governments" tend to adopt the moral virtue of refraining from making war on one another, Kant was only too happy to offer practical reasons. Such governments, he said in 1795 in *Perpetual Peace,* are restrained by constitutions that limit rulers from making war in a capricious fashion without consulta-

tion with those who will bear its burdens; they encourage an understanding of the rights of other citizens and nations; and their economic
ties with other republics make advantageous the peaceful resolution
of conflicts.[8]

Ever since Kant advanced the claim that what we would call constitutional democracies are less inclined to make war (at least on each
other) than authoritarian states, scholars and theoreticians have been
arguing the case. But with the end of the Cold War, the argument has
become particularly intense, with more than a hundred books and articles on the topic appearing in the 1990s alone. What has made the debate especially potent is that with the disappearance of Communism as
a global Beelzebub around whose eradication our foreign policy might
be organized, the promotion of democracy has been seen by some as an
appealing principle in which to anchor U.S. international relations. If
it could be shown that the advance of democracy simultaneously increased the odds of a world at peace, how could anyone doubt the wisdom of its pursuit?

Critics certainly have doubted this wisdom, however, or at least they
have doubted that promoting democracy should stand at the center of
U.S. foreign policy. Those doubts have tended to take one of three
sometimes overlapping forms: (1) a dispute largely among academics
about whether democracies do indeed tend to be more pacific and if so,
under what circumstances and why; (2) a contention primarily by foreign policy "realists" that democracy really doesn't buy us all that its
enthusiasts think it does, and hence that making it the centerpiece of
foreign policy may jeopardize other critical national interests; and (3) a
commercialist argument that democracy is a great goal but that the
best way to reach it, like a crab approaching a mudbank, is sideways or
indirectly through trade and investment. It is worth examining all
three forms in this book, the third of which will be treated in chapter 3,
for all three bear on the relationship between human rights and Americans' own interests.

Whenever I am in London, I pick up *The Times* because I love to read
the obituaries. Those obituaries almost always contain one line that
says everything I need to know about the deceased. My favorite was of
Sir Vincent Wigglesworth, who died at age ninety-four able to claim
that he was the world's leading authority on insect excreta. *The Times*

described him as "a man of exceptional singleness of purpose" and then offered this telling quote from Sir Vincent: "I chose to work on insect excreta for sixty-six years and that has made all the difference."[9]

The scholars who study whether democracy makes nations less warlike would aver, I suspect, that their work has far more profound consequences than Sir Vincent's. After all, if we can show, as the subtitle of one work has it, that "democracy is a method of nonviolence,"[10] then the United States has but to help spread democracy to guarantee a world free of conflict, and the "realist" conviction that war is an inevitable part of relations between nations will have been proven overly pessimistic, if not unfounded.

Over the past three decades researchers have examined international relations going back at least as far as 1789. They have analyzed dozens of wars and a variety of definitions of democracy. They have done cross-cultural comparisons between the Marshall Islands in 1875 with a paramount chief determined by lineage and the Cuna Indians in Panama around 1927 who were governed by a less hierarchical system of elected village chiefs. One study even claimed that civil wars could be predicted by monitoring weapons stocks on the Dow Aerospace and Defense Index! Out of all of this investigation, a widespread, if not unanimous, consensus seems to have emerged that (1) democracies do indeed tend overwhelmingly not to go to war with other democracies, but (2) democracies are nonetheless almost as war-prone as anyone else when it comes to conflict with other types of states.[11] For our purposes this mixed conclusion is certainly not without its significance, for even if only the first proposition is true, that is good news for the United States and its democratic allies. It means that young American men and women are unlikely to be sent to war in any context in which democratic values are at work.

That is one reason it surely behooves the United States to engage as robustly with a potential military adversary like China over the denial of democracy in that country as we do over our commercial interests. For even if greater economic ties increase the likelihood of peaceful future relations (and of course Kant himself agreed they would), the practice of democracy can hardly be dismissed as an unimportant variable in determining how that bilateral future plays itself out. And it is not only bilaterally that China's lack of democracy could well affect us, for Taiwan's former president, Lee Teng-hui, has said that "the authoritarian nature of the [Chinese] communist regime is the key factor alienating the people of Taiwan from the Chinese mainland,"[12] and Taiwan is the principal flashpoint over which the United States and China might come to blows in the future.

Not every conflict in the world need involve the United States, of course. But to discount this country's interest in advancing democracy in any place where we might conceivably become involved militarily (and at least indirectly through the United Nations, NATO, or other international peacekeeping operations, that appears to be just about anywhere) is either to take a huge gamble with American lives or to ignore two hundred years of world history. This reality is borne out by a quick survey of those locales that *have* seen U.S. military action since the end of the Cold War. Among Iraq, Somalia, and Haiti, not one witnessed a baby-kissing politician, a campaign finance scandal, or a negative attack ad because not one was a practicing democracy when the United States intervened.

We Americans are accustomed to disparaging politicians, and many of them deserve it, such as the Massachusetts Democrat who warned on statewide radio one night that "the Republican octopus is spreading its testicles from one end of the Commonwealth to the other." But we rarely stop to reflect that for all of its faults, "politics" as we understand it, in terms of deals and trade-offs and compromises, is part of what helps keep us free and stable. The late political scientist T. V. Smith is once said to have observed that "it is the job of the politician to keep the saints and their respective followers from killing each other over matters of moral principle." But in Iraq, Somalia, Haiti, and Kosovo it was the "politicians" who were doing the killing.

What about Kosovo, though? Is that an exception to the rule? After all, Kosovars were permitted to vote in Yugoslavian elections. And although it is encouraging that democracies don't seem to fight with other democracies, why are they as aggressive as other states on other fronts? Formal democracy alone is clearly not enough to guarantee a peaceful world. As one team of scholars put it, "Governments that are not freely elected have no monopoly on unnecessary and aggressive wars."[13] Could something more complex be going on here than immediately meets the eye?

Just because "the people" have a voice in whether a country goes to war does not mean they will necessarily choose a more pacific path.

For example, war fever pushed President William McKinley into the Spanish-American War in 1898 against his better judgment. It is fairly certain today that were democracy to steal over Arab countries in the Middle East, and certain elements bent on Israel's destruction were to come to power in free and popular elections, Israel's life would be far more difficult than it currently is, with kings in Jordan and Saudi Arabia, and a president in Egypt who holds onto office by arresting his opponents.[14] Which is not to disparage attempts to democratize those countries but only to underscore that although they may not fight among themselves, democracies are not immune to warmongering. After all, they are made up of human beings with all of our attendant pride, swagger, fear, prejudice, and bellicosity.

But if formal democracy alone is not enough to guarantee the peaceful resolution of conflicts, what might increase the odds?

Among the most respected "realists" writing today about U.S. foreign policy is Fareed Zakaria, the managing editor of the distinguished journal *Foreign Affairs.* Zakaria is well known for an essay he published in that magazine in 1997 called "The Rise of Illiberal Democracy." He pointed out that although 118 of the world's 193 countries are democratic, this is hardly cause for unfettered celebration because in too many cases "of what happens *after* the [free] elections." What happens far too often, Zakaria says, is that democratically elected leaders, having gotten themselves in office, proceed to sow unanticipated mischief, from ruling by presidential decree, as did Carlos Menem in Argentina or Alberto Fujimori in Peru, to restricting freedom of speech and assembly, as has the Iranian Parliament, to assuming near dictatorial control, as in the case of President Alyaksandr Lukashenka in Belarus. Zakaria calls such behavior the sign of an "illiberal democracy" and claims that 50 percent of "democratizing" countries—that is, countries that are in the process of throwing off authoritarianism and becoming democratic—are illiberal. What is lacking in such places is not free elections but a commitment to what Zakaria refers to as "constitutional liberalism", which he defines as "the tradition . . . that seeks to protect an individual's autonomy and dignity against coercion, whatever the source—state, church or society." It is dangerous to promote democracy in the narrow sense without first having inculcated constitutional liberalism, he says. The "democratic peace"—the theory that democracies don't fight or don't fight each other—"is actually the liberal peace."[15]

Zakaria's perspective builds on that of two other analysts, Edward D. Mansfield and Jack Snyder, who, writing two years earlier in *Foreign Affairs,* warned against making the promotion of democracy a "pillar of [U.S.] foreign policy." Having reviewed wars that took place between 1811 and 1980, Mansfield and Snyder concluded that countries that are in *transition* to democracy are more likely to go to war, if rarely against each other, than either mature democracies or even autocratic states. They attributed this to many causes, chief among them the tendency of newly elected regimes to build support for themselves by appealing to nationalist sentiments that can easily, in the face of an immature system of governance, get out of hand and lead to hostilities. Newly democratic states, lacking experience with managing diversity and absent established institutions, can often fall prey to such dangers as weak leadership structures, displaced power elites who are eager to reclaim authority, and the temptation to "shore up . . . prestige at home by seeking victories abroad."[16]

Both of these theories help explain why the war in Kosovo is appropriately linked with Iraq, Somalia, and Haiti as nondemocratic contexts in which the United States has found itself militarily involved, despite the fact that Kosovars could vote in Yugoslavian elections. For Yugoslavia was clearly an "illiberal democracy" in Zakaria's terms and, whether in transition to greater democracy or greater repression, certainly exhibited many of the characteristics, beginning with rampant nationalism, that Mansfield and Snyder associate with aggression.

But if Zakaria, Mansfield, and Snyder—"realists" all—point to the limits and dangers of promoting democracy, what do they recommend as a cure? They each endorse one form or another of the commercialist argument, but Zakaria goes on to suggest that we promote "constitutionalism". He describes this as "a complicated system of checks and balances designed to prevent the accumulation of power and the abuse of office" involving "not . . . simply . . . a list of rights but . . . a system in which government will not violate those rights."[17]

Mansfield and Snyder take a similar tack. They say, "The cure is probably more democracy, not less . . . the rule seems to be: go fully democratic or don't go at all". They suggest that in addition to guaranteeing that those who have held power in the past, especially the military, "not wind up in jail if they relinquish power," we should take the following as a top priority:

> Creating a free, competitive and responsible marketplace of ideas. . . . Pluralism is not enough. Without a level playing field, pluralism simply creates the incentive and the opportunity for privileged groups to propound self-serving myths, which historically have often taken a nationalist turn. . . . Mythmaking should be held up to the utmost scrutiny by aggressive journalists. . . . Promoting this kind of journalistic infrastructure is probably the most highly leveraged investment the West can make in a peaceful democratic transition.[18]

What is striking about both of these analyses is that although they start off warning that the United States should be wary about taking the pursuit of democracy around the world as a linchpin of our foreign relations, they end up concluding that a *human rights regimen* can obviate the pitfalls. They end up, in other words, where the great human rights champions of democracy have been all along—with the conviction that democracy requires more than free elections; it also requires a culture of respect for fundamental human rights. For what is Zakaria's "constitutionalism" but a name for Suu's "social and ideological system based on respect for the individual". What is Mansfield and Snyder's call for "full democracy" and a "marketplace of ideas" but a way to denote civil and political liberties? The bottom line is that even based on a "realist" analysis of the relationship between peace and democracy, the conclusion is inescapable that the more respect for human rights we can help engender in a country, the less likely that country is to go to war with us or other like communities.

Of course this is not to say that human rights are the only variable in determining what will predispose a country to war. Trade, territory, plunder, and pride—these and many other interests come into play. That a country encases its democratic practices in a regimen of respect for human rights is no absolute warrant that it will refrain from aggression, but it certainly increases the odds. That alone would make the promotion of democratic communities of rights good for the United States—at least for any American who wants to minimize the chances that his or her child will have to go to war or who fears nuclear conflict in the world.

But wasn't the Kosovo War ostensibly fought to protect human rights? If we make the promotion of human rights around the world a major goal, aren't we likely to entangle ourselves in *more* military conflicts rather than fewer? To encourage democratic communities of rights is not to say by any means that the United States or the West or NATO or even the United Nations is obligated to intervene militarily every time it encounters a country that is committing serious violations of human rights standards. There are many different forms of pressure that can be brought to bear on errant governments short of that, as I examine in chapter 8. Not only would such widespread use of so-called humanitarian intervention be unlikely, but all military action carries with it the danger that it will itself be the vehicle of further human rights violations, perhaps even worse ones than those it was designed to stop.

There is one approach, however, that promises to reduce the number of instances in which military intervention would even need to be contemplated for human rights reasons. It is based on a very simple maxim we rely on every day to conduct our ordinary lives: If you commit a crime, you should do the time. The straightforward principle that society ought to hold criminals accountable for their acts hardly stirs much controversy . . . until it is applied to some of the world's most notorious killers.

I have a lot of respect for Jimmy Carter. I once sat in a meeting he held with a group of business CEOs on one side of the table and a group of religious leaders on the other. The meeting was designed to determine how the two communities could work more cooperatively together. The former president started off by turning to the business leaders and saying in his quiet, steely way, "You in the business community don't really care about poverty in America. If you did, you could end it." And then he stopped. The business folks were nonplussed. We on the religious side did our best to remain passive of face and keep in mind the Apostle Peter's advice that "God resisteth the proud and giveth grace to the humble." Then Carter turned to our side of the table: "And you religious leaders should be even more deeply ashamed. You have far more resources than you allow. You don't care very much about truly helping the poor either." I have a lot of admiration for an equal opportunity insulter.

In one respect I think Jimmy Carter is shortsighted, however. When he negotiated the return of President Aristide to Haiti in 1993, he assured General Raoul Cedras, whose regime had been responsible for hundreds of deaths and thousands of rapes in that tattered country, that Cedras would be whisked away to Panama, where he still lives today, and would suffer no ill consequences. I know, from a subsequent conversation with Carter, that with U.S. jets poised to bomb Haiti within the hour, he believed this plan was the only way to avert bloodshed: get Cedras out and Aristide in. And he may well have been right. Recall that Mansfield and Snyder make it their first rule for preserving new democracies that you assure old leaders, particularly military ones, "that they will not wind up in jail if they relinquish power." And dozens of such leaders have not been imprisoned: Idi Amin, for example, responsible for massive butchery in Uganda in the 1970s, struts the streets of Riyadh, Saudi Arabia, today a free man. Cedras's predecessor, Baby Doc Duvalier, a petty but bloodthirsty tyrant, still lives untouched by the law in France. Even one of the greatest criminals of the modern era, the Khmer Rouge's Pol Pot, managed to die an old man in his bed (although some believe his Khmer Rouge rivals may have killed him there).

Most human rights crimes take place because political or military leaders encourage them, not because a populace rises up in a spontaneous burst of genocidal fury, latent though that fury may be. Somebody with power is responsible for those crimes. That was true in Rwanda in 1994 and in Bosnia in 1995 and in nearly every other instance of widespread violations of human rights. But how many such leaders do we allow to go scot-free before applying the common wisdom that if you commit a crime, you do the time? If we started holding leaders responsible *in a consistent fashion* for human rights crimes committed against innocent populations even within their own countries, how long would it be before other would-be tyrants got the message?

Over the past few years the world has begun to glimpse answers to these questions. In 1993 the International War Crimes Tribunal for the Former Yugoslavia was established, the first such body since the Nuremberg and Tokyo trials and the first ever to be established *during* rather than after a conflict and by somebody other than the victors. In its first six years the Tribunal indicted seventy suspects, took thirty-nine into custody, tried fourteen, and convicted all but one. In 1995 a similar tribunal began its work on the genocide in Rwanda. In 1998, 120 nations voted to approve a treaty to establish a permanent International Criminal Court to make these kind of ad hoc tribunals superfluous. Also in that year the former dictator of Chile, Augusto Pinochet, was taken into custody by the British in response to a warrant issued by a Spanish prosecutor for crimes against humanity, torture, and hostage taking—despite objections by former British Prime Minister Margaret Thatcher, among other leaders, that such action violated Chile's national sovereignty. And in 1999, NATO fought a war in Kosovo prompted in good measure by the execution and mass displacement of tens of thousands of citizens, notwithstanding the fact that Kosovo was still a legal part of Yugoslavia.

A few weeks after Slobodan Milosovic abandoned Kosovo in exchange for a cease-fire, the province of East Timor in Indonesia voted for independence and then erupted in bloodshed, as militias organized by the Indonesian military took revenge on the citizenry. But then a funny thing happened on the way to Timorese independence. Western powers, including the United States, threatened the Indonesian government with economic penalties if the militias were not reigned in. Mary Robinson, the U.N. High Commissioner for Human Rights, extracted an agreement from Jakarta for an investigation of military abuses in East Timor that might well lead, she said, to war crimes trials. "This is really scary for [the Indonesians]," one expert was quoted as saying. "Mary Robinson has raised the specter that for the first time ever—ever—the Indonesian military might be [held] accountable for its deeds."[19] In the face of these pressures the Indonesian military called off the assaults and turned over the province to an international peacekeeping force. Economic pressure played its part without question, but the possibility that impunity might no longer be automatically granted did too. Would Robinson's threats have been credible absent the developments of the previous six years? Would she even have been in a position to make them had it not been for the Tribunals, the International Criminal Court, Pinochet, and Kosovo?

No responsible observer would argue that this recent history promises to banish massive human rights violations from the globe. If the world—over the objections of China, Russia, and the United States—*does* manage to establish a permanent International Criminal Court, that would not put an end to abuses on the international stage any more than the enforcement of our domestic laws against theft or assault or murder puts an end to those practices here in the United States. Yet who among us would argue that, simply because our laws are unevenly enforced or some criminals get away with their crimes, we should give up the prosecution of those laws altogether? It is a great irony that some of those most vociferous in their calls for tough criminal standards and strict law enforcement in the United States go weak in the knees when it comes to miscreants in business suits and military uniforms elsewhere in the world.

Indeed, we may have seen in Kosovo exactly what can happen if laws *do* go unenforced. For although the War Crimes Tribunal for the Former Yugoslavia indicted Bosnian Serb leader Radovan Karadzic and Bosnian Serb general Ratko Mladic and asked that they be taken into custody by international forces (IFOR) stationed in Bosnia, neither man has yet been apprehended, even though for at least many months the troops knew exactly where to locate them. The two escaped arrest because Western leaders feared a violent backlash against IFOR—a concern that, were it cited by police in Detroit, Michigan, to justify a failure to take an indicted murderer into custody from a known hideout, would subject them to endless ridicule, if not charges of endangering the public for fear of their own safety. The refusal to pick up Karadzic and Mladic may well have endangered the world, for their unbridled freedom—even in the face of international indictment and opprobrium—sent a very clear message to Slobodan Milosovic as he toyed with what to do in Kosovo, that he could do just about anything he wanted with those largely helpless people—as in fact he and Karadzic and Mladic had done with the Bosnians—and that he would suffer no penalty. Such a message surely encouraged his adventurism.

If you believe that it is in the best interests of the United States to avoid war whenever it can, it makes sense to support a firm, consistent enforcement of international efforts to establish the rule of law as it applies to those who are suspected of human rights crimes. This is why the decision of the United States not to support the creation of the International Criminal Court for fear that American troops serving abroad may be subjected to unfair prosecution is so myopic. Not only are there innumerable safeguards built into the proposed International Court to guard against politically motivated prosecutions,[20] but it is breathtaking to think that it is in the national interest of the United

States to isolate itself from an unprecedented global attempt to hold human rights criminals accountable for their crimes—and to do so because we are afraid to subject ourselves to the same scrutiny that are Britain, France, Germany, and 117 other countries. What better way than that to lend credibility to claims by the likes of Saddam Hussein that the United States plays by one set of rules for itself while holding other countries to a different set? What better way to weaken the entire scaffolding of international law, to say nothing of our moral authority? Our economic and military might are powerful safeguards of American security, but how much stronger would we be if they were supplemented by a regimen for enforcing the rule of law? Perhaps the most important question is, How many American lives will ultimately be saved if we have an effective mechanism in place for bringing the world's tyrants to justice?

I cannot prove that the old mantra "no peace without justice" is true in every case. Certainly many human rights advocates believe it is. Justice Richard Goldstone, the distinguished former prosecutor of the War Crimes Tribunal, put it this way: "There are just too many victims who can't be ignored. If you sweep [human rights crimes] under the rug, you'll have a cancer in your society. If individuals are not brought to justice, then there is collective guilt. The victims and their survivors cry out for justice against a group."[21] And that just leads to more recrimination, more violence, and more injustice.

But sometimes a society decides to take a different route—as did Chile with its National Commission for Truth and Reconciliation following Pinochet's regime, a commission whose informal slogan was "the whole truth and as much justice as possible"—a recognition that at that point in Chilean history there were limits to what the military would permit.[22] Sometimes greater stability appears to flow from limiting legal action against those guilty of past crimes, as in South Africa and many countries in eastern Europe. If a democratic community of rights chooses that option, so be it.

But the point is people must choose the option and choose it freely. The problem with the Chilean Commission was that its prerogatives were not determined fully free of coercion. Pinochet and his cohorts had insisted that they be given amnesties for their crimes before they were willing to leave office and made it quite clear that they would take back power if they were prosecuted afterward. That alone made Pinochet fair game for international indictment. Reconciliation may be fine for those who can choose it freely, but international structures of accountability are designed for those who cannot.

Would it have been better for Jimmy Carter not to have promised Raoul Cedras safe passage in exchange for his cession of power? How much easier it would have made Carter's decision if he could have told Cedras, "I'm sorry, but I don't have the power to make that promise. As you know, we now have a functioning International Criminal Court, and it may decide to prosecute you." Certainly it is possible that such an answer might have resulted in U.S. bombs being dropped on Haiti and that would have been regrettable. But we have gone the route of impunity for thousands of years of human history, and in this century alone more than 150 million people have paid for it with their lives. How much worse off could our world possibly be if we began systematically to practice accountability? Despite all of the uncertainties and imperfections that would inevitably come with it, it would surely be in our interests to try.

"I've simply *got* to have new toilet paper," my colleague told her husband one night in the presumed privacy of their hotel room in Cluj-Napoca, Romania. "The woodchips in these rolls are doing me damage! I've got to see if we can get some Western toilet paper somewhere tomorrow."

It was 1987 and we were paying an official visit to our co-religionists in Romania, all of whom were ethnic Hungarians based in the country's northwestern quadrant, the land of lore and legend known as Transylvania. Although Prince Vlad Dracul, popularly dubbed by his contemporaries Vlad the Impaler, on whom Bram Stoker's literary character was based, had died in 1476, the dictator Nicolae Ceausescu was still very much alive and in power in Romania. He exerted his maniacal control over an apparently benumbed population and made life for religious groups in general and the two million ethnic Hungarians in particular inordinately difficult. His regime regularly confiscated church property, refused to import Bibles, denied exit visas to citizens, required reports of every contact with a foreigner, required every typewriter in the country to be registered with the government, destroyed villages, imprisoned dissidents, and spied on everyone, not least of all visitors from overseas.

"I've simply *got* to have new toilet paper," my colleague had said in the presumed privacy of her quarters. The next day in her room, but not in mine next door, there was new, Western, woodchip-free toilet paper. "I've simply *got* to have a New York strip steak," I said hopefully that night into my lightbulb, but strip steaks were not on the menu.

Yet despite Ceausescu's twenty-four-year reign of repression, he fell in 1989, in an instant. The spark was a handsome young ethnic Hungarian minister in the Transylvanian city of Timisoara named Laszlo Tokes, who had had enough of intimidation and oppression. When ordered to abandon his ministerial post, Tokes had simply refused. His obstinacy prompted demonstrations on his behalf. Ceausescu overreacted by ordering soldiers into the Timisoara streets; students in Bucharest poured out of their dormitories; Ceausescu's political enemies seized the opportunity to exploit the chaos; the army abandoned the government; Ceausescu fled the capital; and shortly afterward he and his wife were captured and executed. I was back in Romania two weeks after Ceausescu and his regime fell. "His were the fiercest secret police in Eastern Europe," the poet Mircea Dinescu told me, "and yet the dictator lost his courage in only one day."

The Romanian revolution reminds us of lessons we seem constantly to forget: that regimes which rely on total control of a populace may look sturdy from the outside but are often far more fragile than they appear; that human rights violations against ethnic minorities and religious groups (or, in other contexts, against women or sexual minorities) are often early warning signs of that fragility; and that although granting every legitimate social group a voice and a share of power may make life more complicated for a government, paradoxically it is sometimes the only thing that will preserve it.

I first met Laszlo Tokes in the heat of the revolution's aftermath in 1990. He was still smarting from years of adversity and entirely uncertain about the future. Many of Romania's new leaders were former Ceausescu associates; the dreaded Securitate secret police were still rumored to be operating. (Indeed, only a short while later Tokes was involved in a mysterious auto accident on a visit to Budapest that nearly cost him his life.) But today the Romanian government, although far from perfect, is more open than it has ever been before. Today, when I visit Tokes, he is, although still critical of Romania's rulers, playing an important role in winning and preserving rights for religious groups (he is bishop of the Reformed Church) and ethnic minorities. I don't know that the continued state terror under Ceausescu would ever have resulted in massive violence, such as in Bosnia in 1992 through 1995, or in a violent uprising among ethnic Hungarians, such as in Nigeria's Biafran War in 1968 through 1970. But I do know that Romania is a considerably more stable state today, with all of its cacophonous voices and partisan politics, than it ever was under dictatorship.

More democracy does not always equal more stability any more than more democracy automatically equals more peace. In the long run, however, democratic communities of rights do in fact tend to be more "dynamically stable" than autocracies. It is not all that hard to see why.

Safety Valves

Financier George Soros, who has backed up a philosophical commitment to what he calls "open societies" with enormous financial resources, says, "Freedom is like the air: people struggle for it only when they are deprived of it."[23] The post–Cold War period has witnessed an explosion of ethnic and tribal animosity. Many of the globe's worst conflicts have derived from efforts on the part of groups in power to wipe out other groups or at least to discourage those groups from claiming some of that power, reinforcing their own identities or seceding from the state. Much attention has rightly focused on the most violent of these clashes, but there are also examples of states—India and South Africa are two—that have managed largely to accommodate an enormous diversity by providing democratic structures (representative parliaments, a free press, an independent judiciary, a vibrant nongovernmental community, etc.) through which minorities may voice their claims, celebrate their cultures, and resolve their grievances.

Binda Prasad, for example, a lower-caste landless laborer in India, was elected village chief under a constitutional arrangement that guarantees a portion of such positions to the so-called scheduled castes. When Prasad convened his first village meeting, a man from a higher caste yanked him from his chair of honor and administered a terrible beating. Prasad and his allies could have festered in fury or even organized retaliation, but instead they went to the local leaders of their political party, lodged a complaint, and the party pressed local authorities to jail the culprit.[24]

As one scholar of social violence has said, "An important lesson for the management of ethnic [or, I would add, religious, geographic or economic] conflict is that no salient group should be prohibited from a share of effective power."[25] Without that, extremism flourishes, especially where wide income disparities and massive poverty accompany the denial of liberty. As American reformer Saul Alinsky once observed, "Last guys don't finish nice."

This is not to say that all separatist demands can be resolved nonviolently or that a democratic community of rights may not sometimes need to defend itself with arms against dissident factions. But such communities rarely make it government policy to engage in gratuitous domestic violence against groups of their citizens.[26] By providing effective safety valves for equitable, nonviolent conflict resolution, such societies set expectations, create mores, build confidence, extend trust, and some would say, "effectively co-opt" their citizens into more harmonious and stable patterns of living.

Corruption

I lived in Chicago in the early 1970s, when it seemed as if any city or county official not on the take deserved to be fired for failing to be industrious. Democracy and human rights are no guarantors of honest officials. Conversely, not every country that scores well on the independent watchdog organization Transparency International's (TI's) Perception of Corruption index respects human rights, Singapore being the best example. But still, the odds are pretty good that any government or private corporation that escapes careful scrutiny for lack of a free press or an impartial court system or unimpeded monitors or respect for the rule of law—for lack, in other words, of the safeguards that come with a vital civil society—is likely to be tempted by corruption.

We can measure this by comparing the scores countries receive from Freedom House on their deference to political rights and civil liberties with where they fall on TI's index. With the exception of Singapore, every one of the top-ten nations perceived to be least corrupt scores a perfect 1 for freedom (on a scale of 1 to 7, where the lower the score, the better). Of the ten countries perceived most corrupt, the average is 3.9.[27] And although corruption alone may not destabilize a country, it is a powerful contributor, for it undermines trust in government, taints the political system, and speeds economic decay by removing investment incentives for private enterprise.

Rule of Law

Corruption is but one by-product of a system in which respect for the rule of law is absent. "The rule of law" refers to a society's willingness to adopt laws that are broadly consistent with international human rights standards and *to enforce them equitably*. This requires such things as due-process procedures, evenhanded implementation of contracts, court systems free of political bias, and so on. If citizens come to believe that they cannot rely on equitable enforcement of laws, they are far more likely to take the law into their own hands or to turn to extralegal sources of power (paramilitaries, guerrillas, religious or ideological extremists, criminal elements) to protect themselves or meet their needs.

When Mahathir Mohamad, the prime minister of Malaysia, accused his former deputy and handpicked successor, Anwar Ibrahim, of corruption and sodomy in 1998 in a move that was widely perceived to be politically motivated, a trial ensued that fell far below international legal standards. One Malaysian political commentator observed of the events, "I don't like Anwar [the deputy]; I think he's just as much a rascal as the others . . . [but] I support him because I don't want to see my deputy prime minister treated this way. If this can happen to my deputy prime minister, it can happen to me, and there'll be nobody to cry for me."[28] The breakdown or misuse of law lays the groundwork for unrest, upheaval, and terrorism.

Feedback Loops

Chairman Mao was no democrat, but he well understood the system's strengths. "Without democracy," Mao observed,

> you have no understanding of what is happening down below; the situation will be unclear; you will be unable to collect sufficient opinions from all sides; there can be no communication between top and bottom; top-level organs of leadership will depend on one-sided and

incorrect material to decide issues, thus you will find it difficult to avoid being subjectivist.[29]

Thomas Jefferson, who defended a free press by saying that it would be better to have a nation with newspapers and no government rather than a government and no newspapers, couldn't have explained it better. One of the best ways to keep a government stable (or a party in power) is to anticipate the public's needs and opinions.

Even Lenin, when contemplating his vicious campaign against the Russian Church, wrote to V. M. Molotov that such a campaign "must be carried out . . . in the briefest possible time because the masses will not tolerate prolonged application of brutality."[30] Lenin had little to worry about of course, because such feedback loops don't work if people are afraid to speak the truth or if the institutions that provide that feedback—media, political opposition, advocacy groups, universities—are tainted or cowed. A government out of touch with its people will not only make bad ("subjectivist") decisions; it will also seed the ground for its own overthrow. By failing utterly to understand and communicate with his people, "the Shah [of Iran]," says one expert on that country, "was watering [Ayatollah] Khomeini like a slow-growing tree."[31] And when the tree reached its full height, it was not only Iran on whom it cast its shadow. Perhaps we may take some comfort in the fact that it is now Khomeini's successors, clerics who would prevent young people from clapping and cheering at concerts, who may be watering a revolution.

That autocracies tend in the long run to be unstable is hardly news to anyone who has heard of Somoza of Nicaragua, Papadopoulos of Greece, the immutable Soviet empire, or Suharto of Indonesia, to name but a few. There are certainly apparent exceptions—Castro of Cuba, Mugabe of Zimbabwe, Mahathir of Malaysia, the Chinese—but perhaps Chinese prime minister Zhou Enlai's response to a question he was asked in the 1960s about whether the French Revolution had been a success is the wisest course to follow in assessing whether these will remain exceptions. "I'm sorry," Zhou then responded. "It's too early to tell."

What is indisputably true, however, is that whenever the United States allies itself or its interests with a regime that disparages democracy and human rights, it takes a huge risk: of residual resentment in future years, of being aligned with a government whose repression breeds terrorism that could be redirected at the United States, of striking deals with those most likely to renege on commitments.

On a single page in a recent edition of the *New York Times*, these dangers were perfectly illustrated in three stories related to U.S. actions past, present, and future. At the top was a story about how angry the Greeks were at the United States for NATO's bombardment of their Orthodox Serb brothers and sisters in the Kosovo War, an anger reinforced for many Greeks by memory of U.S. support for the Greek junta that toppled a democratic government in 1967. Faced with widespread demonstrations on his visit to Athens in 1999, President Clinton quite appropriately apologized for our 1967 action.[32]

The story in the middle of the page concerned the president's 1999 visit to Turkey, an important strategic ally of the United States in the Middle East, which has long been guilty of profound human rights violations, particularly against its Kurdish minority. Although Turkey has been denied entrance to the European Union several times because of its record, the United States has often been reticent to criticize it. Gradually it has become clearer, however, that Turkey's stability is dependent in part on closer ties to Europe and a cleaner human rights slate at home. So on this particular visit Clinton shunned military leaders, met with human rights activists despised by the Turkish government, and was eloquent in his advocacy of greater liberties.[33] All this is praiseworthy, but whether it has come too late is hard to tell. How much simpler and more effective it would have been for the United States to be clear in the first place.

The final *New York Times* story concerned the proposed pipeline to carry Caspian Sea oil and natural gas from Kazakhstan and perhaps Turkmenistan across Azerbaijan, Georgia, and Turkey to markets in the West.[34] The U.S. and Western oil companies would have an enormous investment in the futures of those countries if the pipeline is ever built, but each is plagued by abuses of their citizens' human rights. In Kazakhstan, opposition leaders have been thrown into jail. In Turkmenistan a critic of the government who aired his views on the U.S.-sponsored Radio Liberty was beaten so severely he was unable to walk. In Azerbaijan a twelve-year-old boy was tortured to extract information about his mother, who had spoken up against a friend's illegal detention. Don't we realize that mistreatment like that breeds festering resentment in a population and instability in a political system? When those systems have tarnished the means for a democratic transition of power from one political leader to the next, as is true in many of these states, the odds of rattling uncertainty, if not political chaos, are increased. All of this hardly invites confidence in the long-term security of the pipeline. How critical that as the United States evaluates its material interests in pipeline countries, it factors in how best to influence their treatment of their own citizens and their experience with democracy.

How the United States influences other countries' human rights practices is enormously complex. Human rights are but one of many aspects of our international relationships. But rights are far more entangled in our self-interest—our interest in a peaceful, just, and stable world—than most realists will acknowledge. When the United States trades arms with human rights violators, as it did with Iraq before the Persian Gulf War or the Mujahedeen in Afghanistan, those same arms may end up being used against us, as they were by Saddam Hussein, or in the hands of terrorists, as happened in Afghanistan in the 1980s.[35] When we avert our eyes from the human rights practices of important allies like Egypt or Saudi Arabia, giving them a pass on their contempt for civil society, we facilitate the possible demise of those governments and their replacement, as happened in Iran in 1979, by regimes far less friendly to the United States. When we stay relatively mute about excesses committed by those on whose behalf we have struggled—about Israel's use of torture or Kuwait's mistreatment of women or Kosovars' retaliation against Serbs—we damage not only our moral standing but our strategic credibility as well.

Foreign policy "realists," I am sure, would at the snap of a finger, if they had the power, spread democratic communities of rights throughout the globe. For the most part, however, they do not believe that the benefit is worth the price. They are convinced that the only safe course for the United States to take is to pursue unilaterally what they call our "national interests" (by which they generally mean our economic and security interests), undistracted by what impact that pursuit has on world opinion or the common interests of the international community. But, as we have seen, our interests are often inextricably bound up with those of others. As political observer David Callahan has pointed out, our "vital interests include the protection of American lives . . . , the security of core democratic allies . . . and the overall stability of the international system"—all of which entail more (rather than less) democracy and greater respect for human rights.[36]

Tell a young American serving overseas in the military that the United States can remain oblivious to world opinion. Tell an American tourist or traveling businessperson concerned about terrorism that we can afford to ignore the common interests we share with other law-abiding countries. Tell an American homeowner worried about the future availability of fuel that the state of democracy in Caspian Sea countries has nothing to do with the United States.

The "realist" approach betokens, at the very least, an abysmal ignorance of how systems work. For it is impossible, in as globalized a society as we live in today, for any single player to pursue its interests without taking into account the interests of others at the table. "Realists" would hate to be considered mystics, but it really is a form of mysticism (comparable to Adam Smith's notion of the "invisible hand" by which free markets produce public welfare) to believe that if the United States merely follows its own narrowly conceived interests, everything else will take care of itself.

Nowhere is that mysticism harder at work than in the areas of trade, investment, and global economics. "The health of the global economy," Callahan quite rightly says, is another one of our vital national interests.[37] But in the United States, more than almost anywhere else in the world, the failure to spot the connection with human rights is widespread. It is not only that the commercialist argument (that the best way to ensure democracy and human rights is via economic growth) has caused endless debate; it is that businesses have traditionally seen human rights concerns to be inimical to theirs. I love *The Economist*'s observation, however, that "if dictators made countries rich, Africa would be an economic colossus."[38] The truth is that not only can business be good for human rights, but human rights are good for business. And for labor. And for any American who cares about the country's economic future. Chapter 3 further explores that topic.

3

The Bottom Line

Why Human Rights Are Good for Business

If you ain't got the ball, you can't shoot the ball.
—MOSES MALONE, NBA basketball player

A NUMBER OF YEARS AGO a sociology professor at Ohio State University discovered that the more frequently people attend church or synagogue, the better their sex lives. At the time this groundbreaking research was carried out, I was president of a religious denomination striving mightily to grow its membership; the professor's correlation was, you had better believe, a welcome one. It was also somewhat counterintuitive, as religious folks are often stereotypically thought of as more straitlaced than average, and yet sometimes benefits are derived from the most unexpected places. As a connoisseur of martinis, I am heartened to learn that Canadian researchers have recently reported that of all alcoholic beverages, martinis score highest in those antioxidants that help fight everything from cancer to cataracts . . . but only if they are shaken!

The observation that human rights are actually good for business falls into the same category of "startling but true." It is not obvious perhaps, and certainly not all business leaders have been persuaded by the formula. But then this is a topic—the relationship between political freedom and economic growth—about which human rights advocates and businesspeople too often talk right past each other. Yet ever since the days of Friedrich A. Hayek's *The Road to Serfdom* (1944), as popularized in Ayn Rand's *Atlas Shrugged* (1957) and catechized in Milton Friedman's *Capitalism and Freedom* (1962), it has been hard-core conservative doctrine that liberty and economic growth, what Rand called "free trade and the free mind," are inseparable. What capitalism requires to thrive, Hayek said, is individual liberty protected by the rule of law, which he defined as "government in all its actions . . . bound by rules fixed and announced beforehand."[1]

In more recent years, however, as American business has found amenable homes in countries little known for their love of liberty, the principle that capitalism and freedom are inescapably linked has been transmogrified into what I have called the commercialist argument. Now influence flows only one way: capitalism and economic growth, we are assured, will eventually usher in democracy, but a free society is no longer a sine qua non for capitalist success.

And maybe that is so. Hayek and company could well have been wrong. But whether the investment of capital is truly secure in a society plagued by fear, threat, and caprice—or, more positively, whether a democratic community of rights carries with it real, practical, bottom-line advantages for investors—is worth some serious reflection.

It is worth that reflection not just for the sake of business, but because the futures of so many Americans are now entangled with international investments. More than $350 billion of our money is now held in mutual funds that invest overseas.[2] At least $160 billion of our retirement funds in the form of IRAs and other such instruments are invested in global stocks and foreign securities; some estimate as much as $530 billion. More than $285 billion in private capital is now invested in developing nations. Our dependence on the economic health of global corporations and foreign countries keeps growing every year.

One observer captured the irony of our newfound circumstances perfectly when he asked, "And who a decade ago could have anticipated . . . how a small-town American whose closest encounter with Thailand before 1997 had been seeing the film *The King and I* could find her life roiled by a previously unknown relationship between the health of her pension fund and the inability of Thailand's finance ministry to monitor its banks' lending portfolios?"[3] But the collapse of such economic and psychological boundaries is exactly what globalization is all about. Exports account for an increasing percentage of our economic growth (foreign trade represents 30 percent of our gross domestic product, up from 13 percent in 1970), and more and more jobs —including high-paying ones, industries dependent on exports paying wages 13 percent higher than the national average—are dependent on the stability of foreign markets.[4] If human rights violations *do* have an impact on international finance, Americans cannot afford to ignore them. Why, then, have so many businesses tried so hard to do just that?

Shell Oil had a tough year in 1995—not financially but in terms of its public image. That year the company was accused of polluting the North Sea with its oil and of being implicated in the Nigerian government's decision to execute the environmental activist Ken Saro-Wiwa, who had led protests against Shell's oil installations in the Niger Delta. I was engaged in a dialogue, first privately then publicly, with Shell in the months leading up to Saro-Wiwa's death about whether the company shared any responsibility for his fate, a disturbing sidelight of which was that the *Houston Chronicle,* the major newspaper in Shell USA's corporate headquarters of Houston, Texas, would not sell Amnesty space to address the issue.

In defending its refusal to intervene in the Saro-Wiwa case, Shell International sent me a letter a few weeks before the activist was killed that contained a classic statement of the position corporations often take when it comes to human rights matters: "[A] commercial organisation [*sic*] such as ours cannot and should not sit in judgment on either political or judicial matters which are the preserve of the state."[5]

What was interesting about this letter was not only that Shell's position contradicted its own behavior a few years before in South Africa, when it and many other corporations, under intense public pressure, finally spoke out against apartheid. By doing so, they helped bring down a morally bankrupt system of government. What was interesting, however, we learned after Saro-Wiwa's death, was that at the very time the letter was written, Shell—recognizing that an execution would be a public relations nightmare for the company—was pleading with Nigerian strongman Sani Abacha to grant clemency.

Vociferously as they often claim that they must remain politically neutral on public issues, no corporation refrains from mixing into its host country's politics if it concludes that its own self-interest is at stake. It is unimaginable that if a government proposed to raise corporate taxes or require additional worker benefits, corporate leaders would refuse to "sit in judgment on . . . political . . . matters which are the preserve of the state"; in fact, shareholders could justifiably accuse them of negligence if they did. In the United States corporations are never reluctant to participate in politics quite directly, political action committees and so-called soft money for the two political parties being their stock-in-trade. Public matters become "the preserve of the state" when companies decide they may be too hot to handle.

Perhaps because their "strict neutrality" argument is at such odds with common practice, corporations have gravitated toward a more acceptable variation—the commercialist argument that democracy and human rights are indeed noble goals but that the most effective way to bring them about is not through direct intervention but economic investment. Such investment, so the reasoning goes, both opens host countries up to the west's liberalizing influence but also, by spreading prosperity, creates a middle class that, freed of the burden of meeting its basic human needs, will have the energy and inclination to demand its civil and political rights. This argument has many advantages over its strict-neutrality cousin. It allows companies to cavort with the angels while pursuing their entrepreneurial ends. It salves guilt while precluding the need to raise uncomfortable questions with one's hosts that just might get a business thrown out of a country. And it has the added virtue that it may even at least in part be true.

Furthermore, all American presidents since Ronald Reagan have embraced this argument wholeheartedly. At a February 1997 press conference, for example, President Clinton was asked to defend his policy, announced two years before, of delinking trade and human rights in light of the fact that the State Department had recently reported that all political dissent had been silenced in China. In his reply the president articulated the determinist philosophy of history that underlies the commercialist stance: "I believe that the impulses of [Chinese] society and the nature of the economic change will work together along with the availability of information from the outside world to increase the spirit of liberty over time. I don't think there is any way that [China] can hold back that, just as inevitably the Berlin wall fell. I just think it's inevitable."[6]

More than one scholar agrees with this sentiment, citing correlations between greater prosperity and greater freedom and pointing to countries like Taiwan and South Korea, which, as they became economically stronger, also loosened their repressive ties.[7] It makes a certain amount of sense that as authoritarian societies are exposed to democratic ideals through business exchanges and the Internet, for example, they may take on a greater coloration of democracy. It may well be true that when people are preoccupied with scratching out a living, they have little energy left over for demanding their liberties. Revolutions are, after all, generally understood to be the making of the upwardly mobile middle class. But is such a development inevitable, as Clinton seemed to think? Karl Marx also preached a deterministic line when it came to capitalism, only he believed it would lead inexorably to revolution. Could it be that the commercialist argument that capitalism inevitably leads to democracy is the twin version (albeit the "good twin") of the Marxist fallacy?

One has but to chew gum on the street, fail to flush a public toilet, or urinate in an elevator in Singapore to learn the answer. For Singapore, with a standard of living second only to Japan's in Asia and voted by the *Wall Street Journal* in 1997 the nation with the world's greatest "economic liberty" (in other words, a capitalist powerhouse), is also one of the world's most autocratic. Gum chewing brings a $1,000 fine; ordering gum from a mail catalog calls for a year in prison and a $6,173 fine.[8] A battalion of inspectors from Singapore's Ministry of Environment roves public toilets in search of aberrant nonflushers, and the major newspaper, the *Straits Times,* has invited calls to a "Toilets of Shame hotline" and published photographs of toilet miscreants such as one of Mr. Amar Mohamed labeled "Caught Without a Flush." Urine detectors are installed in some apartment elevators, which, upon detecting ammonia, lock the elevator doors, activate a hidden camera, sound an alarm at the Housing and Development Board, and dispatch the police.[9] Far more seriously, Singapore's government regularly stifles political opposition and press critics with damaging civil defamation and libel suits; holds prisoners of conscience without trial; imprisons conscientious objectors; bans Jehovah's Witnesses; inflicts mandatory caning for some thirty crimes, including the most trivial; and executes people for even relatively minor drug offenses.[10]

But if the commercialist argument were accurate on its face, Singapore should be a human rights haven. As should Malaysia. Or, in the past, Suharto's Indonesia. Or apartheid-era South Africa, renowned for its hospitality to business, having practically been founded by the Dutch East Indies Trading Company. Or Pinochet's Chile. Or Nazi Germany, given that at least three hundred U.S. companies alone continued operations there even after the war had begun.[11]

Investment of capital may well play a role in encouraging democracy and human rights, but it alone is far from sufficient to guarantee freedom, as level-headed observers like U.S. Trade Representative Charlene Barshefsky has acknowledged: "I am cautious," she said of the link between trade and social change after negotiating China's entry into the World Trade Organization, "in making claims that a market-opening agreement leads to anything other than opening the market."[12]

The relationship between economic incentives and political reform is a complicated one. Were it not, the best way to bring Clinton's inevitable "spirit of liberty" to Cuba, Libya, Burma (Myanmar), Iran, and Iraq, according to the commercialist argument, would be to flood them with U.S. capital rather than starve them through sanctions. But then we all remember what Ralph Waldo Emerson said about hobgoblins and consistency. The reasons sanctions are applied to Burma (Myanmar) and not to China, admitted one Clinton administration official, is because "China's too rich to mess with and Burma isn't."[13]

To be the powerful vehicle it can sometimes be to coax reform out of a government, the partner that economic growth requires is a receptive political dynamic. That can come in the form of more enlightened leadership, as it did with Corazon Aquino and her successor in the Philippines. It can arise out of a powerful constituency for change, such as Solidarity provided in Poland. Or it can be a result of persistent international pressure, as was the case in ending apartheid in South Africa. But whatever its form, respected conservative scholar Samuel Huntington is right: "Economic development makes democracy possible; political leadership makes it real."[14]

"In every country in Asia, including Korea," South Korea's president, Kim Dae-jung, said of the 1998 Asian economic crisis, "the major reason for failure was lack of democracy."[15] Grinding poverty is never a good omen of respect for civil and political rights, but prosperity alone, absent political will, is no guarantor either. That economic growth and political freedom are often found together reveals little about the causal relationship between them. Business may encourage democracy, but it may well be equally true that businesses thrive more in countries that respect human rights. After all, as Alan Greenspan, the chair of the Federal Reserve, has said, "The guiding mechanism of a free market economy . . . is a bill of rights, enforced by an impartial judiciary."[16] If Greenspan is right, the commercialist argument is woefully incomplete and business is far more dependent on respect for human rights than it usually cares to let on.

Not all businesspeople of course are blind to the economic benefits of human rights. I was in Hong Kong a few weeks before it reverted to Chinese control in 1997. The atmosphere was understandably tense. I talked with journalists, academics, students, and politicians of all stripes. I talked with shopkeepers, streetsweepers, and a receptionist in a dental office (the window of which bore the fascinating inscription: "Teeth extracted by the latest Methodists"). But some of the most interesting people I talked with were leaders of the U.S. Chamber of Commerce in Hong Kong.

The U.S. Chamber of Commerce in Hong Kong has often been more outspoken about human rights than its counterparts elsewhere around the world. "Our European and Japanese colleagues always mention human rights when they meet with the Chinese," one American told me. "They have their tea, conduct their business, and then, on their way out the door as they are waving goodbye, shout 'Human rights!' and make a run for it." I was interested to find out why. "The answer," one of the Chamber officials told me, "can be summed up in two names: Xi Jang and Jimmy Peng."

Xi Jang was a Hong Kong journalist who got wind of the fact in 1993 that China was going to raise interest rates. He wrote stories about that and about China's efforts to protect its gold holdings—standard enough business reporting most places and useful information for foreign investors. Too useful apparently, because the Chinese got hold of Xi and sentenced him to twelve years in prison for disclosing "state secrets." He was released on parole in 1997.[17]

Jimmy Peng was an Australian businessman with textile and property investments in the Chinese city of Shenzhen. When the city tried to take over his business, Peng enlisted the help of Deng Xiaoping's niece, who double-crossed him and arranged for him to be jailed. Peng successfully sued the niece but was unable to get the judgment enforced, and in October 1993 he was kidnapped from the Mandarin Hotel in Macao, delivered across the border to China, held without bail for two years, and convicted (under a law enacted a year *after* his arrest) of corruption and embezzlement. Peng was sentenced to eighteen years. Between 1991 and 1996 the Hong Kong government (under British control) lobbied the Chinese on behalf of Peng and some seventeen other businesspeople detained without trial in southern China.[18]

Xi Jang and Jimmy Peng personify two of the reasons why human rights are good for business: business cannot function without a free flow of accurate information and the equitable enforcement of contracts. But there is an even more fundamental reason: respect for human rights contributes mightily to political stability, and conducting business without stability is like playing Russian roulette . . . with all barrels loaded.

Shortly before the Asian Pacific Economic Cooperation (APEC) meetings were held in Jakarta, Indonesia, in 1994, U.S. human rights groups, as they did before every APEC meeting, begged the American delegation to include human rights on the Conference agenda. Especially when it comes to this particular host country with its abysmal human rights record, the groups pressed, issues of economics cannot be divorced from issues of justice. The response from the administration was just as anticipated: "APEC is not the forum to discuss . . . human rights," said U.S. Ambassador to Indonesia Robert Barry. "It's an economic forum," added economist Fred Bergsten, head of APEC's policy committee, "and it's been widely agreed it should limit its discussions to economic matters. If you brought every issue to every forum, you'd never get anything done." It was left to Richard Fisher of the conservative Heritage Foundation, however, to provide the straightforward coda to the administration's official position. Trade is quite simply, Fisher said, "a far more important agenda than human rights." Then he repeated the familiar refrain: "The best way to improve human rights is to increase economic growth."[19]

Three years later the value of Indonesia's rupiah collapsed. The International Monetary Fund demanded stringent reforms in return for a rescue package, but President Suharto resisted changes that would have cut government subsidies, brought the national budget into line, tightened supervision of banks, and rooted out corruption. Widespread layoffs of workers ensued as the value of the Indonesian currency continued its fall. In March 1998, Suharto was reelected as president in a contest in which he was the only candidate. With no other avenues through which to express their frustration, massive numbers of students and workers took to the streets; in May four students were unlawfully killed by the military in Jakarta, prompting rioting in which more than a thousand people died. On May 21, 1998, Suharto resigned after thirty-two years of autocratic rule. The notion that Indonesia's economic future, in which Americans had more than $7 billion invested, could be divorced from its political had been proven pure folly.[20]

One of the people who knew this was Dita Sari. Raised in a comfortable middle-class home, her father a civil servant and her mother an employee of Mobil Oil in Indonesia, Dita was twelve years old before the world's hardships began to impress themselves on her. It was then that her parents were divorced and Dita, realizing how hard her mother had to struggle to fend for herself and her children, began to contemplate the notion that life is not equally fair to all people. But Dita and her parents were fundamentally apolitical people. Although they were aware of the great economic gap between rich and poor in Indonesia, and the hidden conflicts between Muslims and Christians or Chinese and indigenous people, it was not until Dita went to college that she began to take political and economic issues seriously. "I learned in college that intellectuals had an obligation to change society," she reflected later, "and that theory must be put into practice."

Given her growing activist consciousness, Dita abandoned the study of law in which she had at first enrolled. "I saw no way," she recalled, "that law could make any big difference [in Indonesia] when the real question was power." In 1993 she began to participate in student movements for educational reform. It was not long, however, before Dita recognized that the group in greatest need of her energy and leadership were the workers, and so in 1994 she began to organize them—something illegal at the time. Dita's organization was forced to work underground in its efforts to establish a minimum daily wage of $3.30, to stop the employment of children under fourteen, to improve health standards, to gain free speech and the right to strike, and to establish an independent court system to enforce contracts. Over the next few months the charismatic young woman participated in hundreds of job actions, often broken up by the military.

But Dita Sari realized that the deprivation of workers' rights was only one face of Indonesian oppression. She knew that the seizure of land by the Indonesian military on behalf of conglomerates owned by the Suharto family and its hangers-on—a common occurrence—was another instance of the corruption and cronyism eating away at her country. She knew that women suffered disproportionately, not only because they received the lowest wages and were subjected to the worst conditions on the job but also because of cultural and religious mores that plagued their lives in general. She knew that unless broader political reforms were introduced—an end to one-party rule, controls on the police and military, true freedom for an independent press, the right of labor to organize—working people would never obtain their due, and any gains they might make would always be in jeopardy.

This was a country, after all, whose president had presided over the massacre of up to five hundred thousand people alleged to be Communists when he came to power in 1965–66. It was a country that had invaded East Timor in 1975, resulting in the deaths and disappearances of one-third of the population of that land. It was a country in which "insulting" the president brought up to six years in prison; in which it was a crime for the press to express contempt for the government; in which some two thousand books had been banned (including, ironically, books on capitalism); in which the country's greatest writer, Pramoedya Ananta Toer, had been imprisoned for fourteen years; in which those who tried to demonstrate peacefully were arrested and tortured. "Every time I gave an unsatisfactory answer," one student demonstrator said of his police interrogation, "they beat my friend who was sitting next to me. It was . . . much worse than being beaten myself." It was a country in which the regime's political opponents were regularly labeled "Communists" and often assaulted by the police.[21] Even an Indonesian psychic who had predicted that the leader of the opposition party might succeed Suharto was arrested on trumped-up charges of blasphemy. "[Psychics] can make predictions," said a military officer, "but they should not create chaos among the people."[22]

Over the next few years Dita Sari worked hard to unite the regime's disparate opponents. Workers remained the principal focus of her devotion, but as a young, powerful woman who also spoke up for women's needs (she called women "the bravest, most militant, and disciplined" of activists), Dita provided a transforming model in a society in which women had been notoriously oppressed and largely forbidden to take on a political role. The plight of the East Timorese also seized her imagination, for she realized that their mistreatment merely reflected the larger forces of destruction at work in Indonesian society. The affection in which she was held by her supporters and the authority of her leadership continued to grow, as did the attention she received from the military and police. Between 1993 and 1996, Dita Sari was arrested six times, usually held for about forty-eight hours, and sometimes beaten viciously.

It was not until July 6, 1996, however, that Dita's power was sufficient to frighten the Indonesian government into definitive action. That was the day Dita led twenty thousand workers in a job action in an industrial zone in Surabaya, and they attempted to march to the headquarters of Megawati Sukarnoputri, head of the Indonesian Democratic Party and daughter of the former president. Such a demonstration promised to unite labor with the political opposition and conceivably bring down the government. Determined to prevent any such catastrophe, the police and military were out in force, blocking the marchers' path and threatening them with a massive attack. Realizing the potential for disaster, Dita called on the workers to disperse, but as they were doing so, she was arrested once again. Dozens of her fellow demonstrators tried to encircle her to prevent her being taken into custody.

This time Dita was not released. A few days later riots broke out in Jakarta protesting the military's attack on the headquarters of the main opposition party. Despite the fact that she was in jail at the time, Dita and two others, it was alleged in the newspapers, were accused of being the Communist "masterminds" behind the riots and she was charged with subversion. While awaiting trial, she led a protest of women prisoners against prison corruption. At her trial in April 1997, Dita handed out flowers to the judge and prosecutor while hundreds of her supporters packed the public gallery and sang the popular song of struggle, "Hymn of Blood." Needless to say, Dita was convicted, pronounced guilty of undermining state ideology and founding an illegal political party with the intent of bringing about a multiparty democracy. When she arrived in court for sentencing, she wore a red headband reading "Democracy or Death."[23]

At age twenty-three Dita Sari was sentenced to five years in prison. "Every time a letter of solidarity arrives, the rose in my cell blossoms," she wrote from jail to Amnesty activists who had been campaigning for her freedom. She was released in 1999. By that time of course a new government that pledged to support human rights was in place; East Timor had voted for independence; and Indonesia was flirting with economic recovery. But Dita's conviction that Indonesia's economic woes, be they those of the workers or of their employers, were tied up with its political turmoil had long since been proven prescient. "I am a union organizer," Dita said after her release, "but I recognize that for many business owners in the days of Suharto's corruption, competition was not fair. Even if you had a lot of capital, if you had no political power, you could lose your business. And even if you were the worst manager in the world, if you had political power, you could keep it." No one could be secure in his or her economic future as long as terror continued to reign.

A few months after Suharto left office, the World Bank, which had spent more than $25 billion in Indonesia over three decades and had trumpeted the country as a great success story, issued a blistering internal evaluation of its own operations there. Because of its too-cozy relationship with Suharto, the report said, the Bank had turned a blind eye to Indonesia's sick banking system and its refusal to open up politics or to countenance legal reform. "Issues of poor governance, social stress and a weak financial sector were not addressed."[24]

But how could it truly come as a surprise to the World Bank or to the Clinton administration's APEC negotiators, for that matter, that political repression might be economically risky? Even some of the world's most tyrannical regimes think that they must adopt the veneer of democratic reform if they are to attract business. On October 2, 1997, two years after it had executed Ken Saro-Wiwa and while it was still in the grip of Sani Abacha's vicious dictatorship, Nigeria published a full eight-page supplement in the *Wall Street Journal* designed to entice corporations to invest there. The headline of the supplement read, "Country Moves Closer to a New Era of Democracy," a process it described as "still on track, albeit with a few hiccups along the way." The ad failed to mention that one example of that gastric disturbance was that the legitimate winner of the last election for president, Chief Mashood Abiola, was still being held in prison for trying to assume his rightful due.[25]

Countries that abuse human rights, as I detailed in chapter 2, are notoriously unstable, even when they appear solid as rocks. If anything ought to scare away investors, it is political instability with its attendant unrest. In the face of price hikes, growing unemployment, corruption, abusive government officials, unresponsive courts, and increasing disparities in wealth, there are no avenues in a repressive society—no advocacy groups, no unions, no free press—through which citizens may vent their grievances or seek redress. In the middle of the Indonesian crisis, one business owner neatly expressed the problem: "There is no rule of law. There is no way for people to channel their frustrations. The common people feel they are ignored by the law. The Government does not respond to their complaints. So if there's a problem, they quickly become angry and they turn to violence."[26]

Governments face economic crises all the time: sudden drops in the price of a principal export; tight money that sends interest rates skyrocketing; energy shortages; liquidity shortfalls; high inflation; scarcity of foreign exchange; failure of national banks; and dozens of other crises. Many of these result from poor planning or bad policy, and some are for all practical purposes beyond a government's control. But the test for any government—and certainly the test of the extent to which business can have confidence in a government—comes in how it responds to such crises. Dani Rodrik, professor of international political economy at Harvard, thinks he knows one of the key variables that determines success: how a government manages the latent social conflict that inevitably accompanies such shocks. He thinks he knows which kind of governments handle that conflict best: democracies that practice participatory politics, allow the expression of dissent, and respect the rule of law.

In a groundbreaking 1999 study, Rodrik looked at how fifty developing countries, most of which had experienced economic growth between 1960 and 1973, dealt with the turbulence that beset the world economy in the years after 1973. This turbulence included major oil shortages, tighter U.S. money policies, and the abandonment of a system of fixed exchange rates. Rodrik found that those countries that had weathered the storm most successfully were those that had *both* adjusted their monetary and fiscal policies appropriately *and* successfully managed the social conflict those adjustments inevitably generated.[27] Why this is so is not hard to see.

Any economic crisis and its attendant cure will produce a segment of the population that regards itself as being the "losers"—be those workers forced to take lower wages, consumers forced to pay higher prices, or in the most dire situations, citizens forced to scrounge for food. At first glance it might appear that authoritarian governments that "keep a lid on" such discontent are apt to perform most satisfactorily in an economic sense. But Rodrik's study found just the opposite. Democratic communities of rights managed the conflict far better. "Democracy," he explains, "allows discredited policies and politicians to be discarded; it allows for institutionalized modes of participation instead of riots and protests; and it reduces incentives for noncooperative behavior by making it harder for social groups to shift the burdens of adjustment disproportionately on to others."[28]

Other factors are important too, such as the provision of a "safety net" to help the most disadvantaged, but whether it be Botswana (one of Africa's few continuous democracies and one that has managed its diamond resources well and provided high levels of health and education to its people) or South Korea (which has emerged successfully from the Asian currency crisis), the capacity to gain widespread democratic support for government policies has been key. In the midst of the 1997–98 upheavals in Asia, for example, labor unions in South Korea voluntarily called off threatened strikes to avoid endangering the country's recovery. If they want to be fully integrated into the international economic system, the Chinese will be forced to close down more antiquated state-owned enterprises, thereby exacerbating hardships that are already taking a heavy toll on the citizenry. Will that government be able to inspire similar cooperation?

When dictatorships left and right were threatening to nationalize foreign investments in the 1950s and 1960s, the danger of political instability to business was all too obvious. More than once the U.S. government, through the ministrations of its intelligence and/or military services, sought to protect corporate interests—in Central America, for example, and Chile—through subterfuge or intervention. Still today, political turmoil can cost a company dearly. Chevron, for example, which had spent millions of dollars to develop two oil fields in Sudan in the 1970s, was forced to withdraw from that country in 1984 after the civil war erupted there and three of Chevron's oil workers were killed.[29] Malaysia remains terra non grata for much foreign investment and has to pay 1 percent more to borrow money than do its Southeast Asian neighbors, largely because of the sense of political risk engendered by Prime Minister Mahathir Mohamad's illicit pursuit of his former deputy and now rival, Anwar Ibrahim.[30] One well-known business consultant, Marvin Zonis, has even created a "political stability index," which attempts to quantify the odds of businesses running into political upheaval in emerging markets.[31]

But if business (and its allies in government) know that political instability prompted by human rights violations can create a risky investment environment, why does it keep pouring in the capital and giving short shrift to human rights? China, for example, the favorite new locus for American moneymaking—although it has not yet experienced the instability of Indonesia—is so rife with labor and farmer unrest because of corruption and economic disparities, coupled with the absence of vehicles through which to express displeasure peacefully,[32] that the government has had to expand a secretive branch of the military with more than seven hundred thousand troops trained to provide riot control. Although few of the hundreds of demonstrations that take place every year are publicized, this expansion is an acknowledgment, say two former U.S. military attachés in Beijing "that internal unrest is a greater threat to . . . Chinese economic modernization than is foreign invasion."[33]

Whether it be wishful thinking, short-term quarter-by-quarter planning, ignorance ("If [Phillips-Van Heusen] had been sophisticated enough to learn the history [of labor abuse in Guatemala] in advance," said its CEO, Bruce Klatsky, "it would not be in Guatemala."[34]), fear that outspokenness will be punished, or that divestiture is the only alternative to passivity, or simply the fact that contrary to the assumption of classical economics, human beings do not always act in accordance with their best interests, too many companies keep their heads in the sand (and the funds of their investors in danger) when it comes to the implications of human rights crimes.

Of course, the Indonesian economic crisis was not fueled solely by human rights violations. It involved spillover from similar financial crises elsewhere in Asia, inflated currency, irresponsible credit expansion, a host of bad loans by banks, and abysmal economic planning, among other things. But the crisis was certainly exacerbated by the political atmosphere years of repression had fostered, and it turned at least in part on the corruption and "hidden costs" that the lack of the rule of law invariably engenders. The government that succeeded Suharto had apparently taken that point to heart. When chaos broke out in East Timor in 1999, one adviser to Suharto's successor, President B. J. Habibie, was quoted as encouraging a quick end to the violence for fear that lenders would shun the country and business would lose confidence. "If we are not able to overcome this [turmoil], the recovery could slip away and we could fall into another deep [economic] crisis," the adviser said. "We've got to be very careful."[35]

When it comes to business interests, the "rule of law" encompasses three things: combating corruption, providing transparent regulations for the conduct of business, and guaranteeing the fair enforcement of contracts. All three notions are put in jeopardy if human rights are not respected.

When President Clinton visited Africa in 1998, he made a commitment to increase U.S. trade with that continent. The U.S. ambassador to Tanzania, Charles Stith, was doing all he could to fulfill that promise when I paid him a visit in December 1999. He had escorted the Tanzanian president to the United States to meet with business leaders, and he had hosted such leaders in Dar es Salaam. He had published a regular newsletter aimed at corporate leaders and had used his own thick Rolodex and considerable charm to persuade them of the country's virtues. But there was one thing Stith could not do: stop the newsstand attendant at the Dar es Salaam Sheraton from pocketing the purchase price of *USA Today*.

Tanzania has many outstanding features beyond its geography and game parks. For example, its founding president, Julius Nyerere, insisted that Tanzanians avoid the tribal divisions, often exacerbated by the colonialists, that still torment so much of Africa. But Tanzania is regularly counted by the independent watchdog organization Transparency International among the ten countries perceived to be most corrupt in the world.

"How much is *USA Today*?" I asked the attendant in Dar es Salaam's fanciest and most westernized hotel.

"6,000 Tanzanian shillings," she replied. That is about $7.50.

"6,000 shillings?" I asked skeptically.

"Well, then, maybe 600," she said, slipping the bills into her pocket rather than the cash register.

It was the same story at the office of an internationally known shipping firm when I tried to mail a purchase home. "I'm going to write

165,000 shillings on the bill, but you will need to pay me another 30,000 for . . . export fees," said the clerk. And at customs in Zanzibar: "Do you have a wallet?" asked the uniformed customs agent. "Yes, of course," I responded. "OK," he said. "You pay me money."

I really don't resent these little acts of extortion. The average annual income in Tanzania, after all, is something like $200. If I were making $200 a year, I would take every opportunity to supplement my income also. The problem is that this petty corruption reflects a much more serious corruption at the government level, such as that described in a tourist magazine available in every room of the Sheraton that described how Tanzanian officials simply made up numbers out of their heads when a hotel developer tried to pay his taxes. It is that which discourages investment. "If I were a business leader being courted by the ambassador to invest here," I later told Charles Stith, "that attendant, clerk, and agent would have made a far greater impression than all the fancy parties you and the government could throw for me."

Capitalism works not just because money changes hands. It is predicated on a certain set of values, a certain "culture," and, whether one likes those values and that culture, they include, as the economist Amartya Sen has pointed out, mutual trust and respect for a common set of norms, among them respect for the rule of law and, specifically, an understanding that corruption is an illegitimate form of exchange. This doesn't mean of course that corruption is unheard of in the most successful capitalist countries. Corruption is found everywhere. But as Transparency International observes, "The aim is not to achieve complete rectitude but to realize a fundamental increase in honesty—and so [in] the efficiency and fairness of government."[36] And as I detailed in chapter 2, corruption is generally less pervasive in communities that respect human rights.

Why this is important to business goes right to the bottom line. Investing in a corrupt country, one economist has calculated, is the equivalent of adding an additional 20 percent tax on an investment.[37] A survey among businesses in Hong Kong in 1994 revealed that they automatically factor 3 percent to 5 percent into every deal in China as the cost of corruption.[38] American businesses, which under the Foreign Corrupt Practices Act are forbidden from paying *baksheesh* to obtain favorable consideration, are at a particular disadvantage. Between 1994 and 1999 the State Department received reports of bribes being offered on 294 international contracts, totaling $145 billion, and in 77 of those cases U.S. firms lost contracts worth a total of $24 billion.[39] And these are just the cases reported to the department.

All this is to say nothing about how damaging corruption can be to a company's image. In Indonesia the corruption took the form not only of *pungli,* or cash payments for favorable treatment from the government, but of tax and tariff breaks and other advantageous concessions to businesses associated with the Suharto family. Since Suharto fell, some of those companies aligned with the Suhartos have come under close scrutiny. In January 2000, for example, auditors hired by the new Indonesian government accused Paiton Energy Corporation, an electric power company owned in part by Edison Mission Energy Company of New Jersey and General Electric's GE Capital (as well as by the brother-in-law of one of Suharto's daughters), of marking up the cost of building a new power plant by more than $600 million, presumably for payoffs and kickbacks. The auditors urged the Indonesian attorney general to investigate, hardly burnishing Edison and General Electric's public reputations, even if they are innocent.[40]

So instrumental is corruption in creating financial disarray that the World Bank and the International Monetary Fund (IMF) now sometimes use their leverage to stamp it out and promote better governance. In 1997, for instance, the IMF suspended a $220 million loan to Kenya after President Daniel Arap Moi, renowned for sanctioning both corruption and human rights violations, refused to appoint a powerful new anticorruption authority, as the IMF had demanded.[41] At last those two influential bodies seem to be inching toward recognition that accountability and transparency—which almost always require such human rights regimens as a free press, an independent judiciary, an unfettered political opposition, and an unmuzzled independent sector—are prerequisites to long-term economic health.[42]

There is more than one way to be corrupt, of course. Kickbacks and payoffs are but the least imaginative. Far more creative was a well-known artist who sold "zones" of "immaterial pictorial sensibility," which turned out to be his nomenclature for air. It has also been speculated that the Viking Erik the Red was a property developer who named a dubious piece of the Arctic "Greenland" in an early real-estate swindle.

Like any country, China imposes safety-licensing standards on certain imports. To be licensed for sale, personal computers, printers, television sets, and stereos, among other products, must pass a safety inspection. This by itself is not unreasonable. The catch is that it is often difficult for manufacturers to learn what the applicable standards are for a specific product. Or China will arbitrarily set different standards for products from different countries. Or it will set different standards for domestic products from those it holds for foreign. Or it will adopt standards that bear no relationship to international norms but provide no reason for them.[43] Perhaps this is merely a contemporary version of the old Chinese saying that "only those who can appreciate the least palatable of root vegetables can know the meaning of life." But if it is, business isn't biting.

One of the reasons the business community so ardently supported China's admission to the World Trade Organization is to solve puzzles like these. To maintain the kind of disparities and obfuscation evident in China's safety-licensing procedures reflects a tendency on the part of countries unfamiliar with traditions of transparency and accountability to stack the decks, cook the books, and employ just about every other inequitable or misleading device for which there is a corresponding cliché to maintain a home-team advantage. But behavior like that violates economist Amartya Sen's "common set of norms" for the operation of free enterprise. As Arthur Leavitt, chair of the Securities and Exchange Commission, said: "In today's global economy, where capital crosses borders almost instantaneously, there is an unprecedented need for openness and cooperation. . . . [T]he enduring trait of all markets is that in exchange for capital, they demand information."[44]

And reliability. "If capital is to flow freely," says one former Commerce Department official, "disclosure rules must be the same, settlement procedures consistent and redress transparent."[45] To achieve that entails financial decisions, to be sure, but it also requires a culture of respect for the rule of law, the rights of shareholders, the availability of public information, the protection of investigators and whistleblowers, and the maintenance of an independent judiciary. Without those, the interests of both individuals and corporations are put in jeopardy.

For example, Kmart learned, much to its embarrassment and after initial vigorous denials, that it was selling seventy-three tons of rain gear that was manufactured by a business owned by the Chinese military, the People's Liberation Army (PLA). It subsequently switched suppliers.[46] But millions of Americans' pension funds may also be supporting PLA operations, because the PLA has offered more than $6 billion in bonds to U.S. investors. In this case it is not only that Americans may find the "company" with which they are doing business distasteful; it is also that such bonds rely on the faith and credit of Chinese banks that are widely considered unstable and mired in debt. The World Bank says 20 percent of Chinese bank loans are bad, but without full and reliable disclosure how can we know the full extent of those banks' exposure or exactly how reliable the people are who are running them? (The chair of one bank issuing bonds once tried to smuggle $4 million worth of AK-47s into California to sell them to street gangs there.[47]) Or consider that although the United States negotiated a Memorandum of Understanding with China in 1992 to prevent the import to this country of goods made with prison labor, the head of the U.S. Customs Service told Congress in 1997 that because of the unreliability of Chinese data and practices, "it is impossible to know how much of [the $800 billion in imports to the United States] came from prison labor facilities."[48] Conscientious as we may try to be, it is easy to be duped absent a commitment to transparency.

One of those who knows what it is like to be duped is Ronald McDonald. When McDonald's opened its first outlet in Beijing to great hoopla a number of years ago, the move was hailed as an important symbolic breakthrough for Sino-American relations. But in 1994 the Beijing government decided that despite McDonald's twenty-year lease on the property about a mile from Tiananmen Square, it would seize the site for a developer who wanted to erect a huge office and retail complex on that corner. McDonald's fought the seizure and eventually won compensation and the right to build two more restaurants nearby, but not before it had had a thorough taste of China's respect for contracts—something the Australian businessman Jimmy Peng could have told them about as well.

In many ways McDonald's was lucky. Other U.S. companies have lost millions of dollars, thanks to China's business practices. As *Business Week* reported in 1997, "Companies are shaken down by local officials, whipsawed by policy swings, railroaded into bad partnerships and squeezed for technology. McDonnell Douglas, Peugeot, BellSouth and the Japanese retailer Yaohan have all been burned on big investments." In the case of BellSouth, the company signed an "agreement of principles" to build cellular-telephone systems in China in consort with Unicom, one of China's state-owned telecom operators. But no sooner had BellSouth doled out about $50 million in expenses than Unicom demanded a $10 million cash advance. The U.S. company refused and learned later that it was but one of dozens of other corporations with which Unicom had signed similar "agreements."[49]

But then what else might we expect in a country in which lawyers are often prevented by authorities from meeting with their clients or denied access to court material and sometimes even themselves are thrown in jail?[50] The United States has been very tough in trade negotiations with China over intellectual property rights, the protection of copyrights on such things as videos and CD-ROMs against piracy from crooked Chinese entrepreneurs. We in the human rights community admire the government's fortitude and clever negotiating and have often asked why the United States refuses to be as tough when it comes to human rights—but let that go for the moment. There is nothing wrong with protecting property rights if you are going to play in a capitalist system. What *is* wrong is failing to see that the theft of property is merely the flip side of stealing political freedom: they both reflect disdain for law. Respect for contracts is growing in China, but uniform enforcement of agreements is still far from secure and that cannot help but be bad for business. What reason do we have for expecting that China will respect international trade agreements if it doesn't respect simple contracts?

If you doubt that restrictions on the free mind affect free trade, perhaps economist Joseph Stiglitz's experience will convince you otherwise. When Stiglitz was a member of President Clinton's Council of Economic Advisors, he received a letter from a Chinese publisher asking him to write a special preface for an economics textbook he had authored. Trouble was that the publisher had pirated the textbook and was selling it without paying royalties to Stiglitz. As foreign affairs journalist Thomas Friedman, who reported this story, asked, "How do you say *chutzpah* in Chinese?"[51]

In almost any context in which scorn for law predominates, business interests are at a disadvantage and economic health precarious. This is not only true for Asia. Despite the enormous economic potential in South America, for example, former U.S. Treasury Secretary Robert Rubin warned in a 1999 speech that corruption "may be the single most important impediment to economic growth [there]." Rubin went on to say that U.S. investors are wary of "organized crime, extortion and street violence," as well they should be. The threats are not just the obvious ones—more than 972 people were kidnapped in Colombia in 1999, at least 83 of them business executives[52]—but the more subtle as well. "The culture of Brazil," says that country's federal secretary for human rights "has been the culture of impunity, especially for criminals in suits and ties."[53] If there is one factor that appears to mitigate, if not inoculate, against such corruption and impunity, it is a robust and independent press, by which I mean all elements of the media, including the new electronic media.

Although some scholars, as I have discussed, have argued that economic growth leads to more democracy, others have tracked the ways in which greater respect for human rights, particularly as it is manifested in citizens having a "voice" in the public sphere, contributes to economic development. Two World Bank economists, for example, have found a "strong and consistent link between . . . the extent of civil liberties in a country and the performance of World Bank supported [economic] projects." They estimate that if a country were to move from having the lowest levels of civil liberties on their scale to the highest, it would improve the economic rate of return on the projects by 8 percent to 20 percent. They attribute this to the greater voice and "investment" citizens have in economic development when they are granted greater liberties.[54]

No institution is more critical to that voice than a free press. When you add to that role the part independent journalism can play in exposing corruption and conveying financial information, its value to business is enormous. "Without it," said one Hong Kong banker, "you are left divining sheep entrails."

What could have been more ironic than Sumner Redstone, chair of Viacom, the owner of MTV and CBS, proclaiming at a September 1999 conference in Shanghai that news organizations should not exercise their "journalistic integrity . . . in a way that is unnecessarily offensive to the countries in which [they] operate?" Perhaps only Gerald M. Levin, chair of Time Warner, toasting China's President Jiang Zemin at the same conference as "my good friend" at the very moment that Chinese authorities were removing a special issue of *Time* magazine, Time Warner's flagship publication, from local newsstands because it included essays by the Dalai Lama and dissident Wei Jingsheng.

Could it be that Redstone and Levin were unaware that the 1997 Asian financial crisis was set off in part because Thailand and South Korea had refused to disclose how much their foreign currency had dwindled, thus making them vulnerable to currency speculators, and that there had been no financial reporting strong or well-placed enough to pry the information loose? Were they unaware that a dearth of hard financial information had set off a riot outside of brokerage houses in major Chinese cities a few years before, when unnecessary panic had gripped the Shanghai and Shenzhen stock markets because *The People's Daily*, China's official paper, filling the void caused by the lack of business reporting, had opined that prices were overblown? Did Redstone and Levin just not care that Murray Hiebert, Malaysian bureau chief of the *Far Eastern Economic Review*, had been tossed in jail a few months before by Prime Minister Mahathir, charged with "scandalizing the court" for exposing corruption in the judiciary? Or would Redstone consider Hiebert to have unnecessarily offended his host?

"U.S. life insurance companies have been reluctant to finance 'the Asian miracle,'" says a director of the pension fund giant TIAA-CREF, "[because] institutional investors don't get the data they need."[55] And in a speech to Shanghai's financial community, Daniel Henninger of the *Wall Street Journal*, added, "A big investor who didn't have access to a lot of information and to people who could tell him what the information meant for his investment would be regarded as a fool."[56]

If political instability, corruption, lack of transparency, contempt for contracts, and limitations on the free flow of accurate financial information are not enough to convince investors that the human rights situations in the countries with which they do business are relevant to their corporate plans, perhaps a few matters even more directly related to the bottom line will. A wider array of human rights, for example, can open up new markets.

The longer China is closed to new ideas and free thinking, the longer it will be before *Time* magazine, CBS, MTV, the Internet, and the advertisements these venues carry for other products are available in uncensored form to that full eight hundred million–strong population. As John Kamm, former head of the U.S. Chamber of Commerce in Hong Kong, has pointed out, when the Chinese government allowed people in Guangzhou to own television sets that could tune into Hong Kong television, that opened up a huge market to television manufacturers. When it relaxed the freedom to travel, the aircraft market in China boomed.[57] Today the products at stake range from fax machines to controversial movies to satellite dishes to personal computers to Internet providers. This relationship between more human rights and a larger market will not apply to every product, of course (except as they benefit from enhanced advertising). Microwave ovens generate little political heat. But if ours is indeed the information age, then whatever restricts information has got to be bad for the growing numbers of people whose business is transmitting it.

There is another way respect for human rights contributes to economic growth. Despots tend to maximize the revenue they can obtain from citizens through taxes or confiscation for the benefit of a small oligarchy. Therefore the right to property, be it real or liquid, can never be assured, and discretionary income available for investment or consumer purchasing is often at a premium. Democracies may adopt exorbitant tax rates, but not only do the citizens have a say in that taxation (and hence the right to property is more secure), but tax proceeds are generally shared with a larger segment of the population. The incentive for government to grab as much as possible for the benefit of the few is muted, and hence the base for wider economic growth established. This is why it is no coincidence, says economist Mancur Olson, that the pattern of economic growth in Europe over the past three centuries was linked to the development and expansion of democracy.[58] Ignore human rights and you ignore a major stimulus of economic opportunity.

When Lu Guizhu, the Chinese representative of a Hungarian subsidiary of the U.S. firm the Duke Group, was arrested in 1996 after Duke Hungary refused to accept delivery of a late, poorly made clothing order from a Chinese supplier, Lu lost his freedom and the firm lost the services of a presumably valuable employee.[59] Persecution of employees brings the question of human rights violations directly to the doorsteps of business and places employee productivity at imminent risk.

Gao Feng, a Christian activist in Beijing, was detained for a month in police custody in 1994 for planning to hold a private worship service to pray for the victims of the Tiananmen Square massacre. Beijing Jeep, a Chrysler Corporation joint venture and Gao's employer, threatened to fire him for being absent from work without permission; under pressure from human rights groups, however, it later relented.[60] But the local employees of foreign companies are often at risk—"Chinese who work for foreigners are traitors," chanted a crowd in Lanzhou when a new department store opened there—and even American citizens doing business in China have been detained and harassed, particularly if they are of Chinese extraction.[61]

Arresting employees may be an extreme way to render their services useless, but companies that maintain poor working conditions, mistreat their workers, neglect their health, underpay them, and in general violate fundamental labor rights have found an equally effective way to reduce productivity. Doug Cahn, vice president of Reebok International, says straightforwardly that "good-quality products are made in good-quality workplace conditions." Bruce Klatsky of Phillips–Van Heusen elaborates:

> You need to foster good relations with [low-wage workers] to create efficiencies, to create more effective methods of production. The workforce you develop in one place is a valuable thing. After we show up in a developing country . . . GE shows up with more high-tech and the means to pay a higher wage. Right away they knock at the doors of our facilities, as they once did in New England or in the southeastern United States, to steal our employees. So it's very important . . . to create a good working environment in an effort to motivate and retain employees. It doesn't make sense in those conditions to suppress wages.[62]

Businesses can ill afford to render employees sick, angry, and impoverished if they expect to receive the benefits of workers' loyalty and most effective work. Little wonder, then, that although it may be far more counterintuitive to some CEOs than the notion that martinis improve health, the *World Bank Development Report* concluded a few years ago that respect for workers' rights is good for economic performance.[63] Even the slaveholder George Washington knew that slavery was an inefficient labor system, not because of some defect in the slaves but because they had no incentive to establish what Washington called "a good name" as laborers.[64]

Furthermore, if you keep workers enslaved and impoverished, if you keep children tied to looms rather than earning an education, you retard a country's economic development. This further defers the day when those workers themselves will constitute a market for the products they are making and those children better-educated wage earners with the capacity to spend more money.

As executive director of Amnesty International, I speak regularly to college audiences, and I am almost inevitably asked about sweatshops, often in the same breath with the word "Nike." Now this is no longer entirely fair, because Nike, which has been working hard to redress its image, having joined the Fair Labor Association, has agreed to some monitoring of its factories, and has been one of the few companies to disclose the names of its subcontractors. But it does point to how damaging it can be to corporate marketing if a company becomes associated in the public's mind with human rights violations.[65] Although the number of student activists may be relatively small, the percentage of consumers that claim they would take into account the impact of human rights violations in their purchasing is significant. In a 1995 survey, 78 percent said they would prefer to shop at retail stores committed to ending garment worker abuse, and 84 percent said they would pay an extra $1.00 on a $20.00 item to ensure that the garment had been manufactured in a worker-friendly environment.[66] Just as we banned child labor and atrocious working conditions in the United States many decades ago, so Americans do not want to wear clothes or buy products manufactured under conditions that violate our values. Socially responsible investing has grown from $639 million in 1994 to more than $1.2 trillion today; its funds earn returns competitive with other types; and 76 percent of Americans say they would switch brands or retailers if they learned that a company is associated with a good cause.[67]

Reputation is an invaluable commodity to a company. Remember how DuPont's name became indelibly connected with napalm during the Vietnam War or DeBeers diamonds with apartheid, or more recently Kathie Lee Gifford's name with sweatshops in Honduras that were manufacturing her clothes? (Anyone could tell Gifford was in

trouble when even talk-jock Howard Stern went after her.) Many companies have learned to cut their losses in the face of potential public
relations debacles. Retailers and brand-name companies like Levi
Strauss and Reebok, which are particularly susceptible to consumer
opinion because their products are targeted to a young, more politically conscious market and are readily identifiable, have taken the
lead in trying to dissociate themselves from violations and present a
clean human rights face to the world. Others companies, like PepsiCo
and Atlantic Richfield, have divested themselves of holdings in Burma
(Myanmar) under pressure from consumers and shareholders. Rug-
makers have adopted a label (Rugmark) to ensure buyers that their rugs
were not made by children, and soccer ball manufacturers have jointly
agreed to shun child labor and contribute to the education of their subcontractors' former "employees."

But other companies appear not to have learned the lesson. The Canadian oil company Talisman Energy, for example, experienced a drastic fall in stock price after a massive sell-off of shares (including 261,000
held by TIAA-CREF and 100,000 by the Texas Teachers Retirement
Fund) when its oil operations in Sudan were associated with the Suda-
nese government's brutal campaign against the largely Christian tribal
population in the country's southern half.

Even when a company may be innocent of active complicity with human rights violators, it can suffer damage to its image simply by being
linked to violators. Mobil Oil in Indonesia, for example, was charged in
1998 by seventeen Indonesian human rights organizations with
allowing a plant in Aceh to be used by the army for torture and political
killings during the Suharto era and supplying earth-moving equipment for the digging of mass graves. Although only a few companies
ever become the targets of widespread consumer action, those that do
are often forced to take the issue seriously. "All it takes," observed David
Birnbaum, a consultant to the U.S. garment industry, "is one disaster
to damage a . . . reputation."

"You who harmed a simple man," warned the Czech poet Czeslaw Milosz, "do not feel secure: for a poet remembers." But the sobering lesson
for business is that it is not poets' memories they have to fear but victims' and their lawyers. Just ask General Motors and about two hundred other American companies with German subsidiaries how costly

human rights disasters can be, and not just to reputations. These are the companies currently in negotiation with class-action lawyers to avoid lawsuits arising out of their use of more than two million people for forced labor in the Nazi era more than sixty years ago. It could ultimately cost these companies more than $5 billion. Some American companies that profited during the war by manufacturing war material for Germany later received compensation from the United States because their arms plants had been destroyed by Allied bombing, so it only seems fair to ask the guilty to pay.

That ought to give some pause to a company like UNOCAL, which may not have to wait sixty years to pay for its use of slave labor. In 1996 fifteen Burmese plaintiffs filed a claim in U.S. District Court against UNOCAL and Total (France) for collaborating with the brutal military regime in Burma (Myanmar), then known as the SLORC (State Law and Order Restoration Council), in the use of forced labor for the construction of a gas pipeline in that country. Once it is completed, the pipeline will yield the government an estimated $400 million a year—critical to a country that had hard currency reserves that year sufficient to sustain it for less than three weeks. UNOCAL and Total had agreed to hire SLORC soldiers to provide security and ensure a steady supply of labor for the project. This made SLORC the companies' agent and, under U.S. law, companies are responsible for any reasonably foreseeable actions on the part of their agents. Moreover, under the Alien Tort Statute of 1789, anyone who is not a U.S. citizen may still sue any defendant in U.S. court for violations of international law.

Over the past few years, the suit alleges, SLORC soldiers have forced villagers in the pipeline's vicinity to work at the site for days on end against their will, often carrying backbreaking loads too heavy to lift; beaten them mercilessly for resistance; extorted money to buy the laborers' freedom; seized villagers' property and forcibly relocated homes; kicked a baby into a fire after which it died; and raped young girls. Even if their employees were not directly a party to these actions, UNOCAL and Total bear responsibility for the actions of their joint venture colleagues. The suit seeks compensation and asks that work on the pipeline cease, pending an end to these abuses.

No matter how this case is resolved (and a Federal District judge has ruled for the company, though that ruling will certainly be appealed), it reflects the potential liabilities companies may face when they crawl into partnership with abusers. The final reason businesses need to take human rights seriously is because they may be held responsible in U.S. courts if they don't. The side agreement to NAFTA on labor rights, as well as the growing body of international law related to business practices (through regimes such as that of the International Labor Organization), offer added incentives to businesses to fly right. Some corporations are beginning to get the message. In a survey of Fortune 500 companies conducted in 2000, one-third of those surveyed reported that they had "decided not to proceed with a proposed investment project because of concerns over human rights."[68]

The notion, then, that financial interests can be neatly severed from human rights issues, proves at the least to be a quaint one. Whether the commercialist argument that economic investment improves a country's human rights record is true, what is hard to dispute is that respect for human rights is good for business. Yet to this point I have addressed the interests of a limited, albeit substantial, segment of the population—those wealthy enough, for example, to have equity in companies doing business overseas or whose jobs, pension funds, or other assets are affected by the fate of such corporations, or those whose livelihoods may be export-dependent.

There is one group of Americans who have known for a long time that human rights violations directly affect them and that is those workers whose jobs have disappeared thanks to low wages and poor working conditions in foreign countries. To these folks several of the rights guaranteed by the Universal Declaration of Human Rights—the right not to be held in slavery or servitude (Article 4); the right to freedom of association (Article 20); the rights to just and favorable work conditions or to form and join unions (Article 23); the right to reasonable limitations on working hours (Article 24); the right to an adequate standard of living (Article 25)—are far more than academic matters, not just as they apply to themselves but to other workers around the world. Their concern for others' rights, although it may well contain an element of altruism, bears also and unashamedly a relationship to the bread on their own tables. For these people Samuel Gompers, John L. Lewis, or Walter Reuther are not the only labor leaders worth heralding as heroes. Dita Sari (whom I introduced earlier) and Han Dongfang (whom I will introduce shortly) deserve their plaudits too.

Even more than the debate over the relationship between investment and democracy, disputes over the impact of increased global trade on jobs and wages are legion and endless. Although a larger percentage of the U.S. population was employed in 2000 than ever before, and some twenty million net new jobs have been created since the beginning of 1993,[69] the Economic Policy Institute claims that NAFTA resulted in a loss of more than 440,000 American jobs between 1994 and 1998.[70] Does trade with developing countries depress wages, or do reduced consumer prices fostered by lower production costs offset any loss? Most economists believe that trade with the developing world accounts for only about 20 percent of the wage declines among less-skilled workers compared with highly skilled,[71] but it's also true that we haven't seen a lot of price-slashing on goods made by foreign workers.

In any case many big, Western companies will soon have more employees in poor countries than in rich ones.[72] Over the past two decades at least 6 percent of U.S. manufacturing jobs have been lost as corporations move overseas in search of better labor markets.[73] In 1998 and 1999 alone the Bureau of Labor Statistics estimates the United States lost 483,000 manufacturing jobs, and even where jobs are not lost, wages may well decline.[74] Not all wage depressions or factory closings can be blamed on cheaper labor supplies by any means, but when it comes to low-skilled workforces, it's hard for American companies to resist average hourly wages of $.43 in Honduras, $.23 in China, $.10 in Indonesia, and $.01 in Bangladesh.[75] Do corporations get as much productivity out of a $.01-an-hour worker in Bangladesh as they do an $8.31-an-hour unionized worker in New York? Probably not, but you can sacrifice a lot of productivity at $.01 an hour before the differential starts to catch up with you. Everyone can sympathize with the *Newsday* headline: "NAFTA's Toll Minimal (Unless You Got Laid Off)."[76]

What everyone can understand, regardless of which side of the Great Globalization Debate they are on, is that if workers are laid off or wages depressed because an industry cannot keep up with changing times or workers' skills become obsolete, that at least is a problem that can be addressed through economic conversions, retraining, and safety nets. At some level that is the story of capitalism, and unless you want to topple the entire system (which the vast majority of Americans do not), it is something we just have to live with. But if some workers are asked to endure economic hardship because children are being put to work at age eight, or workers in developing lands are consistently being denied even the most elementary labor rights, thus undercutting the labor market, that is not "fair trade." The anger such actions generate is entirely justified, whether in the long run WTO does more good than harm. Part of economist Amartya Sen's "culture of capitalism," please recall, is trust—trust that the same rules apply to everybody. As Harvard's Dani Rodrik puts it:

> How comparative advantage is created matters. Low-wage foreign competition arising from an abundance of workers is different from competition that is created by foreign labor practices that violate norms at home. Low wages that result from demography or history are very different from low wages that result from government repression of unions.[77]

In this sense all the esoteric arguments about statistics are less important than the simple fact that children and poor people are being exploited, and they are not the only ones paying the consequences. It almost doesn't matter exactly how many American jobs have been lost to the *maquiladoras* of Latin America or the sweatshops of Asia, or whether they have been offset by lower consumer prices or whether foreign workers give as much quality product. If human rights represent a vision of what we want our common life to look like, we certainly ought to be able to agree that we don't want to live in a world in which one group of people is not paid enough to buy milk for their children and that penury contributes to the loss of hope, pride, and wherewithal for another group.

Which is to say nothing about how such exploitation adds to the U.S. trade deficit. Or how 24 percent of employers admit they use the threat of moving operations to a more "favorable" labor clime as a bargaining chip with which to finesse wage demands in their own backyards.[78] You need not, in other words, be in danger of losing your job to a foreign worker in the so-called race to the bottom to be affected adversely by his or her ill fortune. But many people are.

Julia Esmeralda Pleites worked in the Formosa Textiles factory in San Bartolo, El Salvador, sewing shirts for Nike and Adidas brands. She was paid $.60 an hour, or $4.79 a day. If she failed to make her quota of seven hundred shirts a day, her identity card was confiscated and she was forced to stay overtime—beyond the theoretical working hours of 6:30 A.M. to 5:00 P.M.—without pay or risk losing her full day's wages. This happened almost every day, and Julia was also often required to work on Saturdays without pay. The temperature in the factory frequently reached 100 degrees; workers were allowed no more than two drinks of water per day and allowed to go to the bathroom no more than twice—those times only with a ticket and under a security guard's supervision. Almost 75 percent of the workers were women, most between the ages of twenty and twenty-five. They sat on long benches without back support all day, were not allowed to talk or wear lipstick, were never given permission for a sick day, and were searched by guards every night when they left. Sometimes their supervisors struck them and often they yelled at them. If any worker dared express interest in joining a union, he or she was fired; indeed, although there are some sixty-five thousand apparel workers in El Salvador, there is not a single functioning union in the entire country.

On October 9, 1998, Julia Esmeralda Pleites stayed home from work because she did not have the $.68 for bus fare and her daughter was ill. The next day when she reported for work, she was sent home and later that week she was fired.[79] The shirts Julia was sewing sell for $75.00. Such stories have put a snarl to students' lips when they say the name "Nike." (Julia is fortunate she was not employed by a maquiladora in Honduras, where young women are injected with the contraceptive Depo-Provera to prevent pregnancy—shots they often believe are administered to prevent tetanus![80])

Impossible as it is to imagine, workers in Latin American maquiladoras sometimes have it good, compared with those in some Asian sweatshops. At the Liang Shi Handbag Factory in Guangdong, China, for example, where in 1998 handbags were made for Wal-Mart, sewers earned between $.18 and $.23 an hour. Out of that they had to pay for their food and lodging, because most of them, 70 percent women, were migrants from the countryside. Housed in cramped dormitories under twenty-four-hour surveillance, they slept two to a bed in filthy rooms with broken windowpanes. Even more alarmingly, given the history of sweatshop fires in China, the factories in which they worked had no fire exits and two partially blocked front doors. Naturally unionization was impossible. Ironically enough, although Kathie Lee Gifford had committed publicly in 1996 to put an end to these kinds of conditions in a

Honduras factory manufacturing her products, Wal-Mart attached the Kathie Lee label to the handbags made at Liang Shi and boasted in its advertisements that a portion of the proceeds from their sale would go to children's charities. Unfortunately, Wal-Mart is but one of dozens of U.S. retailers that have countenanced such conditions. Not all of them are as honest (or perhaps as stupid) as Irwin Gordon, president of Ava-Line, a company that makes lapel pins, who told *Business News,*

> We have a factory in China where we have 250 people. We own them; it's our factory. We pay them $40 a month and they work 28 days a month. They work from 7 A.M. to 11 P.M. . . . [that is $.09 an hour]. They all eat together, 16 people to a room, stacked on four bunks to a corner. Generally, they're young girls from the hills.[81]

But whether contractors are as candid as that or not, the consequences are similar: no labor rights for workers in China and no job security for Americans. Forty-five thousand American apparel workers lost their jobs in 1997. In that same year U.S. apparel companies imported $4.85 billion worth of clothing and accessories made in China, and our merchandise trade deficit with China alone stood at $49.7 billion, up 26 percent over the previous year.[82] We might very well run a deficit of that magnitude even if China were the world's strictest enforcer of International Labour Organization standards, but why should even a penny be chalked up to that country's mistreatment of its workers?

Little wonder, then, that the work of someone like Han Dongfang of China has implications for the lives of thousands of people in our own country.

Many of the leaders of the Tiananmen Square democracy movement have left China to pursue their lives in the United States, but Han Dongfang has remained, albeit in Hong Kong. A few weeks before the massacre in the Square, Han helped workers organize China's first independent labor union. China's labor laws are in some respects quite progressive. They call for an eight-hour day, a forty-hour week, and two days of rest a week. They require overtime to be voluntary and to not exceed nine hours a week.[83] Unfortunately, these laws are rarely honored, and even worse, sometimes the treatment of workers is downright medieval. A migrant worker in the Pearl River Delta in southern China, for example, was locked up in a dog cage with two Alsatians for five hours after he was allegedly found stealing toys from his workplace.[84] Four Chinese farmers who ventured to the northern city of Xi'an were taken into custody by the police, who then sold the farmers for $121 to the owner of a quarry, where they were forced to work sixteen hours a day.[85]

This is to be expected once you know that the only union allowed by law in China is the government-recognized All China Federation of Trade Unions (ACFTU), which, as Han describes it, "does not hesitate to take the side of the employer or management and willingly serves as a tool . . . to talk workers into passivity." In 1989, Han tried to change that with the establishment of the independent Workers Autonomous Federation, but it was quickly squelched and Han jailed for twenty-two months. Having contracted tuberculosis in prison, he was released, sent to the United States for medical treatment (where a surgeon removed a lung that Han said "looked like tofu"), and he was then refused entry back into China when he tried to return.

But Han Dangfong had always had a stubborn streak. While in the army after his high school years, he had complained about corrupt officers and was promptly denied promotion. When he had learned after the Tiananmen Square massacre that a warrant had been issued for his arrest, he went to the police station to argue his innocence and was summarily arrested. Refused entry to China after he had been sent to the United States for medical treatment, Han then tried to sneak in. When he was caught, he was expelled to Hong Kong, where he took up residence and founded the *China Labour Bulletin* to keep information about labor abuses in China alive. He began broadcasting on Radio Free Asia from Hong Kong even after the station's two Hong Kong staffers left their jobs to avoid punishment pending China's takeover of the territory in 1997. Unlike other dissidents in Hong Kong, Han refused offers of political asylum before the city reverted to Chinese rule and remains active there today. Four thousand copies of his *Bulletin* are sent regularly to the Chinese mainland, where the police just as regularly confiscate them. But Han is not discouraged. "Even the police can read," he has said. "They need an independent trade union too. If they can be the first to organize . . . , it would be a very good thing."[86]

Lower wages and abysmal working conditions overseas are not the only reasons American workers are laid off—many are replaced by machines, for example—or that companies seek more fertile labor markets elsewhere. Nor is protectionism either wise or possible in as globalized an economy as ours. But the conclusion is inescapable that of all segments of the population, the U.S. laborer ought to be one of those most concerned about the impact of human rights violations on his or her paycheck and future. Furthermore, to the extent to which human rights violations contribute to higher trade deficits, they can harm every American by costing us capital, depressing prices for U.S. goods, lowering wages, and diminishing our competitive advantage. In February 2000 the United States' overall trade deficit stood at $267 billion, $69 billion of that in relationship to China.[87] Between 1979 and 1994 deficits increased in real terms by about $100 billion, costing, by one calculation, 2.4 million jobs, including 290,000 among college-educated workers.[88] When American workers are out of jobs or their salaries are depressed, it costs us all—at the very least in support for the safety net required to take care of them.

The relationship between business and civil and political rights is an extraordinarily complicated one. It is not enough, for example, for human rights activists to shame or bully one company into compliance with human rights standards if an entire industry is going to keep on violating them. It is downright counterproductive to cut a cooperative company no slack and let intransigent companies go free from criticism. It is not enough for one country to place economic sanctions on an offensive regime if, by restricting the access of its own companies, it is simply making it easier for other countries' businesses to fill the trade vacuum with that oppressive customer. It is not enough to put an end to child labor if the child and her family then starve or are forced into sexual slavery. If we protect the jobs of American workers at the expense of Salvadoran or Chinese, we have accomplished worse than nothing, because the safety nets in the United States are far superior to those in El Salvador or China. At the same time, if the champions of economic integration fail to see that, left utterly unbridled, globalization threatens to upset the balance between capital and labor, the common understandings on which the capitalist system is predicated and, combined with the growing gap between rich and poor, invites explosion, they have been stupefied by the glint of lucre.

Perhaps nothing is more damaging to productive dialogue between the business and human rights communities than the assumption on both sides that the only way to use economic power to further human rights is to apply economic sanctions, be those in the form of divestment, denial of Most Favored Nation trade status, closing off membership in the World Trade Organization, making loans from the World Bank conditional on specified improvements or any other. Social justice advocates often leap to this conclusion because it seems the simplest. Business leaders often leap to it because it seems the most frightening. Sometimes of course coercive sanctions are indeed the most effective strategy. But economic sanctions are usually a zero-sum game and, when it comes to the complexity of international relations, zero-sum games, paradoxically, often create two losers, as they have, for instance, in relationship to Cuba, where U.S. embargoes have merely kept average Cubans impoverished while failing to accomplish their ostensible goal of weakening Fidel Castro's hold on power.

Which leads us finally to the question of the relationship between globalization and human rights violations. Much has been written and even more has been shouted from both the right and the left of the political spectrum about the evils of globalization, its sacrifice of labor and the environment for the sake of even grander concentrations of wealth than J. P. Morgan in his most orgiastic of dreams could ever have imagined.

To dismiss globalization so cavalierly, however, is not only chimerical but it is to ignore the ways in which a more technologically integrated world (which globalization both depends on and feeds) has wrought a revolution in the struggle for human rights. It is virtually impossible today for human rights crimes to be committed in even the most remote corners of the globe without the rest of the world knowing about them almost instantaneously. Any country that would be a part of the world's economy must be hooked into it electronically and that means into information systems the content of which is almost impossible to control. E-mail and the Internet can pass along rights-talk as readily as recipes, news of atrocities as swiftly as purchases by e-commerce. With China having 8.9 million Internet users today (up from two million in 1999), it will eventually be impossible, hard as the government is currently trying, to regulate that burgeoning use. I am not the only person to have visited a Maasai village hard in the Rift Valley that was outfitted with shallow latrines, a broken chalkboard for the schoolchildren and a personal computer and whose chief greeted me with the query "How are Bill and Monica?"

As more and more business is done on-line, as growing numbers of individuals become invested in the international bond market, either directly or through pension funds, as corporations move their investments faster and faster from one country to another, the stability of those countries, their willingness to provide accurate financial information, to crack down on corruption, to regulate the market squarely, to respond creatively to economic shocks—in short, to respect human rights—becomes the hard-core, bottom-line financial concern of more people, corporations, and international financial institutions. That has to be good for human rights.

But they and every other globalized investment are put at risk not just by the fact that the vast majority of the world still has no access whatsoever to the Internet (the so-called digital divide) or by the forces of reaction to modernization but by the human dynamics of inequity. Globalization can work immense hardship on vast numbers of people if it becomes a pawn of repression and a purveyor of even greater poverty. As a sign outside the 1999 APEC meeting in Auckland, New Zealand, read: "What good is economic growth if you can't enjoy it?" As a Bulgarian writer observed following a description of the new-found presence of beggars in Sofia streets and pensioners living on $24 a month: "What is the West offering us in return for this misery?"

Some of the clamor may be sour grapes, and some of it the inevitable fallout of economic transformation. But just as the market reforms, labor agreements, and safety nets of the turn of the twentieth century salvaged the United States, and with it U.S. capitalism from class warfare that might have split apart the country, so those who promote a globalized economy would be wise to match their enthusiasm for earnings with a corresponding commitment to free minds and fair play. The details of how that balance is constructed are beyond the bounds of this book, but the burden of my argument is that whether capitalism fosters freedom or freedom provides the loam for capitalism is ultimately of less interest to either the chicken or the egg than that if you want economic growth, you had best pay heed to human rights. Indeed, it is not too strong to say that just as the solution to imperfect democracy is more democracy, if globalization is to be rescued from itself, it will be rescued by a stronger dose of human rights.

Rail against capitalism as you will, but recognize that since we are stuck with it, the test now is to make it work for the largest number of people. Columnist Thomas Friedman believes that by using the Web's organizing power and consumers' purchasing power, corporations can be enticed, if not bullied, into virtue.[89] The International Monetary Fund has made some of its loans to Russia contingent on the nation taking steps against corruption and toward greater openness—a model that could well be emulated by it and other financial institutions in relation to other issues.[90] American unions have made clear that it is not globalization per se that they resist but the dearth of rules, participation, and conscience in its "governance."[91]

If globalization is to be humanized, however, prophets and profiteers must find those points where their interests intersect. They cannot do that if one continues to speak Finnish and the other Hindi. Banish the moralisms and the machismo, however, and we just may be able to agree that human rights have a relationship to *everybody's* economic welfare. Let that happen and everybody profits.

In 755 the Tang dynasty poet Tu Fu wrote about the corruptions of Chinese court life:

> In the central hall there are fair goddesses ... [who] clothe their guests with warm furs of sable, entertain them with the finest music ..., feed them with the broth of camel's pad, with pungent tangerines and oranges ripened in frost. Behind the red-lacquered gates, wine is left to sour, meat to rot. Outside these gates lie the bones of the frozen and the starved. The flourishing and the withered are just a foot apart.[92]

In economic times as hearty as these in the United States, it takes a bit of perspicacity to see that the flourished and the withered remain little more than a foot apart. The fates of the two are, however, even more complicatedly entwined now, thanks to that globalized economy, than they were in 755. Sometimes it is hard to know exactly how, what with conglomerates and leveraged buyouts and subsidiaries of subsidiaries, our money is being used or who is exploiting whom. One of the features of globalization is that nobody seems to understand it all or to be in charge.

That there are no easy answers, however, is no excuse for making the questions appear even more obscure than they really are. Is there a relationship between civil and political human rights (to say nothing of social and economic) and our financial futures? You bet there is. People wither not just because they starve but because they have no voice with which to call for food; economies fail when they break the political promises required to make them work. By denying the connection between economic health and human rights, corporate apologists and their "realist" government allies make finding solutions even more difficult and in the process put our own economic futures in jeopardy. That goes for the stockholders as well as the garment workers.

If an isolated economy fails, the damage may be limited. But if a globalized economy fails, every one will pay the consequences. Like it or not, our lives depend on other people's wisdom and other people's welfare. Much like they depend on the topic of chapter 4: the water we drink and the air we breathe.

4

Forest and Ice

....

Human Rights and the World around Us

The environment is man's first right.
—KEN SARO-WIWA, environmentalist
and leader of the Movement for the
Survival of Ogoni People

ALEXANDER NIKITIN had never been in trouble before. Throughout the eighteen years he had served as a nuclear engineer in the Soviet navy, he had been considered a model military man. The recipient of many awards and a member of the Communist Party, Nikitin, who was married to the daughter of a Russian admiral, had risen to the rank of captain by 1985 in the Soviet Union's Northern Fleet, that distinguished branch of the armed forces which, during World War II, had kept open the ports of the Kola Peninsula, including Murmansk, through which the Allies supplied the resources the Soviets needed to carry on the war effort against the Nazis. During the Cold War the Northern Fleet had been the Soviet Union's most important naval bastion, especially when it came to the country's nuclear-powered submarines, two-thirds of which were assigned to it. So trusted was Nikitin by military authorities that in 1987 he was appointed senior inspector in the Nuclear and Radiation Safety Inspection Department of the Ministry of Defense, a position privy to information the Soviets considered highly sensitive. He served as senior inspector until his voluntary retirement in 1992.

But Nikitin's years in the Safety Inspection Department were unnerving. The more he learned about Soviet (and later, Russian) handling of nuclear materials, the more worried he became. Those worries prompted him, after his retirement, to join the Bellona Foundation, a Norwegian nongovernmental organization dedicated to exposing the formidable environmental problems of Russia's northwestern region, hard on the Norwegian border, many of them related to nuclear fuel. As a specialist with firsthand knowledge of radioactivity and the practices of the Northern Fleet, Nikitin was an invaluable source of information and guidance.

The information Nikitin supplied the Bellona group was frightening indeed. In a report he coauthored in 1996, Nikitin described the incompetence of nuclear submarine crews, dangerous techniques used to refuel nuclear reactors, the frequency of cracks in the reactors while in operation, leakage of nuclear fuel into the ocean, and unsafe storage practices involving highly contaminated control rods.[1] Moreover, Nikitin detailed nuclear submarine and reactor accidents, four of which had resulted in the sinking of ships and one of which almost resulted in an attack on three U.S. cities.[2] He claimed that more than five hundred people had died in such accidents since 1961, and he noted that more than one hundred decommissioned submarines, reactors intact, had simply been left to rot because Russia could not afford to clean them up.

Even before Nikitin's Bellona report was published, the Russian government took steps to repress it. In October 1995, Bellona's Murmansk office was ransacked by the Federal Security Service (FSB), successors to the notorious KGB, which confiscated all research for the report. Over the next few months the Bellona Foundation worked on reconstructing the report from public sources, thus demonstrating that the material Nikitin had provided was in the public realm. Nonetheless, on February 6, 1996, Alexander Nikitin, retired naval officer, was summarily arrested and charged with high treason and the divulging of state secrets—crimes punishable by up to twenty years in prison. "It was very scary when they took him away," Nikitin's daughter Julia Tchernova said later. "But my father is a calm, determined man and at first he thought it was a mistake. He was astonished when they put him in prison."[3]

And with good reason. For not only had the Bellona Foundation proven that Nikitin had not told them anything the foundation could not have discovered independently (a fact subsequently confirmed by three retired Soviet navy admirals), but knowledge of the risks of radiation are so commonplace in Murmansk (which sits, after all, in a region in which 18 percent of the world's nuclear reactors are located) that a sign in the center of town lists the time of day, temperature, and current radiation level.[4] Furthermore, the report quoted the commander-in-chief of the Northern Fleet as saying in 1995, "The problems of storing spent nuclear fuel, radioactive waste [and] inactive submarines . . . are a problem not only for the Northern Fleet but also for the Russian state. . . . If measures are not taken to address the situation today, over a period of time the situation could become critical and lead to an ecological disaster."[5] Still more germane was the fact that even if Nikitin *had* revealed state secrets about environmental contamination, his right—even his obligation—to do so is protected explicitly in Article 7 of the Russian Federal Law on State Secrets, adopted in 1993. This article holds that no information on the conditions of the environment or on extraordinary incidents that endanger human life may be classified as state secrets.[6]

Nonetheless the FSB declared the Bellona report "banned literature" and forbade its import into the country, apparently unaware that the report had been posted for months in Russian on the Bellona Web site.[7] Thus began a bizarre odyssey for Nikitin through the Soviet legal system. He was initially denied independent counsel and offered a former KGB officer as an attorney on the catch-22 grounds that only someone in whom the FSB had confidence could receive a security clearance to deal with a case involving state secrets. Charged with violating secret laws and held in custody for ten months, Nikitin's tires were slashed after his release pending trial, and he was followed by "men in black" who threatened his attorney.[8] In order that they not be targets of FSB intimidation designed to demoralize the former naval officer, Nikitin's wife left Russia for Canada, and his daughter for Norway and subsequently the United States.

Over the course of the ordeal the charges against Nikitin, Russia's first "prisoner of conscience" in the post-Soviet era, were revised no fewer than eight times as various intermediate court judgments found prosecutorial procedures at fault. Restricted to Saint Petersburg, he was permitted on only one occasion to leave the city (to visit his grandfather in Ukraine) but was removed from his homebound train by Ukrainian security officials and detained at a remote border outpost before finally being allowed to return to Russia.[9] Russian officials, from the Minister for Nuclear Energy to advisers to President Boris Yeltsin, were at pains to convict Nikitin even before trial, some going so far as to call him a "foreign spy."[10] But for the international community Nikitin became a cause célèbre, a potent symbol of the connection between human rights (including free speech and the protection of due process) and the preservation of a livable world.

No doubt in part because of the international notoriety, Nikitin was finally acquitted of the charges in December 1999, and in September 2000 prosecutors lost their final appeal. "I am convinced," Nikitin has written, "that ecology cannot be secret. Environmental openness is an inalienable human right. Any attempt to conceal any information about harmful impacts on people and the environment is a crime against humanity."[11]

If the Nikitin case were a singular example of Russian antagonism toward environmental defenders, it might be no more than a curiosity. But the fact is that Russia's tendency to discourage truth telling about its environmental record is hardly a new phenomenon. The most notorious example of this syndrome was the 1986 nuclear accident at Chernobyl. Serious accidents at nuclear plants have of course occurred in many countries, including such democratic ones as the United States (Three Mile Island in 1979) and Japan (Tokaimura in 1999). But the Chernobyl accident was not only the most dangerous, involving more than one hundred tons of fissionable material and having a measurable effect as far away as the United States[12]; it was also caused in part by the lack of government accountability to a free press characteristic of the Soviet Union, the absence of an independent sector of voluntary organizations capable of monitoring government practices, and the silence of a public deprived of a free vote among contending parties.

Chernobyl was far from the first nuclear accident in Russia, but as Grigory Medvedev clearly described in his 1989 book *The Truth about Chernobyl,* "The concealment from the general public of accidents at nuclear power stations had become a standard mode of behavior under the Minister of Energy and Electronification, P. S. Neporozhny." The secrecy did not stop with the public, however. The accidents were hidden

not only from the general public and the government *but also from people who worked at Soviet nuclear power stations.* This latter fact

posed a special danger, as failure to publicize mishaps always has unexpected consequences; it makes people careless and complacent.

Neporozhny's successor as Minister, Anatoly Ivanovich Mayorets
. . . maintained the tradition of silence. Only six months after his ap-
pointment, he signed an order . . . stipulating as follows: "Information about the unfavorable ecological impact of energy-related facilities (the effect of electro-magnetic fields, irradiation, contamination
of air, water and soil) on operation personnel, the population, and
the environment shall not be reported openly in the press or broadcast on radio or television." In his first few months as minister, Mayorets made this morally dubious policy the foundation of his ac-
tivities.[13]

The tradition of secrecy so prevalent in a totalitarian state, the absence
of free debate occasioned by fear of reprisals for speaking out, and the
lack of an independent press capable of discovering and publicizing the
fact that the public and even certain segments of the government were
being deprived of critical information with which to make decisions
made Chernobyl a disaster waiting to happen. Without accurate information about past mishaps, those in charge had no means by which to
prevent future disasters. Here was a case in which the absence of rights
protection very nearly produced a global catastrophe. For although
many governments try to hush up their mistakes and silence their
whistle-blowers, only those that lack countervailing institutions capable of calling those governments to account will be able to keep those
secrets indefinitely. Even after the Chernobyl accident was public
knowledge, the Soviets downplayed its significance enormously.[14]

The mind-set that motivated the prosecution of Nikitin, then, was
not without precedent. Although many things have changed in Russia
since the Soviet days, an unwillingness to brook criticism of environmental policies is not one of them. For Alexander Nikitin is far from
the only environmentalist to run afoul of Russian authorities. Another
notorious case involved Grigory Pasko, also a naval captain but with
Russia's Pacific Fleet. As part of his duties, Pasko served as a reporter for
the Fleet's newspaper, *Boyevaya Vaktha (Battle Watch)*. He also worked
as a freelancer for NHK, Japan's largest television station.

In 1993, Pasko filmed a Russian navy tanker dumping radioactive
waste into the Sea of Japan. This film, under the title *Extra-Dangerous*

Zone, was eventually shown by NHK in Japan. In a series of articles in *Battle Watch* and in the Japanese newspaper *Asahi Shimbun,* Pasko, like Nikitin, described the environmental threat caused by decaying nuclear submarines and went on to reveal that the Russian navy had illegally dumped liquid and solid nuclear waste off the coast of Vladivostok. Angered by these revelations, the Federal Security Service took Pasko into custody in 1997, confiscated documents from his apartment, and charged him with passing classified information to Japanese agents. Although officials admitted that none of the documents they had confiscated was classified, they claimed that, taken as a whole, the series of articles and television programs published and aired over the previous three years posed a threat to national security.[15]

"All Russian citizens," Pasko later wrote, "can be divided into two categories: those who are already in jail and those who will soon be there." He then described being arrested and held by the police:

> They can come at any time . . . [but no matter when they come for you] there is one thing they will always have in common: they will be brutal. They will handcuff you and take you to the police station, where they will begin the psychological pressure. Then they will beat you and put you in a cell. . . . Then they will take you out, beat you again and interrogate you. Expect regular beatings. My advice: do not resist but . . . always remain silent.[16]

For twenty months Pasko was imprisoned, much of the time in solitary confinement. Like the good journalist he was, he recorded his prison experiences and posted them on a popular Internet site.[17] Finally in July 1999, after a prolonged international outcry against Pasko's arrest and incarceration, the court dropped the charge of treason and convicted Pasko of misusing his authority as a military journalist, a conviction for which it granted him amnesty.

Although both Pasko and Nikitin were ultimately acquitted, it was not before a pointed message had been sent to Russia's environmental community: "Speak out and you too may end up charged with treason." It is a message that Vladimir Putin, then FSB chief and now Russia's president, was only too eager to underscore: "Sadly," he has said, "foreign secret service use not only diplomatic cover but also all sorts of ecological organizations."[18]

This message is apparently getting through. According to the Sierra Club, their Russian counterparts in the environmental movement are running scared. "Russian journalists who have written about the [Nikitin] case have been fired, their papers fearing FSB retribution. Russian environmentalists have shied away from working on these critical, albeit controversial, issues. The director of the FSB, Nikolai Kovalyov, even said at a press conference that he considered fighting environmental lobbies a national priority."[19] Scientists are now feeling the pinch too. Just as Pasko was being released, Vladimir Soyfer, a professor of marine radiology at the Pacific Oceanology Institute who has devoted a forty-year career to studying radioactive contamination of Russia's oceans, was arrested and charged with high treason.[20]

It is not just Russian journalists or environmentalists or scientists whose lives may be disrupted by the violation of their rights, however. The rest of the world has a rather large stake in the outcome of these matters too.

Most monks of the sixth century lived their entire lives in a single place, a single monastery, isolated from the rest of the world. But one set of monks in the time of the Early Church could not sit still. These monks in fact were seized by a terrible wanderlust and proceeded to travel through the desert, lodging at one monastery after another for no more than a few days at a time. They came to be known as "gyratory monks" and Saint Benedict disapproved of them heartily. "They are restless servants to the seduction of their own appetites," he wrote. "It is better to be silent as to their wretched lifestyle than to speak of it."

The ocean currents of the Northern Hemisphere are like those monks. They just can't sit still. In fact, they develop a circular pattern called a gyre that determines the flow of the ocean and all it contains. Those cold-water currents in the Northern Hemisphere, so-called eastern boundary currents, that flow from high latitudes toward the equator are named North Atlantic–Canary and North Pacific–California. The North Atlantic–Canary current tracks out of the Arctic Ocean down the coast of Labrador, across the North Atlantic on the North Atlantic Drift, then down the east coast of Africa (hence "Canary"), back across the Atlantic at the North Equatorial and into the Gulf Stream up the east coast of North America. The North Pacific–California moves out of the Bering Sea across the North Pacific where it splits, some moving north up the Canadian West Coast to Alaska and some south down the California coast toward the Equator.

The Russians have been dumping radioactive waste into the Arctic Ocean since they tested their first nuclear-powered submarine in 1959. In the early years it was commonplace for the waste containers not to sink and for the naval crews to blithely fire on them with machine guns, thus causing water to seep in and the containers to gradually submerge. In more recent years the problems have involved accidents, deterioration of containers, inability to extract fuel from damaged reactors before they are dumped, and widespread violation of the country's own rules about ocean contamination.

Twelve other nations, including the United States, have dumped nuclear waste into the seas at one time or another as well, but the Soviet/Russian dumping, in contrast to that of other countries, has taken place in shallow waters and on the continental shelf. Furthermore, over the course of the past forty years the Russians have dumped high-level waste (the most highly radioactive variety, which decays the most slowly and remains radioactive for hundreds or thousands of years); they have dumped it in liquid and solid form, and they have dumped far more of it than the other twelve nuclear nations put together. Nor is Russia a signatory to the London Convention of 1993 that prohibits the use of oceans as a depository for any nuclear waste.[21] All this has led Nikolay Yegerov, Russia's deputy atomic energy minister, to call the situation "a Chernobyl in slow motion."[22]

And just like the fallout from Chernobyl, which reached the United States on air currents, so too the ocean wastes deposited in the Arctic region, thanks to the action of the gyres, reach U.S. waters.

How serious is the problem right now? The truth is that nobody knows, in part because civilian scientists have not been permitted since 1967 to conduct research tests closer than fifty to one hundred kilometers to the Russian dumping sites.[23] What we do know is that more than 11,000m$_3$ of radioactive waste have been dumped in the Barents and Kara Seas.[24] From studies of discharge from nuclear power plants, we know that radioisotopes dissolved in seawater can travel to regions vastly remote from where they entered the water. We know that such discharges have had a negative effect on fish reproduction and that in general fish are highly sensitive to environmental changes, be it water temperature or pollution. We know that skin lesions have been spotted on fish from the North Sea to the eastern seaboard of the United States. We know that radionuclides can contaminate salt marsh and tidal pasture areas used for grazing. We know that the isotope cesium is easily absorbed into the food chain. And we know, on a larger scale, that Arctic oceans are particularly susceptible to environmental damage and that changes in glacial ecosystems can have a ripple effect around the world.[25] At the very least it seems safe to say that U.S. fishing interests in northern waters are at peril, and all American consumers are at potential risk.

However serious the problem, it is dire enough that Norway has pledged $30 million and the United Kingdom $4.5 million to help clean up the mess. It is serious enough that U.S. government and business interests have spent more than $1.25 million to help upgrade Russia's only liquid radioactive waste-processing facility to provide an alternative form of disposal to dumping. As one U.S. navy official has said, "The US . . . cannot afford the risk of [nuclear] waste migrating beyond the Murmansk region."[26]

No one would argue of course that violations of civil and political rights are the sole cause of Russia's environmental nightmare. Many other factors are at work—from poor training of nuclear workers to an economy unable to afford proper environmental safeguards to weak regulatory oversight. But by intimidating those who try to hold the government accountable or to press it to address the hazards, by mimicking Saint Benedict's posture that "it is better to be silent [about the danger] than speak of it," Russia deprives itself (and hence the world) of a critical element in civil society that can help correct the problems.

If we know relatively little about the effects of radioactive waste on the oceans, we know a great deal about the impact of so-called greenhouse gases, particularly carbon dioxide (CO_2), on the Earth's atmosphere. As the use of fossil fuels has grown over the past century, so too has the amount of CO_2 (and other gases that trap heat) released into the atmosphere. Such human-generated emissions account for about 4 percent of all greenhouse gases, and that in turn is calculated to have increased the Earth's average temperature by 0.3 to 0.6 degrees Celsius. If that doesn't sound like much, consider that this rate works out to approximately a 2-degree-Celsius increase over the next century—and it was a decline of only 2 degrees Celsius that triggered the great Ice Age 115,000 years ago.[27]

Some would dismiss the threat of global warming as inconsequential. "Heat waves, droughts, famines and extreme cold: our predecessors suffered just as we do," editorialized anthropologist Brian Fagan, author of *Floods, Famines, and Emperors: El Niño and the Fate of Civilizations:* "Climatic extremes . . . are part and parcel of human existence."[28] While others, including the more than two thousand scientists associated with the Intergovernmental Panel on Climate Change that advised the Kyoto Climate Change Conference in 1997 to draft a treaty limiting greenhouse emissions, take the problem far more seriously. Among the dangers that models of climate change predict are:

- More frequent and severe heat waves with a corresponding increase in climate-related deaths, including in the United States where Chicago, for example, could see an increase of 260 percent in such deaths over the next fifty years.
- Extreme weather events, such as flood or drought, resulting in increased desertification and threats to safe drinking water.
- Growth in infectious diseases as insect-borne maladies such as malaria, encephalitis, and dengue fever spread into the Northern Hemisphere.
- Continued melting of glaciers and rise of sea levels with accompanying loss of land.
- Reduction in biological diversity.[29]

Regardless of whether all of this comes to pass, however, few people would dispute that we would be wise to limit greenhouse gases as much as possible and no one would deny that one of the most effective natural allies in helping us do that are the Earth's forests. By storing and absorbing carbon dioxide and transforming it into clean oxygen, forests—particularly tropical ones—help ward off the greenhouse effect. But half of the world's tropical forests have been destroyed in the past two hundred years, and with 33.8 million of the remaining 3.5 billion acres being lost every year, it will not be long before we run out of tropical forests altogether. In the Amazon alone a forest area the size of Massachusetts is felled every twelve months. Uncontrolled logging and burning of tropical forests accounts for one-third of the world's carbon emissions, thus contributing enormously to the Earth's greenhouse problems.[30]

Our forests would appear to be in every respect an invaluable resource, to be cherished and protected. But one of the groups most frequently targeted for human rights abuses are those environmentalists in developing countries who try to preserve the forests. Because these activists are often leaders of indigenous communities whose campaigns for forest protection are closely linked with their efforts to defend their people's land, the importance of their environmental witness is sometimes lost on outside observers. In many cases, however, these environmental defenders are the John Muirs of today. Because we recognize even more than in John Muir's time how dependent our own environmental health and safety is on the planet's health and safety, these defenders are in a very real sense fighting for the future of our own communities just as surely as their own.

If you have ever sat in rattan furniture or carried your keys in a rattan purse, you probably have the Bentian people of Indonesia to thank for it. From the vines of the forests in their East Kalimantan homeland, they support themselves by harvesting this well-known product under a highly sophisticated system of rotational agriculture that protects both the forests and their livelihood. So respected is their sustainable system of forest management that they were awarded the prestigious Goldman Environmental Prize for it in 1997.

Not surprisingly, therefore, the Bentians were not happy when they learned in 1993 that a corporation owned by a close associate of Indonesia's ruler, General Suharto, was bulldozing their forests and intending to clear-cut them. When their chief, Loir Botor Dingit, reported the destruction to the government and asked for compensation, he and his supporters were interrogated and harassed by the security police. Finally, not able to silence Chief Dingit by intimidation, the government charged him with forgery. It seems that when the chief had submitted to the government a list of land plots destroyed by the corporation for which he was seeking payment, he had referred to the lands by their ancestral names, as is the Bentian custom. The authorities took this as the pretense to charge him with forging the names of long-dead ancestors. Not until Suharto fell was Chief Dingit finally cleared, in October

1998.[31] He is but one of many environmentalists who have been targeted by authorities in Indonesia—a country whose ancient rain forests are in desperate need of protection. The fires of 1997 and 1998 that ravaged up to ten million hectares of forest in Kalimantan and Sumatra were called "a planetary disaster" by the World Wildlife Fund for Nature and are estimated to have contributed a 5 percent increase in global greenhouse gases through their massive outpouring of carbon.

In many ways, however, Chief Dingit was one of the lucky ones. No one did more to bring the destruction of the rainforests to world attention than the leader of the Brazilian rubbertappers, Chico Mendes, and he paid for it with his life, murdered in 1988 by those connected to timber and logging interests. Wangari Maathai, leader of the Greenbelt environmental group in Kenya, has been subjected to years of harassment, imprisonment, and beatings for her demonstrations against the handover of public forestland to developers and her attempts to plant young saplings on land already clear-cut. In Guatemala Carlos Coc Rax organized his Q'eqchi' people to stop illegal logging on indigenous lands, and in April 1999 he disappeared.[32]

Or consider the dramatic case of Rodolfo Montiel Flores and Teodoro Cabrera Garcia, two campesinos in the southern Mexican state of Guerrero who formed the Organization of Ecologists of the Sierra de Petatlan to peacefully protest Idaho-based Boise Cascade Company's destruction of one of North America's last old-growth pine and fir forests. Mexico has eliminated half of its forests in just four decades, and the government actively encourages rural residents to fell trees or sell forestland to loggers.[33] The longer the logging continued in the Sierra de Petatlan, the peasants noted, the more the region's springs and streams began to dry up and the production of crops to dwindle. In 1995 a group of farmers on their way to stage a demonstration in the state capital were stopped by hundreds of police; seventeen farmers were killed. Intimidated but not defeated, Montiel, Cabrera, and others formed their organization to demand that the Mexican government evaluate the ecological effects of logging on the Sierra.

Eventually Boise Cascade pulled its operations out of Mexico, infuriating landowners who had profited nicely from selling hardwood to the corporation. Seeking revenge, the landowners accused the campesinos of planting marijuana and belonging to leftist guerilla movements, and they enlisted their allies in the Mexican army to track down the community's two leaders. On May 2, 1999, Montiel and Cabrera were arrested, beaten, tortured with electric shocks to the genitals, held for two days partially submerged in a river, and forced to hold marijuana plants and rifles for photographers and to confess to crimes they insist they did not commit. Shortly after their trial, their defense lawyer was herself kidnapped and beaten by assailants. Today Montiel and Cabrera remain in prison and hardwood logging has resumed at an even faster clip under the direction of Mexican logging companies. Without anyone to defend them, the last old-growth forests on the continent are rapidly disappearing and with them one of the most valuable resources with which to defend the planet's health.[34] As Montiel has said so poignantly, "The earth without trees becomes a desert because the soul of the water lives in the cool of the forest."[35]

These are just a few examples of the intimate connection between the protection of human rights and the preservation of the Earth's environmental interests. There are many more examples. Environmental dangers abroad often have consequences in the United States. As one observer summarized,

> Landless farmers can bring about political and economic instability, the overthrow of democratic governments and the loss of U.S. markets. Mass migrations, triggered by soil erosion, flooding and hunger, can burden neighboring states and threaten peace. Competition among nations for scarce water resources carries risks of warfare. A large change in climate equilibrium could profoundly affect prosperity, politics and security around the world.[36]

Environmental dangers like these are always exacerbated when environmentalists are under threat.

Chief Red Cloud of the American Oglala Indians once said of the American government, "They made us many promises, more than I can remember, but they never kept but one; they promised to take our land, and they took it."[37] One of the reasons the government could get away with these many broken promises was because in those days there were no independent organizations like the Indian Law Resource Center or the American Civil Liberties Union to sue the government. Similarly, when a treaty on biological diversity was signed a number of years ago, one national representative remarked that although his government would sign, they wouldn't pay much attention to the treaty's terms. The reason they could afford such cynicism is because they knew that they had frightened their own environmentalists into silence. China, for example, is a major contributor to global climate change, ozone depletion, and illegal trade in endangered species and tropical timber, but its record of enforcement of international environmental treaties, absent a vibrant independent sector and respect for the rule of law, is abysmal.[38]

If the Earth is to avoid ecological degradation, it will require a level of transparency about environmental conditions, including mistakes and failures, and a degree of respect for global environmental standards that most repressive regimes will have a hard time meeting.[39] Of course, environmental damage can be sustained under any kind of political system. I was born in Pittsburgh, Pennsylvania, before that city cleaned up its act and well remember that a white bedsheet hung on the line to dry in the morning would be as gray from soot cover by midafternoon as the perpetually gray Pittsburgh steel mill skies. But Pittsburgh recognized its crisis and learned from it. Politicians knew they would be voted out of office if they did not fix the problem, and citizens had a voice with which to demand reform. In contrast, anyone who traveled through Ceausescu's Romania with its perpetually choking children and blackened heavens at the height of day will not take lightly the prescription one scholar offered right before the fall of Eastern European Communism: "The most environmentally productive thing the West could do," said Barbara Jancar in the summer of 1990, "would be to invest in democracy in the East."[40] That democracies tend to be "greener" than dictatorships is no coincidence. Those who treat human beings as things are hardly likely to be more respectful of things themselves—"things" like birds and trees and streams.

Aware of how closely global environmental trends are tied to U.S. interests, the U.S. State Department has within the past few years introduced the concept of "environmental security" into the mainstream of American foreign policy making. "Addressing natural resource issues," then Secretary of State Warren Christopher noted in a speech at Stanford University in 1996, "is frequently critical to achieving political and economic stability and pursuing our strategic goals around the world." One of the causes of the economic collapse in Haiti that sent so many

Haitians fleeing to this country in the mid-1990s, for example, was the fact that nearly all of Haiti's forests had been stripped, making erosion inevitable and leaving the country with few natural resources with which to support the people economically. You can bet that in Haiti under the restrictive rule of General Raul Cedras there were no environmentalists effectively protesting the destruction of the country's ecosystem.

Willard Libby, a former U.S. Atomic Energy Commissioner, once built what he called a "poor man's [fallout] shelter" in his backyard made out of sandbags and railroad ties at a cost of $30 to prove that with even the most humble protection, Americans could survive a nuclear war. A few weeks after its construction, however, it was destroyed by a brush fire, leading Leo Szilard, the famous scientist and disarmament campaigner, to remark: "This proves not only that there is a God but that He has a sense of humor."[41] In explaining why environmental security is such an important concept that the United States would help finance the upgrading of the Russian radioactive waste-processing facility in Murmansk, William A. Nitze of the Environmental Protection Agency said, "Our goal was to . . . [protect] the Arctic ecosystem. . . . Political borders are not barriers to environmental problems. To protect the health of citizens, the environment of the U.S. and our foreign policy interests, we must pay attention to what is happening to the environment on a . . . global scale."[42]

Nitze is absolutely right of course, but to try to protect all of that without protecting those local environmentalists who are the first line of defense against environmental devastation would be like building a $30 fallout shelter out of sandbags and railroad ties. It would be to fool ourselves into taking the "realistic" view that human rights have nothing to do with our national interests. The trouble is that when it comes to the planet's health, the stakes are enormous, and this time God might not be laughing.

5

Only a Plane Ride Away

....

Public Health and Human Rights

The microbe that felled one child in a distant continent yesterday can reach yours today and seed a global
pandemic tomorrow.

—Joshua Lederberg,
Nobel Laureate, Rockefeller University

I N ONE RESPECT environmental activists Alexander Nikitin and
Grigory Pasko were lucky. As former naval officers whose cases attracted international attention, they were not "average" Russian
prisoners. How they were treated is important to Americans because of
who they are and what they tried to warn the world about, but surely
this cannot be said of the many "common criminals"—more than one
million of them—who occupy Russian penal facilities. What could
their fates possibly have to do with Americans?

"When the door to a [Russian] prison cell is opened," remarked Sir
Nigel Rodley, the U.N. special rapporteur on torture in 1995, "one is hit
by a blast of hot, dark, stinking (sweat, urine, feces) gas that passes for
air." Rodley went on to describe rooms so crowded that their occupants
had to take turns lying down; so unsanitary that water had to be boiled
by the prisoners themselves with makeshift heating wires; so lacking in
light and air that it was almost impossible to breathe; so cold in the
winter that prisoners had to huddle together for warmth; and so hot in
the summer that even stripped to their underwear, prisoners sweated
profusely. "The Special Rapporteur would need the poetic skills of a
Dante," he concluded, "adequately to describe the infernal conditions
he found in these cells."[1] Since 1995, human rights violations of this order in Russian prisons have only gotten worse.

But it was another remark Rodley made that has proven especially prophetic. "These cells," he reported, "are disease incubators." Indeed, that is exactly what they have turned out to be. Four years after the publication of Rodley's report, the Public Health Research Institute issued this warning:

> The tuberculosis epidemic in Russia, particularly in Russian prisons, has reached alarming proportions. The prison system acts as an epidemiological pump, releasing into society tens of thousands of active TB cases and hundreds of thousands of infected individuals every year. The high rate of multi-drug resistant tuberculosis among them is especially threatening.[2]

The incidence of TB in Russian prisons is 40 percent to 50 percent higher than in the civilian population; approximately one in ten prisoners is infected, and the bacilli that transmits that infection cannot be contained within a prison wall. After all, tuberculosis is a highly infectious airborne disease spread by coughing. Lack of ventilation, overcrowding, and perpetual darkness allow the disease to thrive, and HIV, which runs rampant in prisons, accelerates the disease. Guards, prison visitors, and lawyers go in and out of prisons every day; prisoners make appearances in court, and thousands with TB are released every year back into their communities.[3] It is little wonder that Russia is facing a health crisis.

But how could such a distant crisis possibly have an impact on the United States? Very simply. We live in an era of increased travel and trade. The medical relief organization Doctors Without Borders has predicted that the threat from uncontrolled tuberculosis in Russia "will become the principal epidemic of the next century."[4] Twenty-seven million Americans visit developing countries every year, to say nothing of more common tourist and business destinations.[5] They bring back photographs, tchotchkes, and memories. They also bring back diseases. Every year 190,000 flights from developing countries land in the United States. Passengers bring with them hope and new energy. They also bring a myriad of microbes. Furthermore, the World Health Organization reported in 2000 that drug-resistant cases of TB had increased by 50 percent in Denmark and Germany.[6] If previous studies of TB's origin in Germany are correct, as many as two-thirds of those cases originated in the former Soviet Union,[7] and close to two million Americans visit Germany every year.[8]

But Americans do not need to go abroad to be susceptible to TB. Almost twenty thousand cases were reported in the United States in 1997, including those of thirteen passengers on a Paris to New York flight, who contracted the disease from an infected Ukrainian passenger.[9] The United States is a favorite destination for Russian émigrés. Says health researcher Barry Kreisworth, "On the basis of molecular typing of tuberculosis among Russian cases in both the civilian and prison populations, we have identified a highly prevalent multidrug resistant clone that has now been observed in cases of tuberculosis among Russian immigrants in New York City. This resistant strain, and others like it, could easily spread in secondary settings."[10] In fact, New York City already saw a serious TB outbreak, which originated in its own prisons, in 1989. And even when the health of Americans is not put in jeopardy by imported diseases, our pocketbooks certainly are. The treatment of drug-resistant TB costs $250,000 per patient, compared with $25,000 to treat a victim of conventional TB.[11]

Tuberculosis is resurgent once again for many reasons: poverty and inadequate medical regimens are but two of them. But providing the perfect environment in which TB can thrive dramatically facilitates its spread. The notion therefore that Americans have no self-interest at stake when it comes to how Russian prisoners are treated—that we need not care, beyond a certain vague moral queasiness perhaps, that tens of thousands of young Russians are held for years in pretrial detention centers (where disease is most rampant) without even having been convicted of any crime—is pure folly. For as the chief of Russian prison hospitals put it, "If Westerners don't . . . help treat TB in Russia [now], in two or three years the problem will be theirs and then it will cost them billions."[12] One of the most effective ways to treat the disease would be to insist on respect for human rights.

Given the dangers of the transport of disease around the globe, some might speculate that the solution to the problem is simply to shut our borders more firmly. But quite apart from the fact that an even tougher immigration policy than recently adopted in the United States would contribute to even more human rights violations, there are practical reasons why such a "solution" is infeasible. Because the time between infection and appearance of disease is quite lengthy for many illnesses—the incubation period for some diseases may exceed twenty-one days and, in the case of HIV, many years—it is impossible with any degree of certainty to screen travelers who may be carrying dangerous infections.[13] "[Even] having one inspector for every person coming in would not prevent disease from coming in," says New York City's assistant commissioner for communicable diseases.[14] Short of shutting down the worldwide tourist industry, cutting off international business travel, and closing down U.S. borders completely, letting no living soul in or out of the country, we must face the fact that human-borne disease is capable of spreading around the world with remarkable rapidity, carried by anyone, be it the rich or the refugee. In 1991 an Aerolineas Argentinas flight made a scheduled stop in Lima, Peru, picked up a load of passengers, and efficiently delivered cholera to Los Angeles. It doesn't take a planeload of people to transmit disease, however. The Spanish conqueror Hernán Cortés managed to decimate the Aztec population in 1520 when one slave from Spanish Cuba arrived in Mexico infected with smallpox.[15]

Nor are human carriers the only transporters of illness. The growth in global trade with its exchange of goods, including plants, animals, and foodstuffs, is a major vehicle by which vectors—those organisms that transmit pathogenic fungi, viruses, and bacteria—make their way around the globe. A 1985 outbreak of dengue fever in Texas, for example, has been attributed to the arrival of a particularly aggressive mosquito species in a shipment of waterlogged used tires sent to Houston, Texas, from Japan for retreading.[16]

Climate change too—particularly the kind of global warming caused in part by deforestation, as discussed in chapter 4—is responsible for some of the United States' increased susceptibility to disease. Higher temperatures raise the reproductive rates of vectors like mosquitoes and entice them farther north, bringing with them malaria, encephalitis, leishmaniasis (a facial-disfiguring disease for which there is no vaccine), Chagas' disease (which debilitates muscles), and elephantiasis (which currently afflicts some four hundred million people worldwide).[17] Malarial infections are already on the rise in the United States, some cases having been identified as far north as Michigan. Anyone who lived in metropolitan New York City in the fall of 1999 when a breed of encephalitis previously unknown in the area was linked to a number of deaths knows how unnerving the appearance of a new threat can be to a population, to say nothing of the CIA, which examined the possibility that the outbreak was attributable to bioterrorism on the part of Saddam Hussein.[18]

Regardless of how they get here, however, more than thirty new pathogenic microbes have been identified in the United States since 1973.[19] Other maladies thought to be under control, such as cholera and diphtheria, have reemerged elsewhere in the world.[20] The globalization of disease and the possibility of worldwide pandemics is no longer a fantasy in the mind of a science fiction writer. As international commerce and travel increase, the dangers will become still more real. By the year 2020, for example, China, where many strains of influenza have first appeared, will be the world's number-one tourist destination, hosting some 130 million visitors each year and supplying 100 million tourists to other parts of the globe.[21] All this has led the Centers for Disease Control (CDC) to conclude that "the health of the American people is inextricably linked to the health of people in other nations; infectious diseases can and do spread rapidly around the globe" and to warn that "once considered 'exotic,' tropical infectious diseases are having an increasing effect on the American public."[22]

No longer will the relative isolation of the United States' geography, poised as it is between two great oceans, protect us, for pestilents know no national boundaries. If nothing else can convince us that our interests are tied to those of the rest of the world, perhaps a few errant microbes will.

No matter how or where a disease originates, it is unlikely to spread widely in the absence of one or more "amplifiers," that is, one or more factors that exacerbate and multiply the impact of the initial pathogen. Sometimes these amplifiers are impossible to control, such as cyclical changes in weather, flight patterns of disease-carrying birds, or the evolution of new strains of microbes. But often the amplifiers that spread disease are related to human behavior, and frequently that behavior is related to the issue of respect for human rights.

Wars, for example, have long been known to contribute mightily to the dissemination of disease;[23] in the thirteenth through the sixteenth centuries the Mongol conquerors brought with them bubonic plague. Slavery facilitated the spread of malaria and yellow fever throughout the Americas, and British colonizers in India and Africa denied medical treatment to indigenous people on the racist assumption that they were genetically inferior.[24] If the denial of what we now call "human rights" has historically been so closely linked to the amplification of illness, why would we think it any different today? The Nicaraguan dictator Anastasio Somoza invested in the collection of plasma from the poorest and most pathetic of his citizens for sale on the international market out of a facility that Nicaraguans dubbed "the house of the vampires." Somoza's undertaking may well have contributed to the worldwide spread of hepatitis, but what is certain is that when Pedro Joaquin Chamorro, the publisher of the opposition newspaper, *La Prensa*, tried to expose the operation, he paid for it with his life.[25] When countries such as Congo and Ethiopia, among the world's poorest nations, succumb to war, their governments have even fewer resources than other countries to devote to sanitation and health care. The International Red Cross has estimated that of the 1.7 million excess deaths in Congo that have occurred since the recent fighting there, all but two hundred thousand are a function of disease, malnutrition, and the breakdown of the public health system.[26]

When it comes to social and economic rights, the connection between health and human rights is self-evident and not simply because the U.N. International Covenant on Economic, Social, and Cultural Rights guarantees "the prevention, treatment and control of epidemic, endemic, occupational and other diseases."[27] The relationship between poverty and disease is so well established that were the world to take seriously the covenant's commitment to "the right of everyone to an adequate standard of living,"[28] we would have an abundance of microbes on the run in a jiffy. Such a crusade would also pay economic dividends to investor countries, because healthier populations make for more productive workers and a more vibrant market for goods and services. But it is the relationship between health and the more traditional civil and political rights that is of interest to us here. For although many amplifiers may not have a direct connection to these types of human rights violations, others—and assuredly far more than foreign policy "realists" ever allow—most certainly do.

Dengue fever, particularly in its more acute form, is not a pleasant disease to contract. Viral in nature, transmitted by mosquitoes, it is characterized by high fever, severe headache, disabling muscle pain, and vomiting, but it may also produce hemorrhaging from the nose, mouth, and gums. Not pleasant, potentially fatal, and there is no vaccine.

In May 1991 dengue fever raged through Havana, Cuba, affecting at least 344,000 people. It took six months to get the ailment under control, by which point the Cuban government had spent more than $100 million.[29] By 1994 the Centers for Disease Control (CDC) could report that Cuba was "the only country in the region that has eliminated dengue as a health problem."[30]

The only problem was that the CDC was wrong. Cuban medical doctor Desi Mendoza Rivero, president of the Colegio Medico Independiente de Santiago de Cuba, knew by 1997 that it was wrong. Dr. Mendoza, then forty-three, had been raised in a family of "believers" —believers in Castro's revolution. His parents had been Young Pioneers in the Cuban Communist movement, and Mendoza was raised to honor Communist ideals. But gradually he began to notice the inequities in this presumably egalitarian society, the fact that those like his parents who were close to the government enjoyed more access to goods and services than did the average Cuban. When Mendoza was fifteen, he dared to criticize the way his school was run and was expelled for his outspokenness. "Soon I was warned," he said later, "that the little people can't win against the big people—even in Cuba."

For a good many years Mendoza kept his opinions to himself because he wanted to study medicine and emulate a family doctor he had known since his youth who often treated his poorer patients for free. Finally, in 1986 Mendoza received his degree in medicine, eventually taking a position at a teaching hospital where his wife, also a physician, held a position as well. But his unhappiness with the Cuban system had not abated, and in 1994 Mendoza fled Cuba on a raft. Rescued at sea, he was interned in a refugee camp at the Guantanamo military base for eight months. When it became obvious that he would not be admitted to the United States, however, he returned to Cuba. By now Mendoza's reputation had been permanently soiled in the eyes of Cuban authorities, and he was refused permission to work in the teaching hospital. This led to the establishment of the private Colegio, where he saw patients informally at his home in Cuba's second largest city, Santiago.

While he was treating these patients, he first recognized the symptoms of dengue and the possibility of another epidemic.

But how could he sound the warning? He was, after all, no longer a state-recognized physician. "Many people here were sick with dengue and were being told only that they had come down with a virus," his wife, Dr. Pinon Rodriguez, explained later.[31] Some of them were even dying, but for some reason the government was covering up the disease. Although Mendoza's former colleagues in the public health system confirmed to him that lab results revealed the presence of dengue, the death certificates listed the causes of death as unknown. Fearing that a widespread outbreak might be on the horizon, Mendoza concluded that the only way to get the word out was to contact journalists in Mexico and Spain who would in turn broadcast the news back to Cuba—a communications practice popularly known as "the boomerang."

On June 18, 1997, Mendoza contacted the foreign journalists. Three days later the local Santiago paper printed the news, and four days after that, Mendoza was arrested. It seems that from the Cuban government's standpoint, his warning could not have come at a worse time. Santiago was scheduled to host several large international events, including a cultural festival and trade fair, which thousands of foreign visitors were expected to attend. Rumors of an outbreak of dengue fever could ruin the entire enterprise. Mendoza was charged with spreading "enemy propaganda" with the intention, said the indictment, of creating "uncertainty, confusion and panic in the Cuban population."

For five months the doctor was held pending trial. Finally, on November 18, he appeared in court, where the authorities even acknowledged that bad publicity resulting from his outspokenness could have adversely affected tourism. Nonetheless, Mendoza was convicted and sentenced to eight years in prison.[32] About a year later, after an appeal by the king and queen of Spain, he was released on the condition that he take up exile in Madrid. Finally, in February 2000, Mendoza, his wife, and three children made it to Miami, where they live today. The doctor's experience serves as a powerful symbol to other Cuban health workers of the perils of telling the truth about disease. Mendoza is trying to renew his medical credentials in the United States, but for the time being he is working as a security guard. "I don't really mind," says this proud, determined man. "After all, I have to start somewhere."[33]

Dengue fever is already well established in the United States (86 cases reported to the CDC in 1995; 179 in 1996[34]), much of it contracted from travel to the Caribbean. Given the growing number of U.S. visitors to Cuba, to say nothing of travel exchanges between Cuba and its Caribbean neighbors, economic sanctions cannot prevent the dissemination of this disease.

The first line of defense against epidemics is transparency—a willingness on the part of governments to compile accurate information about infectious diseases, to distribute that information to its citizens, and to share the facts quickly and honestly with medical and research professionals around the world. Many observers, including a White House working group on global threats from pathogenic microbes, have advocated the establishment of a global system of surveillance by which such data might be readily obtained and communicated. But as the working group noted, "Individual governments may . . . be reluctant to share [such] information, fearing losses in trade, tourism and national prestige."[35] How much more likely is that reluctance to prevail in countries that lack traditions of transparency, a free press, independent monitoring organizations, and health professionals who have confidence that they will be hailed, not punished, for telling the truth? As Laurie Garrett, Pulitzer Prize–winning author of *The Coming Plague*, has written:

It is often exceedingly difficult to obtain accurate information about outbreaks of disease. . . . Egypt denies the existence of cholera bacteria in the Nile's waters; Saudi Arabia has asked WHO [World Health Organization] not to warn that travelers to Mecca may be bitten by mosquitoes carrying viruses that cause the new, superlethal dengue hemorrhagic fever; . . . and central authorities in Serbia . . . rescinded an international epidemic alert when they learned that all the scientists WHO planned to send to the tense Kosovo region to halt a large outbreak of Crimean-Congo hemorrhagic fever were from the United States.[36]

What Egypt, Saudi Arabia, and Serbia all had in common, albeit to different degrees, were governments that could hardly be said to have prized the free exchange of critical ideas.

Just as diseases cross borders unimpeded, so the fight to detect and prevent the spread of illnesses around the globe cannot succeed without international cooperation. Had such cooperation been in place when slim disease first appeared in Uganda as early as 1962, it might not have prevented the spread of HIV/AIDS, depending on your theory of its origins. But it certainly could not have hurt to have begun monitoring the virus some two decades before it was first formally diagnosed.[37] That was not the only problem in Uganda that may have amplified the outbreak of HIV/AIDS, however. There was also the little matter of a very big man named Idi Amin.

Whether HIV/AIDS emerged first in Africa or elsewhere, and whether it was transported there through the early testing of a polio vaccine, as one recent controversial book alleges,[38] it is widely agreed, based on seroepidemiological tests, that at some point the African strain of the disease radiated outward from the Lake Victoria region on the Uganda-Tanzania border and spread extensively after 1980 through much of central and southern Africa. The highest infection rates in this period were among prostitutes originally from the Lake Victoria area. Beginning in 1975, the number of cases of aggressive Kaposi's sarcoma (skin lesions associated with AIDS) diagnosed in Kinshasa, Zaire, doubled every year, leading one Zairian health official to observe that "something dramatic happened in 1975."[39]

Idi Amin was president of Uganda from 1971 to 1979. At three hundred pounds he was widely considered one of the continent's most intimidating and ruthless dictators, rumored to practice cannibalism and known to be bloodthirsty in his treatment of his enemies. After overthrowing the government of Milton Obote in 1971, Amin expelled between fifty thousand and eighty thousand Asian Ugandans, many of them Indians, who had, much to the resentment of indigenous Ugandans, constituted the heart of Uganda's commercial sector, having been placed in charge of cotton-ginning and wholesale trade during British colonial rule. Not surprisingly, this mass expulsion of legitimate citizens, itself a human rights violation, led to the quick collapse of the formal Ugandan economy and its replacement by an underground black market largely dependent on smuggling. The young men who plied the smuggling trade led a high-risk life of debauchery and promiscuity.[40] Laurie Garrett picks up the story from there:

> Tiny Lake Victoria fishing villages were transformed overnight into busy smuggling ports. As a business, prostitution was second only to the black market. For most women there were only two choices in life: have babies and grow food without assistance from men, livestock or machinery, or exchange sex for money at black-market rates. . . . The area became a vast lattice of mud roads, brothels and smuggling centers through which flowed a steady stream of truckers carrying cargoes bound for Kenya, Tanzania, Rwanda, Burundi and Zaire.[41]

And with those truckers went HIV.

Over the course of his reign, Amin terrorized the professional population, thereby diminishing the number of health workers; looted Makere University, the primary medical training center for East Africa's doctors, "right down to its electrical sockets and bathroom tiles";[42] created a refugee flow of some three hundred thousand Ugandans fleeing for their lives and carrying their microbes with them to neighboring countries; and during the war with Tanzania in 1977 through 1979, fostered a military in which rape was used as a form of ethnic cleansing. Even his eventual overthrow in 1979 did not stem Uganda's misfortunes as, thanks partly to his policies, famine gripped the country, further decimating the population's resistance to disease. Little wonder, then, that writer Jeffrey Goldberg, in arguing that the United States should take Africa as a continent more seriously than it does, has said that "HIV is a clever microbe—a slow, steady incubator—and it might have spread efficiently even without political chaos. . . . [But] the volatile mix of refugees, soldiers, prostitutes and the attendant lack of disease surveillance [in Uganda under Idi Amin] may have given HIV the jump-start it needed to travel the world."[43]

It is hazardous enough to deny the facts about a public health crisis. Even as late as a 1985 conference on AIDS in Africa, health professionals on the continent had formally confirmed only a few cases of AIDS, and many rejected the notion that they had an epidemic on their hands.[44]

Today Africa accounts for 70 percent of those living with AIDS, 83 percent of AIDS deaths, and 95 percent of its orphans.[45] But couple denial with human rights crimes—expulsion of citizens, intimidation of medical officers, rape, child prostitution, forced migration, and so on—and you create a health situation nothing short of lethal. One of the reasons that orphaned infants in Romania under the dictator Ceausescu were given wholly unnecessary blood transfusions later found to be tainted by HIV is because health professionals feared they would be punished by the government if any of the children died. So they agreed to whole blood transfusions in the mistaken belief that it would offer important nutrients to sick children.[46] Furthermore, when people with HIV/AIDS face discrimination, coercion, and punishment on account of their illness, they are less likely to seek testing and treatment, and the disease is even more likely to spread.

When Idi Amin was in power, the world bemoaned his barbarism but treated it largely as a problem for Ugandans or, at most, for Africans. But the human rights violations contributing to the diffusion of HIV/AIDS today—the subjugation of women, for example, or the creation of refugee camps, or the scourge of war that decimates public health care systems—are finally being recognized as everybody's problem. The question is whether that recognition has come too late.

Regardless of how HIV/AIDS initially arose in the United States, it is now so serious a global problem that in April 2000 the U.S. National Security Council declared the disease a threat to national security. More than forty million people are currently living with HIV/AIDS, and a quarter of the population of southern Africa is likely to die of it.[47] Based on current trends, South Asia and the former Soviet Union could duplicate or even exceed that rate at some point in the future.[48] Such massive mortality rates would threaten international stability, disrupt potential American markets (nonproductive populations spending what discretionary income they have on treatments are hardly a reliable consumer base for U.S. products), endanger American workers overseas, make it impossible for countries to bolster their share of peacekeeping missions, and given how readily HIV/AIDS patients succumb to other diseases like tuberculosis, amplify the spread of infectious diseases around the globe.

Other than Africa, the region of the world in which AIDS is now spreading the most quickly is Asia. Incubated along China's border with Burma (Myanmar) beginning in 1990, thanks to the sharing of needles by heroin users, it is now rampaging through China's Xinjiang province and elsewhere.[49] Estimates have it that 2 percent of Cambodian adults suffer from the disease and at least half a million in Thailand.[50] Here too human rights violations have contributed to the menace.

Burma (Myanmar) suffers today under one of the world's most repressive regimes. Once one of Asia's most medically advanced countries, it has witnessed an explosion of heroin use over the years; the erosion of its health care system under brutal military rule; arrest, execution, or emigration of its medical and nursing professionals; a paucity of information about AIDS prevention, thanks to a junta-controlled media; and the absence of nongovernmental health organizations capable of educating the people about their health care needs. All but the first of these facts entail human rights abuses, and all contribute to the explosion of sexually transmitted diseases.

One of the most direct causes of the crisis is the government's persecution of the ethnic Karen and Shan people, many of whom are forced into hard labor on roads, quarries, and railways. Faced with the loss of their men as well as the common incidence of rape by government troops, Shan women and girls are emigrating in high numbers to Thailand to take up the sex trade. Twenty thousand to thirty thousand Burmese women have become prostitutes in Thailand, and it is estimated that they suffer a prevalence of HIV at the level of 40 percent to 60 percent.[51]

Similarly, in Cambodia there has been little replenishment of the enormous numbers of health care professionals executed by the Khmer Rouge (at one point only twenty-five doctors remained in the Ministry of Health[52]). Hundreds of land mine injuries each month require transfusions with blood that is sometimes tainted. And trafficking of Khmer women and girls into the sex trade is increasing[53]—conditions again involving human rights violations.

The results of all of this are staggering for Asia, but it is not only Asia that has cause to worry. There is evidence that American soldiers and officials assigned to the U.N. Transitional Authority in Cambodia in the mid-1990s, mostly young men, dramatically increased the demand for sex services and brought HIV infections back to the United States.[54]

(Indeed, in a larger sense, it has been estimated that since 1980 more U.N. peacekeeping troops have died of AIDS than in combat.[55]) Moreover, given the growing attractiveness of tourist and business travel to China, Thailand, Cambodia, and even Burma (Myanmar), the likelihood of more Americans contracting sexually transmitted diseases in these countries and transporting them to the United States in their bloodstreams, to pass on to others, increases with each airline ticket.

There could be no more direct link in this chain, of course, than the thousands of Americans who indulge each year in the Asian sex trade, including sex with minors. American travel companies such as Big Apple Oriental Tours of Bellerose, New York ("Real sex with real girls, all for real cheap"), and twenty-five others are known to arrange pre-planned tours.[56] In Thailand, for example, two hundred thousand "sex workers" (a conservative estimate), 50 percent of whom are infected with HIV/AIDS and anywhere from 25 percent to 40 percent of whom are under eighteen, service some five hundred thousand foreign tourists annually, of which some reasonable percentage are bound to be drawn from the fifty thousand to one hundred thousand Americans who visit the country annually. Nor do Americans need to go to Southeast Asia to have contact with women who have been forced into prostitution. As many as fifty thousand women and girls may be trafficked into the United States itself for that purpose each year and held for bondage to pay off their $40,000 debts for passage.[57]

Whether it be a sexually transmitted disease, or any another kind, maladies are frequently amplified by human rights violations. Americans, because of a mosquito's breeding habits or their own, can less and less readily escape the consequences. The connection between ill health and human rights is particularly obvious when it comes to migration, the majority of which is prompted by war, economic deprivation, ecological disaster (sometimes caused by the greenhouse effect), or ethnic cleansing. In 2000 the world contained at least sixteen million refugees, many of them living in camps and settlements that are breeding grounds for pathogens. As one physician has put it, "Should a new disease, such as Ebola, emerge in the setting of a refugee camp, the conditions would be perfectly in place for a global plague"[58]—an observation that sheds more doubt on the notion of U.S. policy makers that the 1994 Rwandan genocide had no relationship to U.S. national interest.

Finally, there is the issue of chemical and biological weapons (which have been called "the poor man's atom bomb"), capable in short order of wiping out entire populations. Such weapons are hardly a new phenomenon. Plague-ridden bodies of Tartar soldiers were catapulted over the walls of the city of Kaffa (now Feodosiya, Ukraine) as early as 1346. Sir Jeffrey Amherst unashamedly provided Native Americans with smallpox-infested blankets during the French and Indian War.[59] Today at least twenty-five countries are thought to possess some level of capability to produce toxic chemical weapons and twelve to manufacture biological weapons that employ disease-causing microorganisms.[60] It goes without saying that many of these countries, Syria and Iraq, for example, have atrocious human rights records.

What particularly worries experts, however—and here I return to the issue of transparency—is that without an organized civil society capable of monitoring compliance with treaties, without independent academics and journalists offering alternative views to the people, without a vibrant political opposition to critique an incumbent government's policies—in short, without a healthy respect for civil and political rights—there can be no effective internal checks on *any* government's predilections to use chemical and biological weapons to terrorize the globe. As what Brad Roberts of the Center for Strategic and International Studies calls a "new tier" of states (from Germany to Egypt, Kazakhstan to India) capable of producing weapons of mass destruction—be they nuclear, chemical, or biological—emerges out of the demise of the Cold War, so the need to ensure structures of accountability for the use of such weapons only grows that much more urgent.[61]

Many factors beyond issues of human rights play a part in the proliferation of weapons or the spread of disease. To ignore the role of power politics or religious fervor in the growth of terrorism or to forget how large a part economic ills, foolish risk-taking, and simple ignorance play in the march of microbes is to see the world through far too narrow a lens. My case is not that human rights violations are the only contributors to global health threats or even the primary ones. My case is that they play a far greater role than our policy makers have generally allowed. To dismiss the interdependence of health and human rights is not only to live in a dream world. To dismiss it is very simply to invite disaster.

6

Saving Money while Saving Lives

....

The Economic Rewards
of Defending Human Rights

We cannot rely upon the silenced to tell us they are
suffering.
—HANAN ASHRAWI, Palestinian leader

WHEN JAIME GARZON, political satirist and host of a
morning talk show on Bogota's powerful Radionet station, set out for work at 6:00 A.M. that Friday in August of
1999, he was feeling more secure about his future than he had felt in a
very long time. True, Carlos Castaño, the much-feared leader of the
right-wing paramilitary United Self Defense Forces of Colombia, had
frequently threatened Garzon for his alleged sympathy with the left-
wing guerrillas, the Revolutionary Armed Forces of Colombia (or
FARC), whom Castaño and his men (known by the sobriquet "Head
Cutters" for their practice of decapitating their victims) had vowed to
eliminate. But Garzon had finally scheduled a meeting with Castaño,
and it would take place the very next day.

As a well-respected broadcaster who had forged connections with
the guerrillas ten years before, Garzon knew only too well how vicious
they themselves could be. Recently he had leveraged the trust he had
engendered in them to free several of their kidnap victims, and he was
currently mediating between the Colombian government and one of
the insurgents' armies. But he was no guerrilla himself, and that he
would make Castaño understand.

Garzon never had the opportunity to plead his case, however. As he
maneuvered his Jeep Cherokee through the early-morning traffic, a

white motorcycle intercepted him and the two men riding it pumped a hail of bullets into the broadcaster's head and chest. Later, many local journalists would blame the killing on the paramilitaries. Others said it was the Colombian army. And still others said that because the two worked hand in hand, what did it matter which group it was?[1] In any case, Garzon's assassins would likely never be brought to justice. He was just another victim of shadowy forces that have ruled Colombia for years—forces that have far too often in the past been aligned with, even supplied by, the U.S. government.

The murder of journalists and human rights defenders in Latin America's most violent country has become all too commonplace over the past fifteen years.[2] When we in the United States think of Colombia, however, we tend to think not of guiltless victims of thuggery but of drug cartels picking each other off with justifiable abandon. There is indeed an abundance of drug-related killing there. But since 1986 more than thirty thousand innocent people have died in Colombia for political reasons alone, and the vast majority have been killed not by the so-called "narco-guerrillas"—despicable as they are for their kidnapping, butchery, and profiting from the drug trade—but by the Colombian army and its paramilitary allies in their quest to root out supporters of the left-wing insurgents.[3] On more than one occasion U.S.-funded security assistance ostensibly appropriated to the Colombian army to fight the cocaine wars has been used instead to commit those crimes.

In 1996, Amnesty International made public a series of secret U.S. government documents that proved that Colombian military units responsible for some of the worst atrocities against civilians had received U.S. military training and equipment.[4] In 1999 a Colombian air force commander acknowledged that U.S.-supplied helicopters and transport planes had been involved in an airborne assault on the civilian population in Puerta Lleras.[5] That same year paramilitaries aligned with the army killed more than two thousand more noncombatants.[6] Yet in 2000 the U.S. Congress voted to supply more than half a billion dollars of additional security aid to Colombia under the theory that the only way to stop the flow of drugs is to help the army and police defeat the guerrillas. Whether that is true (and despite immense amounts of similar U.S. aid since 1990, the cocaine flow has steadily increased[7]), what appears likely, if history is any guide, is that some portion of those funds will go to commit human rights violations; neither government nor paramilitary leaders will be held accountable; and people like Jaime Garzon will continue to die.

It is bad enough that eight hundred thousand people have fled Colombia since 1996, thanks to the violence there.[8] It is tragic that thousands have been slaughtered. It is a scandal that funds intended to stop the flow of drugs have been diverted to commit crimes against the innocent. And it is an outrage that any of this has happened with U.S. taxpayers' dollars. But then Colombia is only one example of the simple truth that human rights violations are often a colossal waste of U.S. money.

One of the first victims of torture whom I met upon joining Amnesty International was Sister Dianna Ortiz. Dianna was a dark-haired Ursuline nun, slight of build with a finely chiseled face, who lived in the little town of Grants, New Mexico, when she decided in 1987 to work as a Catholic missionary among the Mayan people of Guatemala's highlands. Still today, when Dianna tells what happened to her in Guatemala, she is often swept up in tears; it can become difficult to discern her words, and she sometimes withdraws for a while to collect herself. But for all her pain, Dianna has become a champion of the effort to find out what the United States' role really was in the multitude of human rights crimes that took place in Latin America throughout much of the Cold War period.

Dianna's own ordeal began within months of her arrival in Guatemala, when she started to receive death threats. It was not until November 2, 1989, that she was abducted from the backyard of her church retreat house and taken to a clandestine detention center in Guatemala City. There she was held in a room swarming with rats, raped repeatedly, burned on her back by cigarettes more than a hundred times, and finally lowered into a real-life inferno, a pit containing human bodies—some dead, some alive, some decapitated, and all caked with blood. The nightmare seemed to go on forever, but almost as distressing as the torture itself was how it ended. At some point, as her attackers began to rape her still again, a new man entered the room. "Shit," he cried in unmistakable American English and then, in heavily accented Spanish, ordered her tormentors to put an end to her ordeal.

This woman, the man told Dianna's captors, was not Veronica Ortiz

Hernández, the name they had insisted on calling Dianna, and a woman who, Dianna later learned, was a member of one of the guerrilla factions the Guatemalan army was fighting. This was a North American and a Catholic nun at that. "Alejandro," as the torturers called the American, helped her put her clothes on, hustled her into a jeep, and told her he would take her to the American embassy. It would be wise to keep quiet, he said, because her ordeal had been photographed. If she spoke up, the photos would be released to the press. Before they arrived at the embassy, Dianna leapt from the jeep while it was stopped at a traffic light, contacted her Ursuline order, and returned shortly thereafter to the United States. But her captors and Alejandro's true identity have never been revealed.[9]

When I first heard this story, I was dumbfounded. Not by the description of the torture; that was all too familiar. But by the American "rescuer." I was well aware that the United States had crawled into bed with some totally unsavory characters. But would an asset of our government be so foolish as to expose his connection to these brutes? For a few months I harbored just a touch of skepticism. But then I read a special report prepared by the *Baltimore Sun* concerning the seventy-eight-day torture in 1983 of a Honduran woman, Inés Consuello Murillo, by members of Battalion 316, a Honduran military intelligence unit that had been trained and equipped by the CIA. The forms of torture were different from Dianna's but the denouement, though more prolonged, was much the same. Several months into her captivity, Inés was visited by an American whom her torturers called "Mr. Mike." Two days later her treatment improved and she was offered a chance to live. Eventually Inés was released. In June 1988, Richard Stolz, the CIA deputy director of operations, testified before the Senate Select Committee on Intelligence that a CIA officer had indeed visited the jail where Battalion 316 had held and tortured Inés Consuello Murillo. And, just to put a finer point on it, the *Sun* reported, there just happened to be a CIA officer in Honduras at the time named Michael Dubbs.[10]

Since I first heard Dianna's story and read the *Sun's* reporting about Inés, we have learned much more about the U.S. subsidization of atrocities in Latin America—so much, in fact, that President Clinton was forced to apologize to the Guatemalan people in the spring of 1999 for the United States having, in the president's words, "supported military forces and intelligence units which engaged in violent and widespread repression," with millions of U.S. tax dollars during that country's thirty-six years of civil war.[11] The president's expression of contrition came shortly after the Guatemalan Historical Clarification Commission had concluded that the training of Guatemalan military officers in counterinsurgency techniques by the CIA had played a significant role in the torture and killings of thousands of civilians.[12] And Guatemala was but the tip of the interventionist iceberg in Latin America. Operation Condor, for example, provided covert U.S. training and information to repressive regimes in Argentina, Bolivia, Brazil, Chile, Paraguay, and Uruguay throughout the 1970s, including support for Argentina's "Dirty War" and Chile's brutal strongman, Augusto Pinochet. But all this, one State Department official said dismissively in 1999, is "ancient history."[13]

Except that it is not. Although the United States may no longer be consumed by a fear of Communism, which was used to justify years of collaboration with rights abusers, our penchant for providing money to train and supply those who go on to commit human rights violations has hardly been spent. In 1995, for example, the Senate Appropriations Committee received reports "that U.S. military equipment, including helicopters, had been used in attacks against civilians in southeastern Turkey."[14] This was scarcely surprising news because the United States had been supplying hundreds of millions of dollars in military assistance to Turkey each year, and the odds would be long that Turkey had never used any of those resources in its war on its Kurdish population. In 1997 U.S.-trained Rwandan army troops participated in "widespread atrocities against civilian populations in Eastern Congo."[15] In 1999 an elite Indonesian military unit known as Kopassus, which had received years of training in urban warfare, sniper attack, and close quarters combat from U.S. Special Forces, turned those talents to use against the citizens in East Timor, who had just voted in their first free elections.[16]

One need not oppose military assistance itself or be disquieted by the arms trade per se, despite the enormity of its size and its federal subsidy, to be uncomfortable with the fact that U.S. tax dollars go regularly to train and equip human rights violators. Forty-four percent of the countries that received U.S. combat training in 1997, for instance, were nondemocratic, including Algeria and Kenya, two governments whose records of violence against their own citizens are notorious.[17]

Train foreign militaries as we might, trade arms with foreign governments if we will, but no American wants his or her hard-earned money
used to harm innocent people. Surely we have better things to do with
our money either in those same countries or in the United States.

It used to be said that the value of a human body, were its nutrients sold
on the open market, would be less than one dollar. That was before the
Chinese began to fetch high prices for body organs extracted from prisoners they had executed—some of them for such crimes as selling fake
fertilizer and pinching women's bottoms.[18] But even with the sale of
body parts making the human creature a more valuable commodity,
we still hesitate to measure human worth in financial terms. I do not
know a single human rights defender who risks his or her life to protect
others because it is the economically advantageous thing to do. More
likely those defenders hear some version of the line from an Urdu
poem echoing through their heads: "How beautiful must have been the
faces trampled in the dust."

Yet ours is a mercenary world in which many political decisions turn
on questions of cost. That it was worth $91 billion to liberate Kuwait
and has been worth nearly nothing to end slavery and slaughter in
Sudan has more than a little to do with economic calculation. As well
they should, foreign policy "realists" regularly include financial costs
among those factors they take into account when trying to determine
whether support for human rights in a particular situation is in the
United States' national interest. They almost always fail to calculate,
however, the price of *neglecting* to pursue a human rights agenda in the
first place.

The fundamental reason to have tried to stop genocide in Rwanda
and Bosnia, for example, is of course because genocide tarnishes the
very luster of our humanity. But even a cold cost-benefit analysis of
early intervention by an international or regional military force—
something that in both cases was stymied by U.S. fear and recalci-
trance—leads to a defensible, if hypothetical, conclusion that intervention would have been far less expensive than passivity.

In their book *The Costs of Conflict: Prevention and Cure in the Global
Arena,* Michael E. Brown and Richard Rosecrance estimate that early
intervention in Bosnia before the full-scale violence erupted there
would have saved the international community between $20 billion

and $43 billion, depending on the size of the force. Because their book was written before the Kosovo War, those figures are unrealistically low if one countenances the reasonable assumption that early and decisive action in Bosnia might have discouraged Slobodan Milosovic from his foolhardy aggression in Kosovo.[19]

The case of Rwanda is equally instructive. Just twenty-four hours after the first eruption of violence in 1994, U.N. Commanding General Romeo Dallaire requested a small contingent of additional troops and expressed assurance that he could contain the killing quickly, because much of it was being accomplished with primitive weapons like machetes. Given this, there is every reason to believe that had Dallaire's request not been rejected, a modest engagement could have saved not only an enormous number of lives but billions of dollars in economic and humanitarian aid that was subsequently required to maintain refugee camps and stabilize the country.[20] The lesson of Rwanda is not only that quick action can avert catastrophes, but that it pays to prevent them in the first place.

Consider the billions of dollars in foreign assistance the United States has spent over the years, either directly or through such institutions as the International Monetary Fund and the World Bank. Coupled with the private charitable donations Americans give to stop hunger or save children, these funds represent a considerable investment in world development. Why, then, has the United States been so reluctant to promote one of the very things—respect for human rights and the rule of law—that will mitigate against those dollars being wasted? Sometimes money has been wasted because we have been willing to overlook the predilections of tyrants. For example, two years before Iraq invaded Kuwait, prompting the Persian Gulf War, Saddam Hussein diverted food purchased under a $5 billion Agriculture Department aid program to the purchase of military equipment, which he later turned on American troops.[21]

Sometimes U.S. assistance to combat famine or flood is needed because the policies of authoritarian governments bring on the disasters in the first place. The Ethiopian famines of the mid-1980s were a direct result not just of drought but of the dictator Mengistu Haile Mariam's backward social and economic policies and the lack of an independent sector or political opposition to challenge these policies. "I never confronted Mengistu outright," said a high-ranking Ethiopian official of that era. "None of us felt we were able to tell him the truth. It is a guilt I and other public officials must live with for, had we told him what we really thought of him and his policies, even at the risk of our lives, the Ethiopian tragedy might never have occurred." And the United States might not have been out $500 million.[22]

Sometimes money is poured into relief efforts while the human rights–related causes of the crisis are ignored altogether. Humanitarian agencies and the United Nations have supplied more than $2 billion ($700 million of it U.S. money) to feed victims of Sudan's eighteen-year-old civil war, a war in which hundreds of thousands have died and thousands of children have been forced into slavery. Rather than see children starve, the agencies have chosen to supply resources that allow both the government and the insurgents to continue the slaughter. How much wiser and more economical it would be for the United States and its allies to take both sides' human rights crimes seriously (as we have done with our constructive intervention in Northern Ireland, for example, where "only" about thirty-five hundred have died, compared with two million in Sudan) and insist on an embargo on the delivery of arms to both sides and a comprehensive cease-fire.[23]

Even where human rights violations are not the direct cause of the squandering of funds, they are often a proximate cause because of their connection to the most common source of waste: simple corruption. I have pointed out in previous chapters that corruption—prompted often by human rights crimes designed to intimidate the press, discourage a vibrant political opposition, and neutralize an independent civil sector—can destabilize a country politically and cost corporations a bundle. Also true is that corruption in foreign places can cost both taxpayers and charitable donors a great deal of money.

For example, food destined for Somalia during the late 1980s famine there under the sponsorship of CARE regularly turned up, still packed in its original bags, in markets as far away from Somalia as Addis Ababa, Ethiopia.[24] Contributions to aid victims of Hurricane Mitch in Nicaragua reached far fewer people than they might have otherwise because of "corruption and a lack of transparency" in the country, according to President Arnoldo Aleman.[25] Indeed, two Nicaraguan economists estimated that 30 cents of every aid dollar was lost to corruption and inefficiency.[26] The Agency for International Development placed at least $4 million in a Bosnian bank that collapsed in 1999 after lending money to fictional businesses and giving personal loans to friends of its owners.[27] In every case, the lack of human rights–related safeguards, like full transparency and independent monitoring, while not the only causes of the profligacy, certainly contributed to it.

So intimate is the connection between human rights violations and wasted riches that the World Bank has concluded that development aid accomplishes little unless market-friendly policies and openness to foreign investment are matched by the rule of law and low corruption.[28] Where this has happened, in relatively well-run countries such as Ghana and Bolivia, the average annual economic growth rate has reached 3.7 percent.[29] Where it has not happened, development efforts have been for naught. As Sadako Ogata, the U.N. High Commissioner for Refugees, has said, "Governments can mess your life up. . . . You need the rule of law in these countries; if you don't have that, the money will disappear."[30]

Far from providing an argument against foreign assistance or private charity, the conclusion to be drawn from this analysis is that such largesse must be coupled with equally great attention to the human rights context in which it is to be expended. Although respect for human rights cannot guarantee that funds will not be wasted, as witness the financial scandals that arise periodically in almost every big American city, ignoring the connection between human rights and governmental integrity will inevitably lead us to regret our generosity.

In some ways of course the fact that human rights violations cost the United States money, although irritating, is the least of our problems. Depending on where we sit, there may be a host of other ways in which unpunished human rights crimes affect our interests. Take immigration, for example. Today immigrants make up a proportionately lower percentage of the U.S. population than they did at the turn of the twentieth century and their presence in many ways has been found to benefit our economy.[31] But whether one believes that or not, it makes no sense to remain indifferent to the human rights abuses—political or religious persecution, failure of governments to protect women from domestic violence, internal displacement of populations—that motivate political asylum seekers to migrate to the United States in the first place. Such people are often champions of American values in their home countries and, whether we worry about increased immigration or simply believe that no human being should be persecuted for his or her nonviolent beliefs, the human rights context that produces asylum seekers in the first place ought to matter.

If we like to travel and therefore are particularly keen to avoid conflict and terrorism, human rights protections should be high on our list of priorities. Their lack almost invariably leads to dangerous situations for tourists or businesspeople traveling outside the states. Americans should also be infuriated that our own government so often fails to notify the appropriate embassies in the United States when foreign nationals are charged with crimes, including capital ones (despite consular treaties requiring such notification); this only invites reciprocal negligence when U.S. travelers get into trouble overseas.[32]

If we are religious people who regard ourselves as part of a larger community of believers around the world—be they Christian, Muslim, Jewish, Buddhist, or Ba'hai—the persecution of those who share our faith feels very much like an attack on that faith itself.

If we are gay, lesbian, bisexual, or transgendered, tolerance for harassment, torture, and execution based on sexual orientation—no matter how remote the venue—retards the arrival of a day when international standards of accountability can be applied to such acts, whether they take place in Laramie, Wyoming, or in Harare, Zimbabwe.

And if we are worried about population control, the growing gap between rich nations and poor and the seeding of new generations of children born without promise and susceptible to extremism, we would be fools to think that the condition of women around the world has no bearing on us.

When young Samia Sarwar died with the connivance of her own mother in her lawyer's office in Pakistan, she joined hundreds of other women—888 in Punjab in one year alone[33]—who are killed for the "honor" of their families. She joined thousands of women who are victims of bride burning or dowry killings. She joined tens of thousands of women raped in the course of war. She joined hundreds of thousands of women subjected to forced trafficking for purposes of prostitution. She joined between 85 and 114 million women at risk of female genital mutilation. She joined a quarter of the world's female population who are violently abused in their own homes.[34]

What all these women have in common is that their ability to control their own bodies, to say nothing of their lives, and to contribute productively to the economic growth of their societies has been severely curtailed. Dr. Tahira Shahid Khan, director of a women's resource center in Pakistan, has made an observation about honor killings that applies equally well to other violations of women's rights: "Women are considered the property of the males in their family irrespective of their class, ethnic or religious groups. . . . The owner of the property has the right to decide its fate. The concept of ownership has turned women into a commodity which can be exchanged, bought and sold."[35]

How, then, can we expect a commodity to have control over its reproductive decisions? With the world population growing by more than eighty million people each year and the attendant impact of that growth on water scarcity, pollution, poverty, and social conflict, the capacity of women to make choices about their reproductive futures without fear is a matter of direct concern to all of us.[36] But violations of women's human rights are designed explicitly to spread fear, maintain control, and contravene a woman's sense of power.[37]

Similarly, a woman whose body can be violated at whim and whose control over her life choices in such areas as education and employment is ceded to others will make far less robust an economic contribution to her society's development than one who is free of the threat of human rights abuses. Small surprise, then, that one study after another has found a positive relationship between rates of sustainable development and women's empowerment.[38] U.N. Secretary General Boutros Boutros-Ghali put the equation more straightforwardly: "Where women have advanced [in legal status and education and training], economic growth has usually been steady; where women have not been allowed to be full participants, there has been stagnation."[39]

The empowerment of women also tends to encourage nonviolent social change as opposed to disruptive social upheaval. The prevalence of women's enterprises in the economic revolution being shaped by the phenomenon of microloans, to take but one example, signals the way in which women are increasingly taking the lead in rewiring their societies peacefully and progressively. Anything that retards such benevolent social change makes the world a far more dangerous and desperate place than it otherwise needs be. Or consider the impact of women's status on the world's children. When nursed and nurtured by subjugated mothers and enculturated into a system of gender oppression, children merely perpetuate the violence, hopelessness, and economic stagnation their parents and generations before them have always known. What a perfect breeding ground for extremism and terror. What a ripe opportunity to sow the seeds of war.

When Samia Sarwar was felled by a bullet, a young woman lost her life, a young woman few people knew—certainly no one outside of Pakistan—and her death, although assuredly tragic, hardly by itself had any global implications. But as a reflection of a larger phenomenon, the subjugation and ill-treatment of women, the implications of her death reach across continents and oceans. As an individual, Samia deserves our sympathy; as a symbol she ought evoke in us a fair measure of anxiety and command a most sustained and lively interest.

7

No Innocent Place

....

Human Rights Violations
in the Sweet Land of Liberty

We should recruit police in a spirit of service, not in a spirit
of adventure.

        —Lee Brown, mayor of Houston, Texas;
        former chief of police, Houston, Texas;
        former New York City police commissioner

DENNY KAUFMAN IS NOT A BAD GUY, but he does like to shock people. Denny is the president of StunTech, Inc., of Cleveland, Ohio, and manufactures electroshock stun belts for a living. He and I have appeared together on half a dozen national television programs over the past few years debating the merits of his product. Denny is amiable, courteous, a good salesman. If you spotted him on the streets of Cleveland, you would guess him to be what he is: an upstanding, Midwestern, salt-of-the-earth-type small businessman. The only problem is that he sees nothing wrong with sending fifty thousand volts, albeit at low amperage, through a human being at the push of a button.

Electroshock has been around for a long time of course, having at one time been the treatment of choice in many U.S. mental institutions. Electric cattle prods have sometimes been used to control crowds. But electroshock as a weapon for use by police and prison officials really came into its own in the 1970s with the invention of the handheld stun gun and the Taser, which fires electrified darts into a victim. (A Taser was used on Rodney King in the notorious Los Angeles beating case.) Today the general public can purchase electroshock weapons for self-defense, electrified steering wheel braces to secure a

car from theft, and even an umbrella with an electrified tip for good-
ness knows what mischief.

The stun belt is in a class by itself, however. Strapped around a subject's waist, it can be activated by the touch of a button from a remote-
control device held up to three hundred feet away. When activated,
fifty thousand volts course through the body for eight seconds at a
time, inevitably slamming the wearer to the ground to writhe in agony
and sometimes urinate, defecate, or lose consciousness. The application can be repeated as frequently as the controller wishes. Although to
my knowledge no one has yet died from a stun belt discharge, the fact
that the shock can disrupt heart rhythms worries some physicians.

But not Denny Kaufman and not the increasing numbers of police
departments and prisons that employ stun belts or one of their electroshock cousins. Authorities like these devices because they provide a
quick way to establish control and subdue someone, even, in the case
of the stun belt, from a considerable (and hence safe) distance. They
appear ideal for use on chain gangs or in prison transport or, more
and more, in courtrooms. From a human rights perspective, however,
they are far from ideal. Although the manufacturers claim stun belts
are perfectly safe, stun technology has been implicated in dozens of
deaths, including that of a Texas corrections officer who collapsed
shortly after receiving a shock from a stun shield in a test of its effectiveness. Suspects high on PCP who were shot with Tasers by police in
California have gone into cardiac arrest shortly afterward. No doubt
this is why the U.S. Federal Bureau of Prisons warns in its own guidelines that electroshock should not be used on inmates with heart
disease. It hardly seems reasonable, however, to expect a police officer
to administer an electrocardiogram before attempting to subdue an
unruly customer, but the consequence may be to turn a minor skir-
mish into a capital crime, the process of arrest into unintentional execution.

Electroshock's proponents argue that these weapons are demonstra-
bly less likely to inflict serious damage than guns or clubs, and that may
be so. But unlike guns that leave a bullet hole or clubs that leave a
bruise, most electroshock equipment leaves no identifiable traces at all.
That is why they offer such temptation for misuse. Even when the acti-
vation of stun technology is evident for all to see, the ease of its application and drama of the aftermath invites gratuitous displays. A trial

judge in Los Angeles County, for example, ordered a sheriff to zap a defendant wearing a stun belt because she thought he was talking too much.

It is not surprising, then, that electroshock is one of the most popular means of torture around the world, its use having been documented in countries from Mexico to Saudi Arabia and perhaps most notoriously in China. Electroshock manufacturers have been reluctant to submit to voluntary export curbs, and in 1995 the U.S. Department of Commerce went so far as to authorize the sale to Saudi Arabia of what were described on the export license record as "[stun] shields used for torture."[1]

Given all of this, Denny Kaufman's enthusiasm for electroshock technology seems arguably misplaced. "I don't seen any downside to the use of this equipment," Denny said on one of our joint appearances. "Well, you or your cohorts just may see a downside the first time one of you is successfully sued," I replied. A few months later, jail guards in a privately operated Texas prison run by Capitol Corrections Resources were caught on videotape applying electroshock stun guns to the backs and buttocks of prisoners who were forced to crawl out of their cells on their hands and knees. In January 2000 those inmates were awarded $2.2 million in damages, and the state of Missouri, which had housed the prisoners in Texas to alleviate overcrowding, agreed to a five-year moratorium on that practice.[2] Here was a case with multiple downsides: for the prisoners who experienced the agony in the first place; for the state of Missouri, which paid out $104,000 a week to defend itself and now has to house its prisoners in overcrowded conditions again, thus endangering both prisoners and correctional officers; for the shareholders of Capitol Corrections, who will pay this initial award; for advocates of prison privatization, whose cause has been set back; and for the citizens of Missouri, who will eventually have to take most of these embittered prisoners back into society when they are released.[3]

It is not only human rights violations in the international arena that can prove detrimental to Americans' best interests. Abuses here in the United States also contain an abundance of costs that are not always immediately evident. For much of its population the United States does not always live up to its reputation as the "sweet land of liberty." Hard as that is for some Americans to admit.

I have admired the work of the Anti-Defamation League of B'nai B'rith for many years. Thus I was surprised by a letter the League's national director, Abraham Foxman, sent to Amnesty International's secretary general in London when Amnesty launched a yearlong campaign in 1998–99 against human rights abuses in the United States. "We are concerned," Foxman wrote, "that Amnesty's in-depth 153-page account of United States' human rights abuses creates the perception that the United States' human rights record is worthy of the same time and effort Amnesty International has devoted to exposing mostly non-democratic, repressive regimes."

This perspective unfortunately is all too typical of many Americans' views of human rights in the United States. The fact that a country is "democratic," as I discussed in an earlier chapter, in no way guarantees that it is free of human rights violations. But here Foxman implicitly praises the depth of Amnesty's findings and even acknowledges later in the letter that "the United States has human rights problems which must be addressed"; yet for some reason he is reticent to have those abuses exposed. The reasons become evident a little further on. First, Foxman says, to raise these issues of U.S. violations "plays into the hands of those countries whose human rights abuses are systematically abhorrent." Second, "it gives the appearance that the United States belongs in the same category as these other countries."[4]

In one respect Foxman is correct. That the United States fails to conform its own practices to the principles it often advances around the world, at least rhetorically, does "play into the hands of" other human rights–abusing countries. But is the appropriate response to this dynamic to attempt to sweep the violations under the rug for fear of the damage that confronting the truth will cause? Or is it to face these abuses squarely and try to stop them? Surely the Anti-Defamation League, which has built its considerable reputation on exposing bigotry and hatred of all kinds, does not recommend the former strategy as an effective way to bring about social change.

Nor has anyone suggested (and the Amnesty report on the United States carefully did not) that there is no difference between a country that can boast the kind of freedoms we enjoy in the United States and a "non-democratic, repressive regime." But that the United States has many positive human rights characteristics, including a wide range of legal and political mechanisms through which to redress grievances, in no way exempts us from criticism for our failings. Amnesty evaluates about 160 nations every year, and to my knowledge Iceland is just about the only country in the world that has never been cited for a violation.

As it turned out, Foxman's unhappiness about Amnesty targeting U.S. problems was far milder than some others' concerns. The *New Republic*, for example, called the idea that there could be serious human rights issues in the states "preposterous" and "scurrilous."[5] It is hard for some Americans, and particularly for some white Americans, to fathom that the United States often falls short of its ideals and sometimes is in direct violation of international human rights standards. A few people ridicule the idea that we ought to worry about such standards at all. Others, be it out of denial or guilt or ignorance, simply do not see the problems or how they hurt every American.

One sign of hope, however, was contained in a poll conducted by the eminent public opinion analyst Peter D. Hart in November 1997. Three-quarters of the Americans surveyed rated the United States "above average" or even "one of the best" among all nations when it comes to safeguarding the human rights of its people. Having said that, however, 52 percent agreed also that the United States had either a "very serious" or "fairly serious" problem when it came to domestic human rights. That number jumped to 74 percent among African-Americans. After hearing a description of the Universal Declaration of Human Rights, 50 percent said the United States lived up to most or all of it, but an almost equal number (49 percent) said only some, little, or none. When asked to grade their nation, two-thirds or more gave the country a C, D, or F for providing equal pay for women, for showing tolerance of differences, and for combating racism. Americans are more than able to discern that commendable as our political system may be, it offers no guarantees of perfection.

Sanctioning human rights violations in this country not only crushes hopes, stains ideals, comforts tyrants elsewhere, and exposes us to charges of hypocrisy, but as we have seen in the international arena, it can cost us dearly in many practical ways. Those reasons alone would justify risking the dangers Abraham Foxman warned about. Putting our own house in order would refurbish both our society and our self-image. In this chapter I consider three major areas of abuse, beginning with the problem 68 percent of Hart's respondents labeled a clear human rights violation: the practice of police brutality.[6]

Police Misconduct

I have a checkered history with the police. I grew up thinking of them in largely positive terms. This is not only because I, like most children of my generation, were schooled by "Officer Friendly" to think of the police as people you turned to for help. It was also because my father taught law to police officers and felt comfortable around them. We welcomed police into our home for social occasions, and one of my father's favorite students, Lieutenant Stan Gorski of the Pittsburgh Police Department, became a close family friend who would occasionally arrange visits to the station house for me and some of my playmates. The jail, the handcuffs, the uniforms—it was all quite fascinating to a ten-year-old.

But then came the 1960s, when police were "pigs" and the Chicago "police riot" at the 1968 Democratic Convention occasioned Mayor Richard Daley (Daley, the elder) to declare: "The police are not here to create disorder; the police are here to *preserve* disorder." By the time I moved to Chicago in 1971 to begin theological school, my animosity toward police was palpable. This attitude was not helped by an incident that occurred within minutes of my arrival in the city. Parking my car on the street outside the school, I went in to register, only to be told that I was wanted by the police—wanted back outside, that is. "You the owner of this car?" a Chicago police officer asked me accusingly. "Yes, sir, I am," I said, searching desperately for a parking sign. "Is it illegally parked?" "Not that," he said, "but we just rammed a cruiser into it. This side of the car, you'll see, is pretty well crushed." And, sure enough, the entire left side of my car had been damaged. "Now you have two choices," the officer said. "You can file a complaint or . . . you can forget all the fuck about it. I advise you as strongly as I can to take the latter course." And because I was twenty-one and had just moved to a new city and this was Chicago and these were the Chicago police doing their best to both create *and* preserve disorder, I forgot all the fuck about it. But I didn't forget what I now thought of the police.

Gradually over the past thirty years my attitude toward the police has changed yet again. They have a very tough job to do and I do not envy them. They are poorly paid; they catch no end of grief; their job is dangerous and an enormous percentage of them do it well. The fundamental problem is that that huge percentage of "good cops" has allowed the much smaller percentage of "bad cops" to evade accountability for their misbehavior, and that has blemished everybody. Far too often the civilian authorities and the general public have collaborated in that impunity.

Here is an example notable only for its typicality. In 1996, Amnesty issued a report on police brutality in New York City. This followed similar reports on police in Los Angeles (1992) and Chicago (1990) that had been well received and contributed to changes in those departments. Amnesty researchers had been working for several years on the New York City report, but despite repeated requests for data and feedback from the police department, we had largely been stonewalled. This meant that we had to rely on statistics from the Civilian Complaint Review Board (CCRB) and the City Comptroller's office, as well as information from U.S. attorneys, district attorneys, defense counsel, and independent monitors. Among other things, the seventy-two-page report pointed out that the number of complaints filed with the CCRB had been rising, as had the settlement amounts paid by the city to resolve liability claims. It reported anecdotally on ninety cases of alleged brutality, noted the disparate portion of those cases involving people of color, questioned why the racial makeup of the department was at such odds with that of the city, and made recommendations for reform. In short, it was a calm, reasoned description of a problem that few people would deny might very well exist in any big city police department.[7]

When the Amnesty researchers and I went to the police commissioner's office to present the report, however, you would have thought we had concluded that, yes, the moon is made of cheese, after all. Commissioner Howard Safir, surrounded by eight or ten of his top "lieutenants," only one of them African-American, only one of them a woman, had two points to make. First, he denounced the report as statistically flawed because of the absence of police department data—data that had of course been denied us. Second, he asserted that had we had the data, it would show that there was no significant problem, that what we were talking about were the proverbial "few bad apples." "We would very much like to see the numbers you rely upon for your conclusion," we said. "We will send you a letter with all the information you need," was their reply.

Three months later Amnesty received that letter. It contained no statistics, but it did reach this bold conclusion: "The use of excessive force [is] neither [a] common occurrence nor a widespread problem in the New York City Police Department."[8] Eleven months later Abner Louima was sodomized with a stick in a precinct bathroom by officer Justin Volpe, and in February 1999 an unarmed man named Amadou Diallo was killed, shot forty-one times by four officers, touching off weeks of protest.

It took these two incidents to persuade Safir and his boss, Mayor Rudy Giuliani, to concede in 1999 that there might just be something wrong with Gotham's Finest. The commissioner had consistently denied there was a problem. Four months before the Louima incident the mayor had put into words the philosophy police officers knew he lived by when it came to accusations of brutality: "You give the benefit of the doubt to the sworn police officers until and unless there are facts, clear facts, that establish the contrary."[9] With officers reluctant to testify against one another, the commissioner in denial and a mayor, the people's representative, opting not for deferring judgment about complaints until the results of an evenhanded investigation had been concluded but for showing bias from the outset, it is little wonder that Justin Volpe felt safe in repeatedly brutalizing Abner Louima.

How serious a problem is police brutality in the United States? The former chief of the New York City police, William Bratton, often credited with turning around the city's crime rate, has acknowledged that his department had a "checkered history of . . . brutality," that cops are reluctant to "rat" on their colleagues, and that bringing false testimony to court ("testi-lying") is common.[10] But even the Department of Justice's Bureau of Justice Statistics, although mandated by Congress to trace the statistical frequency of police abuse of power, was unable to come up with definitive figures.[11] Many police departments keep no records of excessive-force incidents; many citizens are reluctant to file grievances. But here is some of what we do know.

In a March 1991 Gallup poll 5 percent of respondents said that they had been physically mistreated or abused by the police. Nine percent of nonwhites made that assertion. Five percent of the U.S. population is about 12.5 million people. Even if we presume that 90 percent of those people are lying or exaggerating, that still comes to 1.25 million Americans physically mistreated by the police.[12]

According to the U.S. Census Bureau, in 1996 an estimated 1.3 million people "were handcuffed or were hit, held, pushed, choked, threatened with a flashlight, restrained by a police dog, threatened or actually sprayed with chemical or pepper spray, threatened with a gun or . . . experienced some other form of force" from the police. Of that 1.3 million 60 percent had done something to "arouse police suspicions." That leaves 520,000 so treated who had not aroused any suspicions.[13]

Thirty-eight percent of those surveyed told Gallup in 1999 that they thought there was police brutality in their area of the nation. That was up from 6 percent who agreed with that statement in 1965, a jump of 633 percent.[14]

Regardless of the exact number of incidents, what is telling is how complaints about those incidents are handled; police departments have traditionally had abysmal records in this respect. The St. Clair Commission found in 1992, for example, that the Internal Affairs Division of the Boston Police Department sustained less than 6 percent of complaints it received, and the Christopher Commission put the number at 2 percent for Los Angeles in 1996. Most major cities now have some kind of independent civilian review board that receives and evaluates charges of excessive use of force and forwards the ones they deem valid to their respective police departments for action. But all too often that is where the process stops. All too often the departments take no disciplinary steps against their officers. Between 1996 and 1999, for example, the New York Police Department disciplined officers in only 24 percent of the cases recommended by the review board.[15] In Los Angeles, citizens are discouraged from filing complaints altogether because a citizen who files a complaint subsequently found to be false could be prosecuted.[16]

Yet despite these obstacles to holding police officers accountable, the financial awards that taxpayers are paying to settle civil lawsuits arising out of police abuse cases are enormous. The fact that a suit is resolved with a payment does not mean of course that a city has admitted its officers are guilty. But, not wishing to defend officers' actions at trial, Boston, Chicago, Detroit, Los Angeles, New York, Philadelphia, San Francisco, and Washington, D.C., alone paid well more than $439 million between 1980 and 1999 to settle liability claims.[17] As the former deputy city solicitor of Philadelphia said, "This is not Monopoly money. This is real money. How do we save the taxpayers millions of dollars?" Suing police departments is now so pervasive (and lucrative) that Fordham Law School even sponsored a conference for practitioners on how to do it.[18]

Whatever else we can say about police brutality as a human rights offense, the very least we can say is that it is an utterly avoidable waste of public money. Indeed, if other public officials were responsible for so much prodigality, you can bet that those who pride themselves on being guardians of the public purse, on "cutting pork," sniffing out waste and lowering taxes, would be roaring themselves hoarse in protest. Many years ago a Massachusetts governor got into a terrible pickle when it was discovered that he and his aides had been ordering lobster sandwiches from a local restaurant for their late-night confabs and had racked up a bill for the Commonwealth of something like $700. Why the patience when it comes to police misconduct?

Part of the answer is that white people and people of color often see this problem very differently. Even after Officer Justin Volpe was convicted of torturing Abner Louima in that station house bathroom, only 25 percent of white voters in New York City said they regarded police brutality as a "very serious" problem, but 81 percent of black voters said it was, as did 59 percent of Hispanic.[19] Similarly in the 1999 Gallup poll cited above, 27 percent of whites said that they had "personally . . . felt treated unfairly by the police or by a police officer" at some time or another, while 43 percent of blacks agreed with that statement.[20] Shortly after my experience with the Chicago police back in 1971, I mentioned the incident to an African-American friend. "You're just lucky you aren't black," he said, "because if you'd been black, your parked car would have been responsible for ramming that cruiser."

Communities of color are the victims of police misconduct out of proportion to either their percentage of the population or their incidence of criminal acts. It is not just that three-quarters of the people who lodge complaints with the Civilian Complaint Review Board in New York City, for example, are either African-American or Latino, although they represent only about 50 percent of the city's population. Nor is it even that roughly two-thirds of the victims of police shootings are also people of color.[21] Some have argued that these disparities simply reflect the higher crime rate among African-Americans and Hispanics. But the differential in treatment also holds when comparing encounters with police that do *not* result in arrests.

The state of New Jersey acknowledged in 1999, for instance, that its state police had engaged in systematic racial profiling in deciding which cars to search for contraband, with 77 percent of the cars searched having been driven by blacks or Hispanics and 21 percent by whites, even though the number of stopped vehicles in which drugs or weapons were actually found was roughly the same across race.[22] In Maryland, 70 percent of the drivers stopped on Interstate 95 by state police were African-American, even though only 17.5 percent of the speeders were black. Similarly, the attorney general of New York determined that even adjusting for different crime rates among racial groups, Latinos were stopped and searched by New York City police officers 39 percent more often than whites. For African-Americans the figure was 23 percent more often.[23] Perhaps the most absurd example of such racial targeting, however, comes from Des Moines, Iowa, where a black man named Theophilis Bell was stopped for riding his bicycle without a headlamp. Bell subsequently demonstrated in court that 98 percent of bicycles in Des Moines had no headlamps, but that every person arrested for that "crime" in the month prior to his stop had been black, even though Des Moines' population is overwhelmingly white.[24]

Among those who understand this phenomenon, some of the most eloquent and insightful are black police officers themselves. Ronald Hampton served for twenty-three distinguished years on the police force in Washington, D.C., and is now the executive director of the National Black Police Officers Association. "A large percentage of those who choose to be police officers," Hampton says, "go into the field in order to exercise control and authority over others. They are taught from the earliest days at the police academy that communities of color are dangerous, crime-infested places—the perfect places in which to demonstrate that authority. Combine that with the so-called 'blue wall of silence,' the unwillingness for one cop to break ranks with another, and you have a recipe for explosion."[25]

It is obvious, then, why African-Americans and Hispanics should regard ending the human rights violation of police brutality as a matter of self-interest—life and death self-interest. "I tell my son," says an

African-American mother of a twenty-two-year-old, "when you are stopped by a cop, show your hands immediately and keep showing them. Never talk back. Never act up. No matter how much of an asshole he may be. Your very life depends upon it." But because they rarely experience the same kind of mistreatment, harassment, or humiliation at the hands of police that people of color often do, many whites regard police misconduct, if they acknowledge it at all, to be an unfortunate by-product of efforts to lower the crime rate. Because that rate has been in decline lately, some may even regard the excessive use of force as a justifiable trade-off. But that is a foolish assumption and a Faustian bargain.

Nothing threatens to rip this society apart racially any faster than disparity in treatment at the hands of the police. It has happened over and over before. Have we forgotten that nearly every one of the incidents of urban unrest in 1968 was touched off by arrests of blacks by white officers for minor offenses? Have we forgotten the experience of Los Angeles in 1992 following the acquittal of police in the Rodney King case, a conflagration that did more than $700 million worth of damage in the county? Are we unaware that St. Petersburg, Florida, was the scene of a similar, if less costly, riot as recently as 1996 following the killing of a black motorist by a white officer? Do we really want to gamble that the United States has "put all that behind us?" Shortly after the shooting of Amadou Diallo in 1999, Bob Herbert, the only regular African-American contributor to the *New York Times*'s editorial page, made this observation:

> There is a widespread feeling among black New Yorkers that they are living in a police state.... The anger and resentment over this is growing every day. And increasingly the resentment is being directed not just toward the police and the Mayor but toward white New Yorkers in general, who are not subjected to the same levels of brutality and harassment. "I am scared to death," said a former city official... , "that this division between blacks and whites, this schism, is growing so large that it can't be repaired."[26]

A 1995 Gallup poll found that 77 percent of blacks, compared with 45 percent of whites, think the criminal justice system treats blacks more harshly than whites and they are right.[27] Study after study shows that, be it adults or juveniles, people of color receive harsher punishments for crimes than do white people. Take drug crimes as just one instance. Five times as many whites use drugs as blacks, but 62 percent of those imprisoned for illegal drug use are black, and African-American youth convicted of drug crimes are forty-eight times likelier to be sentenced to juvenile prison than are whites.[28] Police are but one part of the criminal justice system of course, but as the "intake officers" they are a critical part. Surely it is worth getting control over our police if the alternative is further disintegration in the racial fabric of American society.

But there is still another way in which police misconduct hurts us all: it makes the job of law enforcement even tougher than it already is and hence it makes our society a far less safe one. A good percentage of successful police work depends on cooperation from the law-abiding elements in any community. If huge segments of the community are alienated from law enforcement authorities, mistrustful of them or frightened, that bodes ill for the willingness of those community members to extend a helping hand. Social commentator Dinesh D'Souza could never be accused of being a "bleeding heart liberal." His reason for opposing racial profiling is quite pragmatic: "Government-sponsored . . . discrimination has the cataclysmic social effect of polarizing African-Americans who play by the rules and still cannot avoid being discriminated against. Even law-abiding blacks become enemies of the system because they find themselves treated that way."[29]

In his book *No Equal Justice*, Georgetown law professor David Cole cites one example after another of unsolved crimes or likely criminals set free because members of racial minorities mistrusted police and prosecutors and refused to cooperate with investigations. Security guard Isham Draughan of Richmond, Virginia, to take but one example, was shot one morning trying to make an arrest in the midst of an unruly crowd. Despite the presence of more than three hundred people, racial tensions with police in the city were so great that no one trusted the police enough to identify the killer. Far more than the threat of incarceration, what reduces crime, Cole writes, is the extent to which people view the legal system as fair and legitimate and the degree to which a cohesive community conveys disapproval of criminal behavior. But when the police display a double standard, that "robs the criminal law of legitimacy" and, as a result, the voices of those in the community condemning the breaking of laws are compromised and seen as less authoritative.[30]

Furthermore, when police violate rights or mistreat suspects, it increases the odds that the courts will eventually release offenders, even if they are guilty of a crime. One example is the recent "Ramparts" scandal in the Los Angeles Police Department, in which police shot an unarmed man in handcuffs, planted guns and drugs on suspects, and lied in court to frame innocent people. As many as one hundred convictions may have been tainted by such abuses and now must be thrown out. Those convicted who were innocent have obviously been subjected to a terrible miscarriage of justice and will now thankfully be set free, but so will those who were guilty. Some experts estimate the civil complaints arising out of these police actions may cost Los Angeles between $200 million and $1 billion and may even force the city into bankruptcy.[31] Prosecutors note that juries too are becoming more skeptical of police testimony.[32] Jonathan M. Levin was a much beloved teacher of inner-city kids in the Bronx who was tortured and ultimately murdered after revealing the pass code for his ATM card. One of his students, Mountoun Hart, confessed to the killing in the face of strong evidence against him, but jurors acquitted Hart because they found that police had coerced him into confessing.[33]

The notion that police must keep brutality and misconduct in their arsenal to be effective crime fighters is disproved by the drop in crime in such cities as San Diego and Boston, where community complaints against police are also low.[34] Even in New York City, where complaints are high, two precincts in the Bronx studied by the Vera Institute of Justice managed to combine a drop in crime with a significant decline in complaints against officers through strict enforcement of penalties against officers involved in repeat offenses against citizens, careful training and mentoring of new officers, and other measures.[35] The fact is that police brutality is a sure way to make our streets *more* crime-ridden rather than less.

To preserve "law and order" in a society, it is necessary to start by ensuring it among the law enforcers, because brutality and corruption breed on each other, brutality generating cover-ups and compromises, corruption seeding a culture of shortcuts and lies. Police officers told the Mollen Commission investigating corruption in New York City in the early 1990s that "acts of violence against suspects and prisoners were used as a barometer to prove an officer was a tough cop who could be trusted [not to rat on his] . . . fellow officers [about their corrupt practices]."[36] If we want honest cops, we must give police respect and expect it from them. It is also important to hold police officers to the highest standards because we cede them the means by which to take our lives . . . in an instant. No one else has such power. The police, like the rich, are different from you and me. Not in their feelings or needs, but in their authority and responsibility.

When I was in Northern Ireland in 1999 on an Amnesty International mission designed to reinforce the human rights elements of the Good Friday agreement (which, at least temporarily, ended the conflict there), I visited one of the most dangerous and polarized communities in that land, a place called Portadown. We were investigating the death of a young Catholic man at the hands of a Protestant mob, which took place at a street corner in the center of the town while officers of the Royal Ulster Constabulary (RUC), the police force, sat in a Land Rover across the street and did nothing to aid the victim. The police claimed that their trucks are soundproof and that as they were faced away from the melee, they didn't hear the ruckus. When we interviewed the local RUC chief, however, he leaned toward us and, in a hushed voice as if to take us into his confidence, said, "Look, my friends, I don't know what happened at that street corner that night, but I tell my officers this: 'Your lives are as valuable as anyone else's and at the end of the day you have no more need to risk those lives than anyone else does. If you don't make a priority of keeping yourselves safe first, no one else will, I assure you.'"

I found this a strange philosophy for a police commander—not the notion that police officers' lives are as valuable as anyone else's, but that the police's first priority is to keep themselves safe. After all, although it may be true that if police don't protect themselves, no one else will, it is also true that if police refuse to protect innocent people from angry mobs, there is no point in having a police force in the first place. When I asked Sir Ronnie Flanagan, the chief constable of the RUC, if his Portadown subordinate's policy reflected that of the constabulary as a whole, he assured me it did not. "We have a 'contract' to protect the people we serve," he said. It is exactly because we make a "contract" with the police that their misconduct is especially grievous. Because the police have the responsibility to risk their lives to protect ours, they deserve appreciation, cooperation, and higher pay than they generally receive. Because we give them the authority to inflict pain and even death, if it is absolutely necessary, we have the right to hold them to the highest standards.

The solution to police misconduct is multifaceted. It involves more careful recruiting, better monitoring of problem officers, more community policing, more lawsuits by the Department of Justice against police departments in which it has found a "pattern and practice" of abuses (a consent decree agreed to by the city of Pittsburgh to settle one such suit has apparently had beneficial effects[37]), the deployment of video cameras on police cars, and other measures.[38] Before the problem can be solved, however, far more people must recognize that there is a problem. Police brutality costs Americans our lives and our tax dollars. It short-circuits criminal convictions, makes the streets less safe, and fosters corruption. It fractures our society and shreds the police-citizen contract. In short, it is a problem for *all* of us, not just one part of the community. That is an important lesson for citizens to learn. Especially white citizens.

Prison Conditions and Criminal Justice

Robin Lucas is a strong woman. She is physically strong and athletic, having once tried out for the Women's National Basketball Association, and she is emotionally strong and resilient. Educated at private schools, the owner of a hair salon at the age of twenty-one, Robin was leading the good life, driving a nice car, vacationing in Europe, when in 1992 she fell in with a bad crowd and made a bad mistake. She cashed $7,800 worth of stolen travelers' checks and was convicted of conspiracy to commit bank fraud and sentenced to thirty-three months in the Federal Correctional Institute in Dublin, California. Her world had come tumbling down around her. Taking full responsibility for her crime, Robin prepared to serve her sentence. What she was not prepared for was what happened to her inside the prison walls.

At one point during her incarceration, Robin had a minor altercation with another female inmate. As was the practice in Dublin, for punishment she was sent to the "hole," the isolation unit, a unit located within the men's facility at the prison. One night in August 1995, as

Robin lay sleeping on her cot in her cell, she was awakened, as she later described, "by the hot breath of a man, his body pushing against me, tugging at my clothes, demanding that I be nice to him." She was shocked to see that the man was an inmate, and when she refused and the two scuffled, the inmate threw her against the metal bed frame, cracking Robin's head open. Seeing the stream of blood pouring from her forehead, the inmate fled. Needless to say, Robin spent a sleepless night, hardly believing what had happened to her.

The next day she filed a complaint with the captain of the guards. Obviously one of the guards had allowed her attacker into her cell. But instead of dealing with the matter promptly, the captain interrogated her accusingly and wrote up the complaint begrudgingly. Soon Robin learned, much to her consternation, that guards in the unit and inmates throughout the prison were aware that she had talked and were not happy about it. The next few weeks would be a living hell for her: her food was tainted with urine; murmurs of "snitch" and "bitch" echoed into her cell; and she anticipated another attack at any moment.

Three weeks after the first attack, another one followed. This time the experience was far worse, however. Three inmates were allowed into Robin's cell in the predawn hours. Knocking her to the floor, they handcuffed her, forced open her legs, and repeatedly raped and sodomized her. When it was finally over, one of her attackers, whom she recognized as her original assailant, urinated on her. Even then her ordeal was not at an end. Despite being in enormous pain and bleeding continuously from the rectum, Robin Lucas would not receive medical examination for thirty-five days.

But Robin is a strong woman, and she was determined to overcome her fear and regain a modicum of dignity. "When I went into prison," she said, "I was supposed to give up my liberty but not my soul." Rape had not been part of her sentence. For the remaining months in prison, Robin gathered evidence of other women who had been similarly victimized. As it turned out, guards at Dublin were running a prostitution ring, literally selling male inmates access to women prisoners. Upon her release in November 1995, Robin and two other female inmates filed a lawsuit against the federal government. On March 3, 1998, the Justice Department settled the cases for $500,000 and agreed to institute a host of reforms designed to prevent a recurrence of what happened to Robin and her sister prisoners.[39]

Today Robin Lucas runs her own women's clothing store, dresses fashionably, appears regularly in the media and at conferences, and has become an articulate spokesperson for prison reform. Far too many women in U.S. prisons are still subjected to the kind of violence and indignity Robin experienced, however. The cost to the rest of us is not only financial; the cost is measured in lost, embittered lives and in the impact that this loss and bitterness has on the children of these abused women.

Thanks largely to far harsher drug laws, the number of women in prison has soared in the past decade, burgeoning from 39,000 in 1991 to close to 150,000 today, a leap of more than 250 percent. Of those 150,000 women, 70 percent are first-time offenders and 80 percent have been convicted of nonviolent crimes. Most women will be released back into the community within a matter of years, where they will try to rebuild their lives and reconnect with their approximately two hundred thousand children who, with a primary caregiver behind bars, also suffer the consequences of imprisonment.[40] If, during their years of incarceration, these women have been harassed, battered, and raped or, as is too often the case, denied proper medical care or even shackled during childbirth—should they be one of the more than one thousand women prisoners who give birth while held in penal institutions every year—their chances of making a smooth transition back into society or of providing the kind of support their children need are grim. The toll that the incarceration of mothers takes on children and society in even the best of circumstances is illustrated by the fact that such children are as much as eight times more likely to become involved in the criminal justice system than the offspring of nonoffenders.[41] One such child took his desperation to an extreme when in April 2000 he held his sixth-grade schoolmates hostage because, according to the local police chief, "he just wanted to go to jail and be with his mother."[42]

Sexual abuse of women in U.S. prisons is tragically all too common, the consequences of such indignities growing more and more expensive. In 1998, Massachusetts was ordered to pay $80,000 to women prisoners who had been strip-searched and ordered to provide urine samples by masked male guards who roused them in the night shouting abuse. That same year Washington state paid out $110,000 to a former prisoner to settle a lawsuit she had initiated after having been raped and made pregnant by a guard.[43]

Nor are women the only prisoners whose mistreatment costs the taxpayers dearly, as the recent $8 million settlement of the litigation prompted by the savage beating of prisoners by guards following the 1971 Attica, New York, uprising attests.[44] In 1998, Bert Brunson received $3.5 million from Shelby County, Tennessee. He will not be able to enjoy the award, however, for Brunson is in a coma, oxygen to his brain having been cut off when he was hog-tied by a county sheriff. Shelby County alone paid out more than $6 million between 1993 and 1998 in thirty-nine cases where people were either falsely arrested or inmates were raped or beaten. In another case Charles Blount, who was arrested for stealing an eighty-nine-cent bottle of tea, was bitten by a poisonous spider while supposedly under suicide watch.[45] Similarly, California agreed to pay whistle-blowing former prison guard Richard Caruso $1.7 million (part of a total $5 million settlement) for job-related retaliation he experienced after exposing the practice of guards shooting unarmed prisoners at Corcoran State Prison.[46]

One does not have to be blind to the unsavory nature of many convicted criminals nor unsympathetic to their victims to recognize that a society that mistreats prisoners in the name of being "tough on crime" is engaged in a degree of self-destructive behavior that would make the worst neurotic blush. The simple fact about prisoners that many Americans seem to want to ignore is this: *most of them will get out.* The average prison term is twenty-seven months. Some 40 percent of inmates are released in any given year. In 2000 an estimated 585,000 felons were released from state and federal prisons.[47] If incarceration and release rates remain stable, as many as 887,000 will be released in 2005 and about 1.2 million in 2010. Fewer than 10 percent of all prisoners are sentenced to life.[48] Given that an enormous percentage of prisoners, even those convicted of nonviolent crimes, have already been subjected to violence at some point in their lives (between 23 percent and 37 percent of women in prison, for example, experienced some form of physical or sexual abuse before they reached the age of eighteen[49]), additional brutality is hardly the prescription for producing law-abiding citizens. Given that a huge percentage of prisoners are addicted to alcohol or drugs, failing to provide them treatment almost guarantees the perpetuation of their addiction (with its attendant costs and crime) upon their release. Given that a large proportion of prisoners have low levels of education and job skills, the refusal to provide adequate training opportunities contributes enormously to lack of employment (with its attendant crime and costs) among certain populations.

Furthermore, the notion that prisoners' medical problems have no impact on the general population is as spurious as the idea that the United States is immune to foreign-generated diseases. Not only do guards who have sexual relations with women inmates carry sexually transmitted diseases into the general population (and the percentage of women prisoners with syphilis, to take just one such virus, ranges from 3 percent to 22 percent[50]), but, as the St. Louis Post-Dispatch noted in a series of award-winning reports on neglect of prisoners' health: "Simply put: diseases don't respect bars. . . . Without effective medical intervention in jails and prisons, released inmates 'pose a threat to the public health of the community'. . . . Poor health also threatens visitors, guards and other workers in prisons ands jails." As discussed in an earlier chapter, a major new form of tuberculosis resistant to most drug treatment emerged in 1989, with 80 percent of all cases being traced to prisons and jails. At least eight thousand inmates have AIDS, and more than thirty-five thousand are HIV positive; an estimated three hundred thousand have hepatitis.[51] But health care in U.S. prisons is often substandard and almost always underfinanced. In light of this, unless one is prepared to advocate life in prison for all criminal offenses— something that might well make the growing number of private providers of prisons happy but is unlikely to appeal to even the most hardnosed politician when he or she faces the tax implications—the only alternative is to crack down on human rights violations in U.S. prisons. In this case the humane solution is also the best public policy option.

This is even more true with juvenile offenders than with any other part of the population. The rash of school shootings across the country over the past few years has fueled calls for ever tougher treatment of juveniles, despite the fact that the number of arrests of males under eighteen has fallen by 26 percent since 1994.[52] It is not just the apparent sympathy for the imposition of the death penalty at ever lower ages (one Texas legislator proposed lowering the death penalty–eligible age to eleven[53]) or the trend toward trying more juveniles as adults or even the incarceration of youngsters for petty crimes like making harassing phone calls or painting graffiti that is cause for alarm. It is the widespread abuse and neglect of children in U.S. facilities—from the growing use of metal restraint chairs to which children are strapped for hours on end to the excessive use of isolation (one 1992 study found that isolation had been imposed for more than twenty-four hours on almost ninety thousand occasions that year) to systematic neglect of the mental health needs of the 20 percent to 61 percent of youth in correctional facilities suffering from psychiatric disorders and substance abuse. In one juvenile facility in South Dakota, for example, girls held for "status offenses" like truancy or running away from home were forced to lie on their backs spread-eagled, their wrists and ankles shackled to rings embedded in concrete. Guards then cut off their clothing and covered them with a thin piece of material known as a "suicide gown."[54] Horrifying as this is, perhaps even more destructive is the number of young offenders—thirty-seven hundred in 1997 and 1998—under eighteen housed in forty states with the general adult criminal population, where they are 500 percent more likely to be sexually assaulted than if in a juvenile facility and are almost inevitably taught the finer arts of criminality.[55]

Even if one has no sympathy for troubled kids or rejects the theory that the younger the offender, the more deserving of an opportunity to redeem her or his life; even if one dismisses the international strictures contained in the Convention on the Rights of the Child (which of course the United States has not signed), which hold that "the best interests of the child" should be a primary consideration in all government actions concerning children, one ought to be sobered by the fact that the vast majority of juveniles will be released from these facilities in fewer than ten years.[56] To reintroduce into the society youngsters or young adults who have been subjected to brutality, gone untreated for their illnesses and addictions and transformed from angry, confused teenagers, three-quarters of whom come from broken homes,[57] into bitter, hardened adult criminals is breathtakingly stupid, as even the strictest disciplinarian ought to see.

Nor is there any clear evidence that this tougher approach to crime, whether adult or juvenile, has reduced the recidivism rates. A 1996 Florida study revealed a higher rate of recidivism among juveniles transferred to adult criminal court than those retained in the juvenile system,[58] findings that were confirmed in a review of New York and New Jersey cases in which those adolescent offenders sentenced in juvenile court had a 29 percent lower rearrest rate than those sentenced in adult criminal court.[59]

Joe Arpaio, sheriff of Maricopa County in Phoenix, Arizona, bills himself "America's Toughest Sheriff." He has generated immense publicity through his claims that by feeding inmates rotten bologna, making them wear pink underwear, and housing them in tents under Arizona's hot sun, he has made jail life so unpleasant that no one will want to return. The only problem is that when the sheriff commissioned an Arizona State University researcher to prove his claim, Professor John Hepburn discovered that before Arpaio had taken over the jail, the rate of inmate rearrest was 61 percent; five years after he had instituted his tough program, the rate was 62.3 percent.[60] Green bologna was hardly the worst of Arpaio's offenses, however. The Justice Department forced him to stop his deputies from repeatedly zapping prisoners with stun guns and using a metal restraint chair to inflict excruciating agony rather than to calm down uncontrollable prisoners, the purpose for which it was intended.[61] Unfortunately, the 1997 "settlement agreement" Arpaio signed with the Justice Department to avoid a lawsuit didn't come in time to save the life of Scott Norberg, who died in that restraint chair, or to save Maricopa County taxpayers the $8.25 million they and their insurance companies had to pay to settle Norberg's family's claims.

Joe Arpaio would be unimportant except for the fact that his philosophy of criminology has made him the state's most popular politician, thus illustrating how easy it is to confuse Americans about what is really in their best interests when it comes to dealing with criminals. But Arpaio is less interested in criminal justice and protecting the public than he is in advancing his career. I learned this when I appeared with him on the late-night talk show *Politically Incorrect,* which was being taped at his invitation from the Maricopa County Jail in front of an audience of inmates. Throughout the program Arpaio and I went head to head, I pulling no punches about his worst behavior; he insulting me with his cruelest cuts. When we walked off the stage into the back lot, I could not imagine that the sheriff was very happy with me. When I saw him gathering a group of his largest and most intimidating deputies and heading my way, I thought for a moment that I might rather be back in Liberia. But then the sheriff stuck out his hand. "You know," he said, "you and I are putting on a great show. Any chance you can get us on *Larry King Live*?" The fact is, though, that it is not just the prisoners who are suffering from the sheriff's "show" but all Maricopa County citizens, whether they know it or not.

More than two million Americans are now behind bars, the second-highest incarceration rate in the world (645 per 100,000 population), second only to Russia.[62] At least half of those are nonviolent offenders.[63] It is beyond the bounds of this book to tackle the many controversial aspects of the U.S. criminal justice system—from its racism to its inefficiencies to the relationship between the drug wars and the growing privatization of prisons to the fact that many states now spend more on incarceration than education. Nor would I deny that many of those in prison deserve to be there. But none of them deserve to be brutalized or subjected to neglect. Not only does that do us a disservice as a people who like to think of ourselves as civilized, but it also makes our country a more dangerous place for everyone. That is true even when it comes to the most controversial punishment of them all, the death penalty.

Death Penalty

For better or worse I have been speaking publicly against the death penalty since I was thirteen years old. That was the year I was selected to deliver a speech at my junior high school graduation derived from a term paper I had researched and written on capital punishment. The school I attended in 1963 was overwhelmingly conservative, the other students coming primarily from wealthy Pittsburgh business families. The next year a straw poll showed 97 percent of the student body favored Barry Goldwater over Lyndon Johnson for president. In retrospect, it is interesting that my speech against the death penalty caused hardly a ripple. The fact that the school administration, which was not known for challenging the community's prevailing political sentiment, had selected me and my topic for the commencement ceremonies reflected the relatively low level of support for the death penalty in those days, even among conventional conservatives.

Today, of course, the situation has changed dramatically. Upward of 70 percent of Americans say when asked straightforwardly whether they favor or oppose capital punishment that they support it. (The numbers change dramatically when people are asked if they favor the death penalty or guaranteed life imprisonment without the possibility of parole, however.) Nonetheless, the arguments marshaled by both sides have changed very little from the time I researched that junior high term paper. Proponents argue that the death penalty is just reward for the taking of human life; that it reflects how much value we as a society place on life to deprive those who take it of their own; and that the death of the perpetrators lends closure and relief to the victims' families. Abolitionists argue that there is no evidence the death penalty deters future crime; that it violates the sanctity of life, to say nothing of international human rights standards; that innocents can be killed; and that the punishment is applied capriciously and tainted with racism.

It is not my point here to rehash these familiar arguments. What I am interested in at the moment is whether the death penalty makes us safer or rather, as I suspect, perpetuates violence in society at large. Proponents of the death penalty will find such a notion ludicrous. But even the most ardent among them cannot demonstrate that capital punishment makes for safer streets. In fact, a comparison of FBI statistics for murder rates reveals that eighteen of the twenty states with the highest murder rates are death penalty states and that death penalty states have averaged 9.1 murders per 100,000 and abolitionist states 4.9. The state of Texas, which has executed more prisoners than any other since 1977 (more than two hundred), has a murder rate more than 25 percent higher than the national average.[64] Even absent a deterrent effect, however, one might conceivably be able to say that the death penalty, although it may not help reduce crime, certainly does no harm, were it not for three other things we know.

The first thing we know is that dozens of people—eighty-seven as of June 2000—have been convicted of capital crimes and sentenced to death who have subsequently been released from death row. This is a frightening statistic. Even more frightening given that the vast majority of those eighty-seven were released not because police, prosecutors, or judges discovered exculpatory evidence and corrected their mistakes, but because those eighty-seven were lucky enough to have lawyers, investigators, journalists, or college students whose digging and dedication helped free them.[65] Robert Lee Miller Jr. is one such person. In 1987, Miller, a vagrant, told Oklahoma City detectives of a dream he had in which he had raped and murdered two elderly women. Miller also told them that he was the Lone Ranger, an Indian warrior, and that his family had visionary powers. Nonetheless, on the basis of his "confession," he was convicted and sentenced to death . . . until DNA testing in 1995 proved he could not have committed the crime and identified a convicted rapist as the killer.[66]

When police or prosecutor misconduct is not to blame, sloppy defense lawyering often is. For example, Aden Harrison Jr., a black man accused of murder in Georgia, was assigned an eighty-three-year-old attorney who had been an imperial wizard of the Ku Klux Klan.[67] Defense lawyers, who are often state-appointed and paid abysmally low fees, have been known to sleep through trials, show up drunk, be facing disbarment, fail to cross-examine key witnesses, and commit a variety of other offenses that almost ensure their defendants will be convicted. Not surprisingly, then, two-thirds of all death penalty convictions are overturned on appeal, and at least eight death row inmates have been exonerated by the growing use of DNA evidence.[68] But what about the hundreds whose lawyers were not even competent enough to prepare their cases for appeal or where no DNA evidence was available for testing? The problem with convicting innocent people and sentencing them to death, much less executing them, is not only that it represents injustice of the first magnitude, but that such a practice undermines confidence in the entire criminal justice enterprise. That cannot possibly make for a less dangerous country.

The second thing we know is that the race of the victim of a capital crime is a profound determinant of whether the perpetrator of that crime will be sentenced to death or to a lesser penalty. Defendants charged with killing white victims are at least 4.3 times more likely to be sentenced to death than defendants charged with killing blacks, even though the number of black and white victims are roughly the same.[69] This means that the death penalty is indisputably administered in a racially biased way and, as with any penalty meted out disproportionately because of bias (be it sentencing for petty theft, wearing a dunce cap for disobeying a teacher, or being spanked by a parent), such discrepancies undermine the legitimacy of the system itself, be it criminal justice, educational, or parental. *That* cannot possibly make for a less dangerous society.

The effectiveness of U.S. criminal law depends on the extent it is seen to be morally credible, that is, as Northwestern University Law Professor Paul Robinson has said, the extent to which it is seen as "punishing those who deserve it, under rules perceived as just; protecting from punishment those who do not deserve it and, where punishment is deserved, imposing the amount deserved—no more, no less."[70] Under these criteria what could do more to undermine the credibility of the law (and hence of our safety) than risking the execution of innocent people and applying punishment in a racially discriminatory manner? Theoretically, of course, both of these objections to the death penalty could be eliminated if we could be guaranteed that no one innocent would ever again be convicted and no racial bias ever again displayed. But that ethereal realm of possibility would be almost impossibly hard to realize.

In the case of the third objection to the death penalty, however, there is no way we could overcome it, no matter how much we tinker with the practice. The third reason the death penalty undermines the goal of a less dangerous society is because it gives the state's imprimatur to the use of violence as a means of resolving problems. It is a staple of American political philosophy that government serves as a model of those values it wishes to see inculcated in its people. Government should reflect a commitment to liberty, equal opportunity, due process, integrity, fiscal responsibility, and so on. Sometimes social conservatives advocate an even more explicit embodiment of values, as, for example, when they call for posting the Ten Commandments in school classrooms. But every American, conservative or liberal, agrees that how our government conducts itself has an impact on how our citizens behave.

On one level we know this almost instinctively when it comes to the punishments we find appropriate for crime. Consider the biblically based notion of an "eye for an eye and a tooth for a tooth," the *lex talionis*. Almost all proponents of the death penalty eventually put forward some version of this argument, even if it's dressed in secular raiment. Setting aside the fact that many of the ethical imperatives of the Hebrew scriptures (Old Testament) are ones to which we would hardly subscribe today (Leviticus's injunctions against sleeping with menstruating women or in favor of executing all magicians, being but two of them), the *lex talionis*, though it was designed not as its latter-day interpreters believe to justify revenge but rather to set limits to punishment ("no more than an eye for an eye"), would seem on its face to sanction treating one person in an identical way to how he or she had (mis)treated another. Why, then, do we not feel comfortable applying this principle in any other realm of enforcement of our criminal laws? If the *lex talionis* prescribes the death penalty for first-degree murder, why would it not follow that, instead of or in addition to imprisoning a thief, we should rob her of something, or instead of incarcerating a rapist, we should rape him in return? Indeed, following the *lex talionis* would have us not just execute murderers by lethal injection or even electricity but duplicate as closely as possible the method by which the killer killed, plucking out his or her eye, for example, if that kind of mutilation accompanied the crime. And yet even the most hardhearted among us would likely reject such brutality as inappropriate behavior for a civilized government.

If government action, then, provides a model for citizens to follow, what model does the death penalty provide? When the government executes capital offenders, it is sending two contradictory messages to 280 million people. It is sending the message that it presumably wants to send—that is, if you commit a crime of like order, this is what will happen to you—but it is also sending the message that violence is the province of the powerful; that violence signifies victory, success, triumph, retribution, and toughness. An adviser to Governor Jeb Bush of Florida caught this spirit perfectly when he was quoted in state papers as saying of a speeded-up death penalty process, "Bring in the witnesses, put [the prisoner] on a gurney and let's rock and roll."[71] How could any would-be capital criminals possibly ignore the message that violence may very well be a simple solution to their problems too? Inasmuch as most of those convicted of capital crimes have been subjected personally, usually at a young age, to volumes of physical abuse at the hands of parents and guardians, and are, as a result, already prone to see violence as a customary means of asserting power and authority, the use of the death penalty is a perfect vehicle through which to perpetuate that myth. I submit that one of the reasons criminals continue committing capital crimes even when they know they may face the death penalty is because when it comes to the execution drama, they identify not with the "victim" who receives the jolt of electricity or lethal dose of drugs but with the powerful figures who administer them.

Criminologist Joan McCord of Temple University cites multiple studies that show that exposure to violence desensitizes those who view

it to future violence.[72] Many across the political spectrum certainly believe this is true when it comes to entertainment. Why, then, do we not
think the same dynamic is at work when it comes to state-sponsored
violence? Or consider that some studies have even shown that the more
severe the threat of punishment for any particular behavior, the more
attractive the act being punished becomes. If that is true, the death
penalty may well *invite* that which it seeks to discourage. Several studies have indeed shown that homicide rates *increase* when the death
penalty is used. The average annual increase in homicides in California
was twice as high during years in which the death penalty was carried
out than in years in which no one was executed.[73]

Because the application of the death penalty undermines the credibility of the criminal justice system and because capital punishment
models and institutionalizes violence, it is one of the terrible, tragic
paradoxes of U.S. society that the very practice designed to prevent
criminals from committing horrible acts may in fact perpetuate the
very behavior it is intended to eliminate. Do we really think the crime
rates in other industrialized societies, none of which except Japan have
the death penalty, are so much lower than ours simply because the people in those societies are "nicer" than we are? Or might it have something to do with the way the United States administers justice?[74]

I cannot prove that ours would be a less dangerous society if we abol-
ished capital punishment. But given that there is no evidence that the
death penalty deters crime in any systematic fashion, and because the
option of life imprisonment without parole (and with financial restitu-
tion required to the families of the victims) is itself a crushing punishment (I for one might very well prefer death to being locked up with no
hope of ever being released for the rest of my life), why should we take
the chance that we are contributing to making society more violent
rather than less by retaining executions?

At its heart, of course, the argument about the death penalty is more
emotional than analytic. I understand that. I have immense sympathy
for those who have lost loved ones to murder. I love my wife, Beth,
more than anything in the world. If she were to die at the hands of a
murderer, I would be consumed in hatred, swallowed up in grief and
pain and rage. My first reaction would probably be that I too wanted
her killer to die or, better yet, to suffer the most profound kind of agony

imaginable. All those feelings are utterly natural; there is nothing wrong with them. But just as I pray that I would not turn those feelings into action and mimic the killer's crime by killing him myself, so would I not want the state to dishonor the memory of a gentle, loving soul like Beth by killing in her name. It would pay no tribute to she who embodies my highest values, all that is good with the world, to indulge those passions that represent me at my most violent, vicious, vengeful, and destructive. Surely we can pay our loved ones greater honor than that.

That some may get a kind of relief out of knowing that the killers are dead may well be true. But that we ought to base our social policy on the satisfaction of those passions when the death penalty has so many other damaging effects on our society I cannot believe. The death penalty too is a violation of human rights that ill serves the best interests of the United States.

The United States is the venue for human rights violations that besmirch our name and compromise our ability to influence human rights practices elsewhere in the world. The ones I have examined thus far are perhaps the most obvious, but there are others.

When the United States harbors torturers and killers—as it does, for instance, by allowing Emmanuel Constant, the notorious Haitian police chief suspected of overseeing hundreds of murders and rapes during the regime of General Raul Cedras, to live freely in this country—it makes it far more difficult for us to insist that other countries bring their own human rights violators to justice.

When the United States mistreats refugees (including political asylum seekers, many of whom have stood up for democratic values in their countries of origin and suffered for it) by housing them in county jails with the general criminal population, where they are often assaulted and abused, it renders hypocritical our preachments that other countries have obligations to respect the rights of refugees and displaced people. Two Chinese women refugees housed in an Oregon jail, for example, were knocked to the ground and handcuffed when, not understanding English, they failed to respond to an order to switch bunks.[75]

When gay, lesbian, bisexual, or transgendered people are harassed, assaulted, or even killed on account of their lifestyles, it makes it almost impossible for us to preach tolerance of minorities—be they sexual, racial, religious, or any other—in international contexts.

No one expects the United States or any other country to be perfect. The very genius of the American system is that it has built-in mechanisms through which to correct its faults. Abraham Foxman of the Anti-Defamation League apparently believes that U.S. violations of human rights are not worth as much "time and effort" as those of "nondemocratic, repressive regimes." But to stop abuses in the United States not only benefits those Americans who suffer from them; it also serves the national interest by showing the world this country at its best. When the United States conforms its performance to its values, it strengthens its credibility and its clout on every global issue that matters to Americans, from national security to economic growth to human rights. Were we ever to abolish the death penalty, for example, our standing with our European allies would soar.

No one easily abides a hypocrite. Those nations whose words mirror reality command almost universal respect. To this extent a United States free of its own human rights dilemmas benefits everyone whose human rights are in jeopardy elsewhere around the globe. *If* we are willing to use our voice and our power on their behalf. How we might do that is the subject of chapter 8.

8

David Trimble's Tears

What We Can Do to
Promote Human Rights

Let us not underrate the value of a fact; it will one day flower in a truth.

—Henry David Thoreau, *Notebooks*,
December 1837

T HE YOUNG CATHOLIC MAN killed at that street corner in Portadown, Northern Ireland, by a Protestant mob, while the police sat across the street in their Land Rover and did nothing, was named Robert Hamill. I visited his family at their modest row house in 1999. Later, when I had occasion to meet with David Trimble, leader of the Ulster Unionist Party, first minister of Northern Ireland, and one of Protestantism's most ardent defenders, I raised the case with him. The Hamill killing had become emblematic for the Catholic republican community of their mistreatment by Protestant unionists and of the indifference of the Royal Ulster Constabulary. But more than that, the Hamills were Trimble's constituents.

David Trimble is an enigmatic man. A cowinner of the Nobel Peace Prize (with the Catholic leader John Hume), he is given to legendary bouts of temper. A key figure in forging the compromises with republicans, including Sinn Fein, that allowed Northern Ireland to regain self-governance, he built his reputation on his credentials as a member of the rabid Protestant Orange Order and once danced a jig with the hate-filled extremist Ian Paisley. A former law professor, Trimble took no compunction in assuring me that the principle of "innocent until proven guilty" was no more than a "theoretical construct." David

Trimble is a tough, hard-nosed realist when it comes to politics in Northern Ireland.

For this reason, when an Amnesty International colleague and I met with him in 1999, we did not have high expectations that he would make a priority of combating human rights violations against Catholics. Indeed, Trimble put on his customary show of temper at republican outrages (of which of course there have been many) and at one point slammed a book down on a table to make his point. When I raised the Hamill case, the unionist leader was quick to aver that Hamill himself had been guilty of various vague infractions. "You're not saying, are you," I asked, "that Hamill brought his death upon himself by simply walking down that street?"—a question that elicited another tirade. So I decided to change my tack. "Mr. Minister," I said as quietly as I could, putting my hand gently on his forearm, "I don't know the whole facts of the Hamill incident. Perhaps none of us ever will. But I *do* know that there are a mother, father, and sister in that house who are in deep mourning for a beloved child. And I *do* know that as first minister, you are now not just leader of the Ulster Unionist Party. You are the leader of this *entire* country, this *whole* community. If Northern Ireland is ever to heal, it will be because people in your position reach out across the barriers of the mind to the regions of the heart. Can you find it in *your* heart to reach out to a suffering family, even though they be of a different political or religious faith, as simply one frail human being to another?"

With that, something absolutely remarkable happened. The room became still and for an instant David Trimble's eyes filled with tears. The tears didn't spill over; they were so brief that my colleague, sitting across the room, didn't even notice them, and Trimble quickly caught himself and reverted to his more familiar style. So stunned was I at what had just transpired, even uncertain that it had, that I decided to test the matter once again. After thirty more minutes of conversation, just before the meeting was drawing to a close, I once again turned quietly to Trimble. In similar words to those I had spoken before, I asked if he would consider visiting the Hamill family, his own constituents, as just one scarred and suffering human being to another. Once again Trimble's eyes became misty and he averted his head. "Yes," he said, "I will consider it," and the meeting drew to a close.

I have thought of this interaction with Trimble many times since then. If he were asked if our conversation had affected him emotionally, I'm sure he would deny it, assuming he even remembered it had occurred. I don't think he has ever made it to the Hamills' door and I didn't really expect him to. But the incident provoked three thoughts in me, the first being the obvious observation that occasionally it is possible to cut through political and cultural barriers to touch a strain of our common humanity. The second observation is that the reason we must remain so vigilant about human rights, embedding them in law and pursuing them in practice, is because we cannot rely on the persistence of our governors' tears.

The philosopher Martin Buber tells of an emperor who was presented with an edict banning Jews from his country. The emperor took up his pen, was interrupted, took up his pen again, and again was interrupted. Finally he signed, but reaching out for the sandbox to dry his signature, he spilled the inkwell all over the paper. In the face of this final obstacle, the emperor tore up the edict. "Never bring it to me again," he instructed. A just order, we reflect, but can we stake our lives on our "emperors'" clumsiness?

My third observation about David Trimble's tears, however, is the most important. I think his bombast is not so much a sign of insensitivity as it is a protection against feeling all the pain he sees around him—the Hamills' and everybody else's. Of the aphorist E. M. Cioran, it has been said: "He didn't see Auschwitz and despair. He despaired as a way of not seeing Auschwitz."[1] I think Trimble is like many other so-called pragmatists, "realists": he is afraid that if he allows himself access to the true terror of *everybody's* suffering in Northern Ireland, he will be both emotionally overcome and forced to revise his worldview. So when the tears break through, he has to be quick to choke them. Not only would he lose credibility with his unionist allies if he were thought to be going "soft" on republicans but, even more frighteningly, he would come face-to-face with his own limitations—moral limitations ("How have I contributed to this carnage?") and political limitations ("Maybe I don't have the power to stop this").

Trimble's dilemma is that of all political realists, where "realist" refers to those who counterpose "morality" to "national interest" and assure us that rarely the twain do meet. I grant it is not easy to learn of slaves in Mauritania whose legs are tied to the sides of parched camels and whose legs, thighs, and groins are slowly dislocated as the camel drinks and its sides expand.² It is not pleasant to read Harry Wu's description of a Chinese prisoner so famished that he licked soup from a mud floor even after a guard had split open his head so that "bean sauce, blood and mud [were] smeared across his face."³ It is disheartening to know that every twelve seconds in the United States a man beats up a woman.⁴

We are tempted to deny these unpleasant truths, to push them away. When a puff adder plays dead, a tiny trickle of real blood drops from its mouth. Perhaps this human blood too is only pretense. How frustrating that we powerful ones can sometimes do so little, even if we would do much, and how hollow perhaps sound Gandhi's words to those who are accustomed to triumph, "What you do will be insignificant, but it is very important that you do it." How much easier it is to declare this suffering "terrible, terrible, yes," but not as important as other things —our national security, our economic welfare. How complicated life might be if in fact the suffering and the "other things" are one.

The arguments by which foreign policy "realists" try to stave off human rights claims follow a pretty consistent pattern. First, as we have seen, the "realist" will claim that Americans must make a choice between promoting human rights and pursuing our national interest. Then they will warn that promoting human rights is tantamount to imposing our values on other people—something we Americans have been taught never to abide. Third, they will suggest that even if we want to support human rights, there is either very little we can do or, conversely, we run the risk of getting entangled in military ventures that could cost American lives. And finally, when all else fails, the "realist" will issue a dire warning about our American independence, implying that to accommodate an international human rights regimen may ultimately be to sacrifice our own freedom and sovereignty as a people to some vague but terrifying "new world order." It is necessary to respond to each of these arguments in turn to clear the way for a "new realism."

When it comes to characterizing human rights and U.S. national interests as fundamentally at odds with one another, some "realists" resort to caricature. "I maintained," says Alexander Haig of his years as Secretary of State, "that an American foreign policy which is preoccupied solely with the achievement of ephemeral values such as human rights will ultimately . . . offend our sense of reality."⁵ Because no serious observer has ever contended that human rights (which, in Haig's view, presumably include such "ephemeral" values as free speech and the right to a fair trial) should be the "sole" goal of U.S. foreign policy, Haig's comment is as overblown as his personality. Other analysts, however, put the point in more sophisticated terms. Ronald Steel of the University of Southern California has said that "a workable foreign policy . . . cannot indulge in flights of rhetoric, dedicating itself to the pursuit of vague objectives like 'democracy' and 'pluralism' [which he later calls "quixotic goals"] in lands inhospitable to these values and of no threat to the United States."[6] Richard N. Haass of the Brookings Institution has written:

> The principal focus of American foreign policy should be on interstate relations and the external conduct of states—discouraging classic aggression, acquisition of weapons of mass destruction by rogue states, protectionism. . . . These matters have the greatest potential to affect the most important U.S. interests most deeply. . . . Considerations of "justice"—democracy, human rights, human welfare— would . . . ordinarily be of a lower priority. . . . The reasoning here is simple. Order is the most basic concern. One can have order without justice but not the other way around.[7]

As I have shown in this book, "interstate relations and the external conduct of states" are very much related to human rights conditions in those states. If democratic communities that respect rights are less likely to wage war on other such communities, as is almost universally agreed, what better way to prevent "classic aggression" than to encourage the creation of such communities? Does Haass really believe that whether Afghanistan, Iraq, Libya, or any other "rogue state" acquires weapons or uses terrorist tactics bears no relationship to their degree of respect for human rights? Foreign policy analyst Steven R. David has warned that "as central governments weaken and fall, weapons of mass destruction may fall into the hands of rogue leaders and anti-American factions," but the stability of "central governments" rests in good measure on whether they create a rights-friendly atmosphere.[8] Furthermore, the extent to which a country adheres to the rule of law and other human rights-related variables has a direct bearing on how open it will be to economic relations that truly benefit U.S. interests. Tell the former leaders of South Africa, Indonesia, and the former Soviet Union, Mr. Haas, how lasting order is without justice.

Indeed, when Steel and Haas list what they consider "vital national interests" (as opposed, presumably, to "quixotic goals"), Steel includes protection of natural resources, quelling regional disorders, and defending U.S. borders against illegal aliens and terrorists. Haas adds such things as preventing disease, promoting U.S. exports, and preventing domination of Europe and elsewhere by a hostile power— every one of which is related to issues of human rights.

Haass for one seems to be uncomfortable with the false dichotomy he has established, for in the very next paragraph following on that quoted above, he writes: "Under this doctrine, the United States would act . . . to shape the behavior . . . of governments . . . so that they are less likely to act aggressively either beyond their borders *or toward their own citizens*."[9] But what does it mean to act aggressively toward one's own citizens but to violate their human rights?

Haass's self-correction is a wise one of course. A failure to take internal repression seriously can indeed have drastic consequences for the United States. When Saddam Hussein saw that he could get away even with using chemical weapons against his own Kurdish citizens in 1988, it emboldened him to think the world would little balk at an invasion of Kuwait. More than one former political dissident has ended up a leader of his country—Vaclav Havel and Nelson Mandela are the most prominent—and it hardly makes for warm relations if the United States has supported their oppressors. "Were the Persian Gulf oil fields destroyed in a Saudi civil war," says Steven R. David, something that might well eventuate from the Saudi Arabian government's brittle repression of its political opposition, "the American economy . . . would suffer severely."[10] And then again, as British Foreign Secretary Robin Cook has testified, "Countries which observe the rule of law at home are more likely to accept their international obligations to fight the drugs trade or halt weapons proliferation."[11] To insist that we must choose between supporting human rights and defending our national interests is not only a phony choice but a foolish one.

What Churchill said of Munich applies far more often today than we think: "The moment came when honour pointed the path to duty and when . . . the facts . . . reinforced its dictates."[12]

The "realist's" second line of defense is one that superficially appeals to many Americans. Because we are taught to be tolerant of other cultures, the argument that to advance human rights around the globe is to try to impose American values on other people and hence should be avoided has a certain logical ring to it. Mao was raised in the Chinese tradition. The Chinese tradition has no concept of human rights. To expect Mao to abide by them, therefore, is not only unfair but reflects an attempt to foist Western values on a different culture. The Chinese Communist Party may decree, as indeed it has, that Mao's merits outweigh his mistakes by a proportion of 7 to 3, but making judgments like that is not up to outsiders.[13]

This argument has been popularized by Singapore's Lee Kuan Yew, who has claimed that "Asian values" place the interests of the community ahead of those of the individual and that economic development requires sublimation of personal liberties to the achievement of the collective good. Many Americans found themselves quite sympathetic to Lee's approach, when in 1994 an American teenager, Michael Fay, was caned four times for allegedly spray painting graffiti on cars and traffic signs in Singapore. I appeared on dozens of talk shows about the Fay case, and many a caller would insist that "it is not up to us to tell Singapore how to run its civic life," expressing a tolerance for brutality Fidel Castro and Saddam Hussein would no doubt be thrilled to hear. I always asked such interlocutors whether, since they supported the caning of Fay because they so respected the sanctity of law, they also supported the caning of vendors in the Sudan whose licenses had expired or the stoning to death of women in Saudi Arabia who are accused by men of adultery, since those punishments were prescribed by those two nation's laws. The best I ever got for an answer was that those situations were (somehow) different.

The idea that contemporary concepts of human rights, including the fundamental notion that governments ought not practice cruelty, have no basis in non-Western traditions is nonsense, as economist Amartya Sen has gone to great lengths to show.[14] Confucius himself asserted that "an oppressive government is worse than a tiger."[15] Moreover, it has always struck me as odd that when Lee and his disciples speak on behalf of Asians and what Asians presumably value, they seem always to have in mind only those Asians who are wielding the stick and never the ones on the receiving end. Do we truly believe that all those Chinese who were tortured or died in Mao's prisons would agree that they deserved their ill treatment because it was consistent with "Asian values"?

The fact is that human rights, as articulated in the Universal Declaration of Human Rights, are not "Western values," no matter what their origin, but universal values that transcend any particular culture. "Realists" seem to have no problem promoting the Western value of "private property," even though that concept may be a foreign one to millions of the world's people. Why, then, are they so reluctant to support values (like the right not to be tortured or imprisoned for one's nonviolent beliefs) that have been affirmed by nearly every nation in the world?

Human rights represent the boundaries of the acceptable, the limits beyond which an international consensus agrees that we may not go, regardless of the proclivities of a culture or tradition. "If you practice slavery, torture suspects, castrate girl children, we will not abide or sanction it no matter how loudly you proclaim it a custom of your society"—that is the message human rights deliver. The strict cultural relativist has no grounds for criticizing any practice undertaken in the name of tradition. The human rights advocate believes not necessarily that values are absolute but that we have in hand a global vision of "best practices" with which to order our common life together.

Some "realists" will acknowledge that support for human rights is a valid goal of U.S. foreign policy but will then go on to argue that there is very little we can do short of trying to become that notoriously dreaded gendarme, "the world's policeman." Richard Haass warns that "promoting democracy and human rights may be important interests, but U.S. foreign policy can only rarely accomplish this."[16] That will be news to the millions of people in eastern Europe, the former Soviet Union, South Africa, Latin America, Korea, Taiwan, the Philippines, Thailand, and now Indonesia, who over the past decade or so have experienced, in relation to their own histories, unprecedented levels of respect for human rights and democratic institutions. It is true that sometimes U.S. foreign policy has actually thwarted the emergence of those new impulses (as, for example, in parts of Latin America or in our stubborn support for Suharto). But unless Haass is prepared to say that we are nothing but a sleeping giant, the idea that the United States played little or no role in those developments is surely wrongheaded.

I remember a cartoon that was very popular back in the "radical 1960s." It showed a much-beribboned U.S. general talking on the phone to some hapless dictator. The general was saying, "Become a democracy tomorrow or we bomb the shit out of you." But the U.S. government and its allies have wide-ranging resources with which to entice, cajole, badger, and boost other countries into greater respect for human rights short of bombing them, and those resources begin with the diplomatic table. Imagine how different the situation in Sudan might be, for example, if the United States put as much effort and prestige into resolving that conflict as it has into settling differences in Northern Ireland or the Middle East. (One cannot help but speculate that racism may play a role in our choice of priorities, or worry what impact those choices have on the confidence of African-Americans in the U.S. government.) Imagine what impact we could have on Burma (Myanmar) or even China if we put as much energy into cracking the information shield in which those countries have enveloped their citizens as we did in Cold War Eastern Europe—something that with new communications technologies is far easier to do today than in the 1950s. Training in how to institutionalize the rule of law and other elements of civil society is far from inconsequential.

In as globally interdependent a world as ours, we need not rely only on such relatively paltry goals as academic or cultural exchanges to define our leverage over other countries. Controlling the trade in arms or in those commodities that support that trade (such as diamonds in West Africa) can be a highly effective tool to further human rights. Travel bans and support for extradition of those who may be guilty of human rights crimes to countries where they will be put on trial are other measures. Most countries are desperate for international respectability. Why else would the Chinese spend millions of dollars in foreign aid each year to bribe developing countries that sit on the U.N. Human Rights Commission to vote against resolutions of censure of China's human rights record—resolutions that carry little, if any, practical consequences at all? Playing on that desire for respectability can be a productive ploy. Those same countries are desperate for economic integration with the global economy, be it through private investment or grants and loans from international financial institutions with which the United States holds considerable sway. Clever use of economic carrots and sticks can bring remarkable change, as we discovered most dramatically in the case of apartheid South Africa.

But to play with carrots and sticks is to be willing under certain circumstances to withhold the carrot or wield the stick, and it is exactly because they shy away from employing or withholding economic incentives that "realists" are sometimes reluctant to admit the degree of influence we can wield over human rights developments if we choose to. Their modesty parallels the tongue-tiedness that strikes many corporate executives when they are asked to help promote human rights overseas. At some point a CEO will inevitably say, "We'd like to help, but we just don't have the power you think we do." I always get a kick out of watching a mighty CEO play the shrinking violet. We know that of the world's one hundred largest economies today, fifty are corporations, not countries, and that if we combine the sales of the top two hundred corporations, that figure exceeds the combined economies of one hundred eighty-two nations—all nations in the world, in fact, except the nine largest.[17] We also know that many corporations are more powerful even than intergovernmental organizations—and a lot wealthier. The total United Nations budget in 1995 and 1996 was $18.2 billion, while Lockheed Martin alone took in more than $19 billion that year.[18] One of the few advantages of running a trade deficit with China is that we buy up about 40 percent of China's exports, and it wouldn't be a piece of cake for China to make that loss up overnight from others. That is clout the United States has proven to have in its negotiations over piracy of intellectual property.

But more telling than many of these statistics is the fact that much of what corporations are asked to do to promote human rights requires no confrontations with government; only decisions about how to run their own businesses. They can be mindful of human rights when it comes to setting wages, working conditions, and production standards for subcontractors and suppliers or granting labor rights (including even where trade unions are forbidden, recognition of workers' associations that can negotiate with management) or meeting environmental protection requirements. They can insist that security forces working in tandem with the corporation respect human rights or pay attention to the company's impact on a community. Indeed, dozens of corporations, to their credit, have adopted codes of conduct and terms of engagement without risking government ire (though their willingness to allow independent monitoring of these codes often leaves much to be desired). Furthermore, many retailers or mail-order houses that may not operate directly in repressive countries can support human rights simply by insisting that their products be free of the taint of child labor or slavery.

Even when a human rights–friendly approach requires resistance to a government (when, for example, an employee is arrested for free expression or a company objects to the holding of political indoctrination sessions on its premises), it is more than possible in most circumstances to raise objections, preferably with the support of one's own government and others in the industry, without risking fatal animus. Some business leaders have even gone so far as to advocate release of prisoners of conscience without ill consequence. Former president of the U.S. Chamber of Commerce in Hong Kong, John Kamm, for example, has done so on numerous occasions and swears his business connections have never suffered for it. In 1999, Paul Fireman, president of Reebok, wrote a moving letter to President B. J. Habibie of Indonesia, citing his company's decade-long investment in Indonesia and seeking the release of human rights activist Dita Sari—a gesture that may well have played a part in winning her freedom. There were no negative repercussions for Reebok's operations.[19] Of course nothing precludes corporations from being far more generous and supportive of human rights organizations themselves, both domestic and international, thereby accomplishing indirectly what the corporations may be hesitant to do themselves. The U.S. government can certainly be proactive in encouraging steps like these.

When it comes to economic sanctions, the record of success is decidedly mixed. Economic sanctions alone rarely, if ever, topple a government and often lead to humanitarian catastrophes, but sanctions as part of a larger strategy, particularly sanctions targeted to affect the power brokers, may well have a salutary impact, as they did in ridding Cambodia of Khmer Rouge influence and in helping bring an end to apartheid in South Africa. The key is whether those sanctions are strictly enforced and, because they so rarely have been, it is hard to know just how effective economic sanctions would be if they were taken seriously by all parties involved.[20] The larger point is, however, that both governments and businesses have far more options than "realists" generally acknowledge with which to bend other parties to the international will.

One of those options of course is military intervention. English critic Cyril Connolly once said, "If attacked by a lion, thrust your arm down his throat. This takes some practice." "Realists" find the notion of using military force for human rights purposes equally impractical and are quite adept at invoking the specter of Somalia to prove it so. Unless there is a direct and obvious connection with U.S. national security or economic interests, "realists" oppose intervention to stop slaughter. Commentators of that ilk fell all over themselves declaring the Kosovo War unwise and unwinnable. Even after the war had ended and most of the Kosovars returned to their homes, journalist Michael Hirsh could write, "By the middle of May, despite two months of bombing . . . , it should have been obvious to even the dullest observer that, no matter what the strategic outcome, America had lost the war in Kosovo."[21] Hirsh will presumably forgive those thousands of Kosovars whose lives may have been saved by the NATO bombing and who are now back in their homes for being such dull observers as not to have taken notice of NATO's loss. And we will forgive him for not being prescient enough to see how that "defeat" ultimately set the stage for Milosovic's departure.

Advocating military intervention for humanitarian purposes is always a tricky call for human rights advocates. Amnesty International never takes a position on such matters and, although the organization had steadfastly criticized dictator Slobodan Milosovic's actions in Kosovo, it also accused NATO of war crimes after the war was over. But governments and intergovernmental organizations do not have the luxury of such studied neutrality, and to rule out military action even in the face of genocide or its potential is to tread a line both morally ambiguous and imprudent.

No one would disagree that military intervention should always be a last resort, employed only after all other options have failed. It goes without saying that the lives of young Americans are immensely precious. But to wave the red flag of U.S. casualties, to haul out the image of the United States as "the world's policeman," every time the possibility of military action for humanitarian ends is contemplated is tragically misleading. First, it is by no means true that Americans must always be on the battle lines in such ventures. Although the United States must usually encourage or support (and certainly not block) international interventions if they are to be successful, regional powers can often be called on to carry the military responsibility, as witness ECOMOG (Economic Community of West African States Cease-fire Monitoring Group) in West Africa and Australia in East Timor. A standing military force under United Nations control would further decrease the need for unilateral U.S. involvement. Second, even if the United States should commit its own troops, casualties are far less likely if action is taken early before bloodshed gets out of hand. Whether American or other troops had intervened in Rwanda in response to General Romeo Dallaire's call for reinforcements early in the conflagration, it would not have taken many of them. Finally, we must ask ourselves how many foreign lives one American life is worth. National security analyst Alan J. Kuperman has argued that had the United States intervened in Rwanda late in the genocidal rampage, we might have saved seventy-five thousand lives, a number that, compared with the eight hundred thousand killed, he implies, would not have been worth the effort. But on what grounds are we willing to contend that the lives of seventy-five thousand Rwandans are not worth the risk to a few hundred Americans?[22]

Military intervention is never a happy choice, and under some circumstances it would be a disastrous one. No sensible observer, for example, has ever suggested such action by outside parties to put an end to Russia's misadventures in Chechnya. The idea that post-Kosovo the United States is going to run around committing troops willy-nilly to faraway places to combat human rights infractions is a scare tactic of the most scurrilous kind. As journalist Michael Ignatieff has written: "Stopping genocide doesn't commit America to intervene everywhere. It actually sets the bar to intervention very high and justifies the use of force only when large numbers of civilians are facing extermination, mass deportation or massacre and where force can actually turn the situation around."[23]

Ought force remain an option when it comes to supporting human rights as it does when it comes to protecting national security or promoting U.S. economic welfare? Given how intimately linked human rights are to those and other interests, quite apart from our moral obligations, the answer should be obvious. After all, we put Americans in harm's way to topple a ruler in Grenada and to capture a drug-dealing thug in Panama. What kind of people would we be if we were utterly unwilling to consider doing that to stop the massive slaughter of the innocent?

When all other arguments fail, the "realist" will wave the flag of American "exceptionalism," the doctrine that the rules that apply to the rest of the world do not apply to us. "Realists" will claim that if we conform our own laws and practices to international human rights standards, we will be in danger of sacrificing our sovereignty. Thus, in describing a "conservative" foreign policy, Professor Samuel P. Huntington can say, "Conservatives give their highest loyalty to their country. . . . Unlike most liberals, they see international institutions not as good in themselves but good only insofar as they contribute to furthering the well-being of the American nation."[24] And John Bolton of the American Enterprise Institute, in decrying criticism of the use of the death penalty in the United States by a U.N. special rapporteur, warns darkly that "to whatever extent the rapporteur's work has an impact, it represents a shift away from a [U.S.] constitution-based decision-making structure toward one that subjects us to the vagaries of world opinion."[25]

When I hear comments such as these, I often wonder what world their vocalists are living in. On a globe as interdependent as ours, how can American interests possibly be divorced from those of our trading partners, our cyberspace neighbors, and indeed even our would-be adversaries? What breathtaking self-pride to believe that we can reap the benefits of interconnectedness—lower trade barriers, bans on weapons, military alliances, environmental cooperation, holding others accountable for crimes—but refuse, whenever we wish, to play by the rules ourselves, rules that in many cases, including that of the Universal Declaration of Human Rights, we have been instrumental in making. "Realists" like to say that the United States must lead by example, but what kind of example do we set by such an attitude? What kind of a world would we live in if every nation took the tack that "international institutions [are] . . . good only insofar as they contribute to furthering the well-being of [our] nation?" Let Americans just try to solve our environmental and health problems, maintain a healthy economy, and preserve the peace in such a world as that.

The United States is a mighty power, but it is not omnipotent. If history is any guide, it will not remain even a mighty power forever. Wouldn't it be wiser, then, while we have the power, to enter wholeheartedly into the creation of international norms, be they legal or behavioral, that best reflect our values and then respect those norms and their attendant procedures even when we may be found in violation? This is not to sacrifice our Constitution but, at most, to adapt its interpretation to the changing nature and values of the world—something that we have always done, when, for example, we outlawed slavery or child labor. European countries have managed thus far to conform their laws to the strictures of the European Court of Human Rights without abrogating their national identities. How "realistic" is it to think that we can thumb our noses at the rest of the world forever and truly suffer no ill consequences?

If foreign policy "realists" have their illusions, human rights advocates do too, perhaps the greatest of which is an unwillingness to acknowledge the moral ambiguity that often accompanies hard policy decisions. It is simply not true that human rights concerns trump every other. To refuse to negotiate with human rights violators when the consequence may be widespread violence; to refuse to make alliances with distasteful regimes to counter even greater evil; to insist that all human rights criminals must be brought to justice even if that means continuing upheaval for most of a nation's people; to show no sympathy for policy makers who must balance competing interests—this is also to live in a dream world (as playwright Bertolt Brecht famously said of the Spanish Civil War: "My food I ate between battles/To sleep I lay down among murderers"). It is to risk the kind of moral myopia that the Marxist historian Eric Hobsbawn displayed when he was asked whether, had he known in 1934 that fifteen million to twenty million people would die for the Soviet experiment, he would have renounced Communism. "No," he said. "The chance of a new world being born in great suffering would still have been worth backing."[26] It is hard to come up with a better moral compass for decision-making than a utilitarian calculation as to how many people will endure how much suffering. This means that addressing human rights claims will sometimes have to be a lower priority than negotiating an arms control agreement, for example.

The problem of course is that it is often impossible to make such calculations with any sense of assurance that they are accurate. That is why we resort to rules for the protection of human rights and must tread warily on their breach. Nor is it the case that human rights must inevitably be violated to reach our larger objective. Crime can be fought without abusing citizens' rights. Drugs can be interdicted without targeting innocent people. Wars can be fought without committing war crimes. In fact, all of these goals can be achieved even *more* readily if they are accomplished in a manner that honors human rights. Among the reasons to exclude torture from a government's bag of tricks is that the information received under such duress is rarely reliable. The resentment capricious torture spawns in the affected community, to say nothing of the affected individual, inevitably makes relations with the governing authority even worse.

Take an illustration provided unwittingly by political observer Robert Kaplan. In a casual little essay written for the *Atlantic Monthly,* Kaplan inveighs against those who would introduce moral scruples into policy making and praises the ruthlessness of those Machiavellian-like political leaders who adopt a "warrior" mentality on behalf of just causes. He cites Yitzhak Rabin admiringly and specifically Defense Minister Rabin's 1988 order to Israeli soldiers to "go in and break their bones" in response to the Palestinian intifada. It was Rabin's toughness, Kaplan avers, that got him elected prime minister in 1992 and allowed him to start peace talks with the Palestinians.[27] What Kaplan doesn't mention is that as a result of Rabin's order, Israel was convulsed in turmoil when it learned that its soldiers had with no cause at all mercilessly beaten groups of passive Palestinians in the West Bank villages of Beita and Hawara; that an Israeli court found the soldiers' commander, Col. Yehuda Meir, guilty of issuing a manifestly illegal order; and that Rabin subsequently denied having told anyone to break any bones at all.[28] How can Kaplan know that loss of Israeli moral stature—in the eyes of Israelis, of Palestinians, and of the rest of the world—caused by Israeli mistreatment of the Palestinians has not done the country more harm than good? How can he be sure that had the Palestinians been treated more equitably (which in no way excludes their criminal acts from being punished), they might not have come to negotiations even earlier? How can he tell that it was Rabin's association with a policy both the court and he himself had repudiated that changed voters' minds, rather than his status as a war hero? How can

Kaplan measure the degree to which Rabin's endorsement of gratuitous violence may have contributed to the "warrior" mentality in Israeli society that ultimately struck him down when he was assassinated?

So although human rights advocates ought not claim supremacy for
our values in every instance, those who would downgrade their importance risk facing more than a moral quandary; they risk damage to the
very interests (in Rabin's case, Israel's security and stature, peace with
one's adversaries, and the preservation of his own life) that presumably
motivated them in the first place.

Ending human rights abuses is not easy, and it does not happen quickly.
When the guru Sri Ramakrishna was asked why God allowed evil to
flourish in the world, he replied, "To thicken the plot." But the plot is
now quite thick enough, and it takes a long-term commitment to un-
ravel it. What I have offered in this book is not a replacement for "realism" but a corrective to it. That is why I call for a "new realism"—a recognition not that human rights are the only or even necessarily the
primary consideration that either Americans or American foreign policy makers must take into account, but that they are entwined in a far
more complicated way with matters of safety, trade, health, and progress than has ever been acknowledged.

A new realism would insist, for example, that human rights concerns
be understood as matters of morality, legality, *and* utility, rather than
sloughed off as a subsidiary interest unrelated to the truly "serious
questions" of the day. A new realism would take human rights out of
the box marked "preferences" and place it solidly in the box marked
"strategic interests." It would recognize that human rights have implications for nearly every other policy concern our leaders must address.
It would view human rights as more than the release of prisoners of
conscience or an end to torture but as a comprehensive effort to shape
democratic communities of rights that will be peaceful neighbors, fair
trading partners, and collaborators in the effort to preserve a green
planet. It would be flexible in its choice of tactics, recognizing that we
cannot deal with a nuclear power in the same way we deal with a developing state, but it would insist that the same rules apply to all,
including ourselves, even if the enforcement is uneven. It would recognize that short-term expediencies often lead to long-term catastro-

phes, and it would act with an eye cocked toward the future. If a new realism is successful, human rights will come to be understood as a "hard" concern, not a soft one, and its pursuit just as much a function of gumption, fortitude, and courage as any other national interest. Ronald Reagan, after all, was a champion of the rights of those oppressed by Russian Communism and in that sense was an unreconstructed Wilsonian—and no one ever considered Reagan soft on anything.

Are all human rights violations of equal threat to the United States? Of course not and, as I said earlier, some may not directly affect Americans' interests at all. But you can be pretty sure that one set of violations signals the possibility of others. If a country employs child soldiers or persecutes gay, lesbian, bisexual, and transgendered people or intimidates religious minorities or tolerates acid burnings of women, for example, it is a good bet that that country will be guilty of other abuses— that it may tolerate environmental toxins, fail to regulate cyberfraud, or ignore treaty commitments at will. A new realism will understand human rights violations in a holistic fashion.

What is an acceptable living wage? When should sanctions be applied? How "democratic" must an election be to be recognized as legitimate? Is there a reasonable transition phase from authoritarianism to democracy during which limited human rights compromises are appropriate? What are the warning signals of genocide, and at what point is the United States obligated to intervene? These and many other questions about how to implement human rights policies are complicated ones, but we will never answer them satisfactorily if we are content to adopt the traditional "realist" posture that human rights are compelling only when they are convenient.

And we will never transcend traditional "realism" until the American people recognize how abidingly their own interests are entangled with respect for other people's human rights around the world—so abidingly that they cannot be left to foreign policy technocrats alone. Fortunately, many women at least are apparently getting it. A recent poll showed that American women are more likely than men to decide issues based on their global implications. "American women understand," says the director of the project that commissioned the poll, "that the well-being of themselves, their families and their communities are . . . intimately connected with the well-being and stability of other countries."[29]

Foreign policy rarely sways national elections, nor do issues like police brutality, prison conditions, or the death penalty usually affect state and local elections. But even modest-sized numbers of people can have an impact on foreign governments and international corporations as well as legislation, policy making, and a politician's image here in the United States. At least forty thousand political prisoners have been freed thanks at least in part to the letter writing to foreign governments (and now the faxing and e-mailing) of Amnesty International's members. Retailers are supremely sensitive to how they are perceived in the activist student community, and the threat of consumer boycotts can have a major impact. When Senator Patrick Leahy of Vermont inserted a groundbreaking amendment into the Foreign Assistance Act in 1999 that banned U.S. military assistance to any foreign military or police units associated with human rights violations, he rejoiced in the grassroots support that helped get it passed.

To convince jewelers not to trade in diamonds that fuel the grotesque brutality in Sierra Leone, or American diplomats to be as wily in lobbying in *favor* of a U.N. Human Rights Commission resolution condemning China's human rights record as the Chinese are in opposing it, or the U.S. Senate to ratify a treaty establishing an International Criminal Court, or a police commissioner to crack down on the misbehavior of his officers—all this can be accomplished by a determined constituency. The environmental movement provides an inspiring model. Not only are few politicians today willing to be labeled "enemies of the environment," but environmentalists have often made an ally of business. The Forest Stewardship Council, for example, certifies which forests are being logged at a sustainable rate and hence which derivative consumer products support ecologically sound practices. The timber industry (and, increasingly, fisheries as well) supports this program because they want to avoid litigation and bad public relations and because they know that sustainable forests are ultimately in their own best interests. Environmentalists support this program because they know that logging is here to stay and business will be either an ally or an agitator.[30] How has the environmental movement been able to leverage its power with both politicians and corporate chieftains? By connecting the globe's future to our own, by supplementing our love of nature with the need to protect our children's health. The human rights movement will learn to link the moral to the pragmatic as well, or we will remain irritants rather than influentials carrying plenty of passion with but a thimbleful of weight.

Finally, a confession. When I was preparing this book, I summarized its thesis to a friend. "Oh, what a shame!" she exclaimed. "To think that we need selfish reasons to care about our fellow human beings." I understood what she meant. I wish it were enough to tell people that in early-twentieth-century Congo, Belgian labor bosses cut off the right hands of boys who did not meet their mining quotas for diamonds. To show off their strictness, they kept baskets full of those hands on display in their offices. I wish the revulsion that story evokes were enough to motivate people to stop parallel atrocities committed today in Sierra Leone. But it is not.

I wish everybody responded with chills down their spines when they read Loung Ung's reflections on her father's murder by the Khmer Rouge when she was a small child. Her Pa was "loved for his generous heart," "a teddy bear, soft and big and easy to hug," who "smiles not only with his mouth but also with his eyes." After months of hiding from the Khmer Rouge, the Loungs were finally discovered. Two men in black came for Pa. " 'My beautiful girl,' he says to me as his lips quiver into a small smile, 'I have to go away with these men for awhile.' " Ung never saw her Pa again, never knew exactly what happened to him, but she imagines:

> I have heard many stories about how the soldiers kill prisoners and then dump their bodies into large graves. How they torture their captives, behead them, or crack their skulls with axes so as not to waste their precious ammunition. I cannot stop thinking of Pa and whether or not he died with dignity. I hope they did not torture him. Some prisoners are not dead when they are buried. I cannot think of Pa being hurt this way, but images of him clawing at his throat, fighting for air as the soldiers pile dirt on him flood my mind. I cannot make the pictures go away! I need to believe Pa was killed quickly. I need to believe they did not make him suffer. Oh, Pa, please don't be afraid.[31]

I wish that story made everybody shudder, that we each could feel as if we knew Pa too, but it does not.

I wish all of us identified with Aleksandr Tvardovsky, the editor of the Russian journal *Novy Mir,* who, the first time he read *Ivan Denisovich,* Aleksandr Solzhenitsyn's staggering account of life in Stalin's slave camps, got out of bed and put on a coat and tie, saying that it would have been an insult to the victims had he read the book in his pajamas. But we do not.

I have spent a professional lifetime trying to convey the truth about human suffering that it might touch another's heart. I am a reasonably good writer; I can give a fair public speech; I can occasionally call on some skein of authenticity with which to reach into a soul to find that little corner out of which one human can respond to another's brokenness. And once in a while I have been successful, even in evoking David Trimble's tears. All of it is good, I think. But it is not enough. Not enough to rescue the tortured and the dying from the throes of perfidy. On some level I accept my failure and my limitations. It would be the height of hubris if I did not. But what I will *not* accept is those who tell us that it doesn't matter, that other things are more important, that we ought to offer a hand to anguish only in the narrowest of circumstance.

This book has argued that those circumstances are far wider than we think. But it is a mere footnote to the reason we ought offer that hand in the first place: because to look on human agony and consistently remain unmoved is to be dead in all the ways that truly matter, dead to the mystery of pulse and breath, dead to the gifts of grace and kindness, dead to the fragility of Creation.

Ultimately I do not care why we staunch another's suffering. Only that we do what we can to stop it. Only that we not remain indifferent. This book is a polemic against those who would cloak indifference in the raiment of "interests." It is an appeal to Americans to judge their interests wisely. A similar book could be written for every country in the world. But it is meant as nothing more than a supplement to a much more abiding conviction: that if we would live in the world with honor, we must not let misery go unmet. A world worth keeping sleeps ill with the torn unmended.

Appendix: How to Get Involved

If you would like to learn more about how to address the issues dealt with in this book, here are some organizations to contact.

Human Rights Organizations

Amnesty International USA
322 Eighth Avenue, Tenth Floor, New York, NY 10001
Telephone: 212-807-8400 or 800-AMNESTY, Fax: 212-627-1451
www.aiusa.org

Lawyers Committee for Human Rights
333 Seventh Avenue, Thirteenth Floor, New York, NY 10001
Telephone: 212-845-5200, Fax: 212-845-5299
www.lchr.org

Physicians for Human Rights
100 Boylston Street, Suite 702, Boston, MA 02116
Telephone: 617-695-0041, Fax 617-695-0307
www.phrusa.org

Human Rights Watch
350 Fifth Avenue, Thirty-fourth Floor New York, NY 10118-3299
Telephone: 212-290-4700, Fax: 212-736-1300
www.hrw.org

Committee to Protect Journalists
330 Seventh Avenue, Twelfth Floor, New York, NY 10001
Telephone: 212-465-1004, Fax: 212-465-9568
www.cpj.org

International Human Rights Law Group
1200 Eighteenth Street, NW, #602, Washington, DC 20009
Telephone: 202-822-4600, Fax: 202-822-4606
www.hrlawgroup.org

RFK Memorial Center for Human Rights
1367 Connecticut Avenue NW, Suite 200, Washington, DC 20036
Telephone: 202-463-7575, Fax: 202-463-6606
www.rfkmemorial.org

The United Nations High Commission for Human Rights
www.unhchr.ch

Minnesota Advocates for Human Rights
310 Fourth Avenue South , Suite 1000, Minneapolis, MN 55415-1012
Telephone: 612-341-3302, Fax: 612-341-2971
www.mnadvocates.org

Freedom House
1319 Eighteenth Street NW, Washington, DC 20036
Telephone: 202-296-510, Fax: 202-296-5078
www.freedomhouse.org

Environmental Organizations

Sierra Club
85 Second Street, Second Floor, San Francisco, CA 94105-3441
Telephone: 415-977-5500, Fax 415-977-5799
www.sierraclub.org

World Wildlife Fund
1250 Twenty-fourth Street NW, PO Box 97180, Washington, DC 20037
Telephone: 800-CALL-WWF
www.worldwildlife.org

Greenpeace
702 H Street NW, Washington, DC 20001
Telephone: 800-326-0959
www.greenpeace.org

Women's Rights Organizations

National Organization for Women
733 Fifteenth Street NW, Second Floor, Washington, DC 20005
Telephone: 202-628-8NOW, Fax: 202-785-8576
www.now.org

Equality Now
250 West Fifty-seventh Street, Room 826, New York, NY 10017
www.equalitynow.org

International Center for Research on Women
1717 Massachusetts Avenue, NW, Suite 302, Washington, DC 20036
Telephone: 202-797-0007
www.icrw.org

International Women's Tribune Center
777 UN Plaza, New York, NY 10017
Telephone: 212-687-8633
iwtc@iwtc.org

Madre: An International Women's Human Rights Organization
121 West Twenty-seventh Street, Room 301, New York, NY 10001
Telephone: 212-627-0444
madre@igc.org

Women' Environment & Development Organization
355 Lexington Avenue, New York, NY 10017
Telephone: 212-973-0324
ddr@wedo.org

UNIFEM (United Nations Development Fund for Women)
304 East Forty-fifth Street, New York, NY 10017
Telphone: 212-906-6400

WILD for Human Rights (Women's Institute for Leadership Development)
1375 Sutter, Suite 407, San Francisco CA 94109
Telephone: 415-447-4644
wild@igc.org

Gay, Lesbian, Transgender Rights

International Gay and Lesbian Human Rights Commission
1360 Mission Street, Suite 200, San Francisco, CA 94103
Telephone: 415-255-8680, Fax: 415-255-8662
www.iglhrc.org

National Gay and Lesbian Task Force
1700 Kalorama Road NW, Washington, DC 20009-2624
Telephone: 202-332-6483, Fax: 202-332-0207
www.ngltf.org

Human Rights Campaign
919 Eighteenth Street NW, Washington, DC 20006
Telephone: 202-628-4160, Fax: 202-347-5323
www.hrc.org

The Gay, Lesbian and Straight Education Network
121 West Twenty-seventh Street, Suite 804, New York, NY 10001-6207
Telephone: 212-727-0135, Fax: 212-727-0254
www.glsen.org

Gay & Lesbian Alliance Against Defamation
248 West Thirty-fifth Street, Eighth Floor, New York, NY 10001
Telephone: 800-GAY-MEDIA or 212-629-3322, Fax: 212-629-3225
www.glaad.org

U.S. Issues

American Civil Liberties Union
125 Broad Street, New York, NY 10004-2400
Telephone: 212-549-2500
www.aclu.org

Innocence Project at Cardozo Law School
55 Fifth Avenue, New York, NY 10003
Telephone: 212-790-0354
www.criminaljustice.org/PUBLIC/cardozo.htm

National Coalition Against the Death Penalty
436 U Street NW, Suite 104, Washington, DC 20009
Telephone: 202-387-3890
www.ncadp.org

Death Penalty Information Center
1320 Eighteenth Street NW, Fifth Floor, Washington, DC 20036
Telephone: 202-293-6970, Fax: 202-822-4787
www.deathpenaltyinfo.org

Murder Victims Families for Reconciliation
161 Massachusetts Avenue, Cambridge, MA 02140
Telephone: 617-868-0007, Fax: 617-354-2832
www.mvfr.org

Other Organizations of Interest

Business for Social Responsibility
609 Mission Street, Second Floor, San Francisco, CA 94105
Telephone: 415-537-0990
www.bsr.org

The National Labor Committee
National Labor Committee, 275 Seventh Avenue, Fifteenth Floor, New York, NY 10001
Telephone: 212-242-3002, Fax: 212-242-3821
www.nlcnet.org

The American Anti-Slavery Group
198 Tremont Street, #421, Boston, MA 02116
Telephone: 800-884-0719
www.anti-slavery.org

OXFAM America
26 West Street, Boston, MA 02111
Telephone: 800-77-OXFAM or 617-482-1211, Fax: 617-728-2594
www.oxfamamerica.org

Doctors Without Borders
6 East Thirty-ninth Street, Eighth Floor, New York, NY 10016
Telephone: 212-679-6800, Fax: 212-679-7016
www.doctorswithoutborders.org

The United Nations High Commission for Refugees
1775 K Street NW, Suite 300, Washington, DC 20006
www.unhcr.ch

International Campaign for Tibet
1825 K Street NW, Suite 520, Washington, DC 20006
Telephone: 202-785-1515, Fax: 202-785-4343
www.savetibet.org

Transparency International—USA
1112 Sixteenth Street NW, Suite 500, Washington, DC 20036
Telephone: 202-296 7730, Fax: 202-296 8125
www.transparency-usa.org

Notes

The complete text of the Universal Declaration of Human Rights
is available at www.un.org/Overview/rights.
Additional notes are available at www.beacon.org/schulznotes.

Preface to the First Edition

1. From an extensive interview with Hina Jilani conducted March 11, 2000, by William F. Schulz in Providence, Rhode Island; and from Amnesty International, "Pakistan: Violence against Women in the Name of Honor," September 1999, pp. 19–22.

Introduction

1. From the Convention on the Prevention and Punishment of the Crime of Genocide (1951) to the International Covenant on Civil and Political Rights (1966) and International Covenant on Economic, Social, and Cultural Rights (1966) to the Convention on the Elimination of All Forms of Discrimination against Women (1979) and many more, both regional and international.
2. "Proud but Concerned, Tribunal Prosecutor Leaves," *New York Times,* September 15, 1999.
3. "$190-Billion Bonanza for Charity," *Chronicle of Philanthropy,* June 1, 2000.
4. In a 1997 study the Pew Research Center for the People and the Press found that 61 percent of Americans answered "no" when asked whether what happens in western Europe matters in their lives. 36 percent said "yes." For Asia the numbers were 61 percent "no"; 35 percent "yes."
5. Statistics from James F. Hoge Jr., "Foreign News: Who Gives a Damn?" *Columbia Journalism Review,* November/December 1997. *Time* devoted 24 percent of its pages to international coverage in 1985 and only 14 percent ten years later. The figures for *Newsweek* are 22 percent in 1985 compared with 12 percent in 1995. For *U.S. News and World Report* the decline was from 20 percent to 14 percent.
6. Though higher than "helping to bring a democratic form of government to other nations" (29 percent). John E. Rielly, ed., *American Public Opinion and U.S. Foreign Policy, 1999* (Chicago: Chicago Council on Foreign Relations), p. 16.
7. Steven Kull, "What the Public Knows That Washington Doesn't," *Foreign Policy* (winter 1995–96): 113.

8. Steven Kull, "An Emerging Consensus: A Study of American Public Attitudes on America's Role in the World," Center for International and Security Studies, University of Maryland, July 10, 1996, p. 6.
9. Ryszard Kapuscincki, "Letter from Mauritania," *The New Yorker*, August 23 and 30, 1999, p. 99.
10. "Bosnia: One Big Yawn," *Harper's*, February 1996, p. 17.
11. David Rieff, "The Precarious Triumph of Human Rights," *New York Times Magazine*, August 8, 1999, p. 41.
12. Jesse Helms, "And After Pinochet?," *Washington Post*, December 10, 1998.
13. Jesse Helms, "What Sanctions Epidemic?" *Foreign Affairs* (January/February 1999): 2–8.
14. Alan Tonelson, "Jettison the Policy," *Foreign Policy* (winter 1994).
15. Richard Ullman, "The U.S. and the World: An Interview with George Kennan," *New York Review of Books*, August 12, 1999, p. 6.
16. "A Suitable Target for Foreign Policy?" *The Economist*, April 12, 1997.
17. Thomas L. Friedman, *The Lexus and the Olive Tree* (New York: Farrar, Straus & Giroux, 1999), p. 209.
18. "South Carolina High Court Derails Video Poker Game," *New York Times*, October 15, 1999. See also Mary Ann Glendon, *Rights Talk: The Impoverishment of Political Discourse* (New York: Free Press, 1991), for a discussion of the prodigality of rights from a neoconservative perspective.

1. *"Like the Home-Born among You"*

1. For the full story of the creation of the UDHR, see Johannes Morsink, *The Universal Declaration of Human Rights: Origins, Drafting, and Intent* (Philadelphia: University of Pennsylvania Press, 1999).
2. Ibid., pp. 290–96. Italics added.
3. Reports from Amnesty International News Service: "Afghanistan: Amnesty International Condemns International Community for Ignoring Conflict in Afghanistan," December 15, 1994; "Women in Afghanistan: The Violations Continue," June 1997; and "Afghanistan: Public Executions and Amputations on Increase," May 22, 1998.
4. Phillipe Villers, "Dealing with Demons," *Changemakers*, December 1994.
5. Cynthia Ozick, "The Moral Necessity of Metaphor," *Harper's*, May 1986, pp. 30. Or as the Senegalese saying puts it: "If a vulture attacks your enemy's body, remember it could be you and chase it off."
6. deWaal, Frans, *Good Natured: The Origins of Right and Wrong in Humans and Other Animals* (Cambridge: Harvard University Press, 1996), pp. 40–88.
7. William Shakespeare, *The Merchant of Venice*, Act III, Scene 1.
8. Joan C. Golston, "Ritual Abuse: Raising Hell in Psychotherapy; Creation of Cruelty: The Political, Military, and Multigenerational Training of Torturers: Violent Initiation and the Role of Traumatic Dissociation," *Treating Abuse Today* 3, no. 6.
9. The most outspoken exponent of the so-called Asian values argument against the universality of human rights has been Lee Kuan Yew, senior minister of Singapore.

See, for example, Fareed Zakaria, "Culture Is Destiny: A Conversation with Lee Kuan Yew," *Foreign Affairs* (March/April 1994). His view was anticipated in 1948 when the American Anthropological Association opposed the UDHR because they believed that cultural relativism precluded one culture imposing its values on others, a view that is being challenged more and more readily in the anthropological community today. See "Universal Human Rights versus Cultural Relativity," *Journal of Anthropological Research* (fall 1997).

10. Amnesty International, "Uganda: 'Breaking God's Commands': The Destruction of Childhood by the Lord's Resistance Army," September 18, 1997, p. 14.

11. Richard Rorty, "Human Rights, Rationality, and Sentimentality," in Stephen Shute and Susan Hurley, eds., *On Human Rights* (New York: Basic Books, 1993), pp. 133–34.

12. See Thomas L. Pangle and Peter J. Ahrensdorf, *Justice among Nations: On the Moral Basis of Power and Peace* (Lawrence: University of Kansas Press, 1999), pp. 234–38, for a treatment of Morgenthau's views in this respect.

13. Clinton Rossiter, *The Political Thought of the American Revolution* (New York: Harcourt, Brace, & World, 1963), p. 200.

14. Anthony Lewis, "Peace and Justice," *New York Times, November 17, 1997*.

15. Joseph S. Nye Jr., "Redefining the National Interest," *Foreign Affairs* (July/August 1999): 24.

16. Martin Marty, *Context,* November 15, 1989.

17. Reinhold Niebuhr, *Moral Man and Immoral Society* (New York: Charles Scribner's Sons, 1932).

18. "In Breisach, Germany . . . when twenty-seven judges of the Holy Roman Empire sat in judgment of Peter van Hagenback for . . . allowing his troops to rape, murder and pillage." Aryeh Neier, *War Crimes: Brutality, Genocide, Terror, and the Struggle for Justice* (New York: Times Books, 1998), p. 12.

19. Stephen Spender in Richard Crossman, ed., *The God That Failed* (New York: Bantam Books, 1949), p. 231.

20. Amnesty International, "USA: Rights for All," October 1998, p. 126.

2. *"When the Birds No Longer Hide"*

1. Lawrence Wechsler, *A Miracle, A Universe: Settling Accounts with Torturers* (New York: Penguin Books, 1990), p. 86.

2. Milan Kundera, *The Book of Laughter and Forgetting* (New York: Penguin Books, 1980), p. 3.

3. Aung San Suu Kyi, *Freedom from Fear* (New York: Penguin Books, 1991), p. 173. Suu argues also that a democracy will reflect values contained in the Buddhist view of kingship: liberality, morality, self-sacrifice, integrity, kindness, austerity, non-anger, nonviolence, forbearance, and nonopposition to the will of the people.

4. Amartya Sen, *Development as Freedom* (New York: Alfred A. Knopf, 1999), p. 11.

5. Jon Lee Anderson, "The Devil They Know," *The New Yorker,* July 27, 1998; and personal interviews and observations from an Amnesty International mission I led in 1996.

6. Conversation with Natasa Kandic, May 4, 2000, Washington, D.C. See also Humanitarian Law Center, *Spotlight on War Crimes Trials* (Belgrade: Humanitarian Law Center, 2000).

7. "Ignoring Scars, Milosovic Is Stubbornly Pressing On," *New York Times,* October 31, 1999. See Helsinki Committee for Human Rights in Serbia, *Report on Human Rights in Serbia for 1999,* February 2000.

8. Immanuel Kant, "Perpetual Peace," in Hans Reiss, ed. *Kant's Political Writings,* trans. H. B. Nisbet (Cambridge: Cambridge University Press, 1991).

9. Obituary of Sir Vincent Wigglesworth, *The Times* (London), February 12, 1994.

10. R. J. Rummel, *Power Kills: Democracy as a Method of Nonviolence* (New Brunswick, N.J.: Transaction, 1997).

11. See Carol R. Ember, et al., "Peace between Participatory Polities," *World Politics,* July 1992. Alex Mintz and Geva Nehemia, "Why Don't Democracies Fight Each Other? An Experimental Study," *Journal of Conflict Resolution* (September 1993).

12. Lee Teng-hui, "Understanding Taiwan," *Foreign Affairs* (November/December 1999): 13.

13. Melvin J. Small and J. David Singer, "The War Proneness of Democratic Regimes," *Jerusalem Journal of International Relations,* 1976.

14. "A Middle East Choice: Peace or Democracy," *New York Times,* November 28, 1999.

15. Fareed Zakaria, "The Rise of Illiberal Democracy," *Foreign Affairs* (November/December 1997): 22–43.

16. Edward D. Mansfield and Jack Snyder, "Democratization and War," *Foreign Affairs* (May/June 1995): 79–97.

17. Zakaria, "Rise of Illiberal Democracy," p. 41.

18. Mansfield and Snyder, "Democratization and War," p. 96–97.

19. "Army Pullout Shows Indonesia Fault Lines," *New York Times,* September 19, 1999. A few months later the lesson seems to have begun taking hold as an Indonesian general was quoted as saying, "We need to know what is allowed and what is not allowed today. Because we do not want to end up like our superiors who were doing their jobs in East Timor and then were accused of human rights violations." "Under Attack at Home, Indonesia's Military Reels," *New York Times,* February 13, 2000.

20. These include the so-called complementarity standard that allows a country to assert the primacy of its national judicial system for its own citizens; limiting the crimes covered by the ICC to genocide, crimes against humanity, and serious war crimes; limiting the prosecutor's ability to bring unwarranted prosecutions through judicial restraints; and authorizing the U.N. Security Council to defer a prosecution. See "The International Criminal Court: The Case for U.S. Support," Lawyers' Committee for Human Rights, December 1998.

21. Howard Ball, *Prosecuting War Crimes and Genocide* (Lawrence: University of Kansas, 1999), p. 139.

22. As Commissioner Jose Zalaquett put it, "The underlying assumption [of the democratic government that succeeded Pinochet and authorized the Commission] . . . was that if Chile gave truth and justice equal priority, the result might well have been that neither could be achieved. Fearing that official efforts to establish the truth would be the first step toward widespread prosecutions, the mil-

itary would have determinedly opposed such efforts." "Balancing Ethical Imperatives and Political Constraints: The Dilemma of New Democracies Confronting Past Human Rights Violations," in Henry J. Steiner and Philip Alston, *International Human Rights in Context: Law, Politics, Morals* (Oxford: Clarendon Press, 1996), p. 1,107.

23. George Soros, "Toward Open Societies," *Foreign Policy* (spring 1995): 74.
24. "The Lowest Castes in India, Reaching for Power, Shake up the System," *New York Times,* September 23, 1999.
25. David Welsh, "Domestic Politics and Ethnic Conflict," in M. Brown, ed., *Ethnic Conflict and International Security* (Princeton, N.J.: Princeton University Press, 1993).
26. Rummel, *Power Kills,* pp. 91–98.
27. Based in both cases on the organization's ratings for 1998.
28. "Malaysia Autocrat May Win Now but Lose Later," *New York Times,* November 27, 1999.
29. Stuart R. Schram, ed., *Mao Tse-tung Unrehearsed, Talks and Letters: 1956–1971* (Harmondsworth: Penguin Books, 1976), p. 277–78.
30. Quoted in Martin Marty, *Context,* March 15, 1997.
31. Sattareh Farman Farmaian, *Daughter of Persia* (London: Corgi Books, 1995).
32. "Clinton Tries to Subdue Greeks' Anger at America," *New York Times,* November 21, 1999.
33. "Clinton's Vigor in Turkey May Help Speed Up Reform," *New York Times,* November 21, 1999.
34. "U.S. Deal on Caspian Oil Still Faces Problems with Bottom Line," *New York Times,* November 21, 1999.
35. "During [the campaign to drive Soviet forces from Afghanistan in the 1980's], the CIA spent hundreds of millions of dollars training religious fighters and buying them modern weapons. Now [those religious fighters] are using those skills, and in some cases those weapons, to topple what they say are godless regimes." In "Zealots' Latest Targets Are Poor, Remote, and Vulnerable," *New York Times,* October 31, 1999.
36. David Callahan, *Unwinnable Wars: American Power and Ethnic Conflict* (New York: Hill & Wang, 1997), p. 43.
37. Ibid.
38. Quoted in Rein Mullerson, *Human Rights Diplomacy* (London: Routledge), 1997, p. 32.

3. The Bottom Line

1. Friedrich A. Hayek, *The Road to Serfdom* (Chicago: University of Chicago Press, 1944), p. 72.
2. See Robert J. Samuelson, "Global Boom or Bust?" *Newsweek,* November 10, 1997.
3. David E. Sanger, "Global Economy Dances to Political Tune," *New York Times,* December 20, 1999.
4. Laurie Ann Mazur and Susan E. Sechler, *Global Interdependence and the Need for Social Stewardship* (New York: Rockefeller Brothers Fund, 1997).

5. Correspondence from A. J. C. Brak, group public affairs coordinator, Shell International Petroleum Company Limited, to William F. Schulz, October 5, 1995.

6. Excerpts from transcript of presidential press conference, *New York Times*, January 29, 1997.

7. See, for example, William H. Meyer, *Human Rights and International Political Economy in Third World Nations: Multinational Corporations, Foreign Aid, and Repression* (Westport, Conn.: Praeger, 1998), or Robert J. Barro, "Democracy: A Recipe for Growth?" *Wall Street Journal*, December 1, 1994, though Barro must today be somewhat embarrassed by his predictions in 1993 that based on his model of economic growth, countries such as Iraq, Sudan, Syria, and Singapore would all "be more democratic" by 2000.

8. Norman Solomon, "Economic Liberty, Personal Oppression," *Cleveland Plain Dealer*, January 25, 1997.

9. Stan Sesser, "A Nation of Contradictions," *The New Yorker*, January 13, 1992.

10. *Amnesty International Report, 1999* (London: Amnesty International, 1999).

11. "The Hunt Hits Home," *Newsweek*, December 14, 1998.

12. "A Deal That America Couldn't Refuse," *New York Times*, November 16, 1999.

13. "Unocal Signs Burmese Gas Deal; U.S. May Ban Such Accords," *New York Times*, February 1, 1997.

14. "Business Asian Style: A Revaluing of Values," *New York Times*, February 7, 1998.

15. "A New Kind of Leader for Korea and Perhaps the Rest of Asia Too," *New York Times*, February 23, 1998.

16. Fareed Zakaria, "The Rise of Illiberal Democracy," *Foreign Affairs* (November/December 1997): 34.

17. Amnesty International, "China/Hong Kong: Release of Journalist Does Not Alleviate Concern over Handover," Amnesty International News Release, January 27, 1997.

18. Bruce Bueno de Mesquita, David Newman, and Alvin Rabushka, *Red Flag over Hong Kong* (Chatham, N.J.: Chatham House Publishers, 1996), p. 22.

19. "Protesters Draw Focus on Rights Records," *USA Today*, November 14, 1994.

20. As I tried to warn in William F. Schulz, "Where Economic Woes and Political Repression Meet," *Christian Science Monitor*, February 11, 1998. Indonesia also imported $5 million worth of goods from the United States in 1997. See U.S. Department of State, "1998 Country Reports on Economic Policy and Trade Practices: Indonesia," January 31, 1999.

21. Jeri Laber, "Smoldering Indonesia," *New York Review of Books*, January 9, 1997. See also Human Rights Watch, "The Limits of Openness: Human Rights in Indonesia and East Timor," September 15, 1994; Human Rights Watch/Asia and the Robert F. Kennedy Memorial Center for Human Rights, "Indonesia: Tough International Response Needed to Widening Crackdown," August 1996; and Amnesty International, "Indonesia: Arrests, Torture, and Intimidation," November 27, 1996; among many others.

22. Amnesty International, "Indonesia: Predictions of a Psychic a Threat to National Security?" July 1995.

23. Action in Solidarity with Indonesia and East Timor, " 'Jailed for Daring to Strug-

gle': Story of Dita Sari Jailed for Five Years in Indonesia for 'Subversion,'" 2000. Also interview with Dita Sari, June 3, 2000.

24. "World Bank Beats Breast for Failures in Indonesia," *New York Times*, February 11, 1999.

25. "Country Moves Closer to a New Era of Democracy," *Wall Street Journal*, October 2, 1997.

26. "Price Rises Exact a High Cost in Java," *New York Times*, February 8, 1998.

27. Dani Rodrik, *The New Global Economy and Developing Countries: Making Openness Work* (Washington, D.C.: Overseas Development Council, 1999).

28. Ibid., pp. 84–85.

29. "Oil Flowing in Sudan, Raising the Stakes in Its Civil War," *New York Times*, October 17, 1999.

30. Thomas Friedman, "Shakespeare Does Malaysia," *New York Times*, August 24, 1999.

31. Marvin Zonis, "Political Stability Index," *International Political Economy*, 1996.

32. "In China's Boom, Rural Poor Feel a Widening Gap," *New York Times*, October 9, 1999.

33. "China's Secretive Army for Riot Control Grows," *International Herald Tribune*, March 29, 1999.

34. *Business and Human Rights* (Cambridge, Mass.: Harvard University Human Rights Program, 1999), p. 60.

35. "East Timor Chaos seen as Imperiling Indonesian Recovery," *New York Times*, September 8, 1999.

36. Transparency International, "The TI Source Book Executive Summary," September 20, 1996.

37. Daniel Kaufmann, "Corruption: The Facts," *Foreign Policy* (summer 1997): 120.

38. John Kamm, "The Role of Business in Promoting Respect for Human Rights," speech to the Commission on Security and Cooperation in Europe, November 13–14, 1995.

39. Stuart Eizenstat, briefing, OECD Convention on Anti-Bribery, June 30, 1999.

40. "Indonesia Auditor Alleges Bribery in Power Plant Deal," *Dow Jones Newswires*, January 3, 2000.

41. "Global Lenders Use Leverage to Combat Corruption," *New York Times*, August 11, 1997.

42. "A World Seeking Justice Is Running Low on Exemplars," *Wall Street Journal*, October 28, 1996.

43. U.S. Trade Representative, 1998 National Trade Estimate Report on Foreign Trade Barriers—People's Republic of China.

44. "China's Free Market Must Stress Cooperation," *New York Times*, January 17, 1997.

45. David Rothkopf, "In Praise of Cultural Imperialism?" *Foreign Policy* (summer 1997): 44.

46. "How China's Army Stocked American Shelves," *Christian Science Monitor*, June 3, 1998.

47. "You, Too, May Be Funding China's Army," *USA Today*, May 14, 1997.

48. Statement of George J. Weise, Commissioner, U.S. Customs Service, Before the

Senate Committee on Foreign Relations, May 21, 1997. Wiese went on to explain the problem further: "In 1990, the Chinese Justice Ministry official gave us conflicting figures ranging from as low as $300 million to as high as $1 billion for the value of goods produced by prison farms and factories. Some 70%, they say, is consumed within the prison system with the balance sold domestically. However, the 1989 *China Law Yearbook* stated that China exported $100 million worth of goods produced within the prison system. Like most written information we have about the Chinese prison and labor reform systems, these reports on exports are dated and no current figures are available."

49. "How You Can Win in China," *Business Week*, May 26, 1997.

50. "In China's Legal Evolution, the Lawyers Are Handcuffed," *New York Times*, January 6, 2000.

51. Thomas Friedman, "China Syndrome," *New York Times*, January 8, 1995.

52. "A Surge in a Crime That Pays," *Newsweek International*, May 8, 2000; and Cinep/Justice and Peace database showing that "80 commerciantes and three empresarios" were among those kidnapped in Colombia in 1999.

53. "Policing the Policia," *Los Angeles Times*, October 10, 1999.

54. Lant Pritchett and Daniel Kaufmann, "Civil Liberties, Democracy, and the Performance of Government Projects," *Finance & Development*, March 1998.

55. "More Information, More Money," *Far Eastern Economic Review*, August 8, 1996.

56. Quoted from the *Wall Street Journal*, January 18, 1996, in Joseph Scarry, "The Leading Edge of China's Rights Iceberg," unpublished essay, October 27, 1997.

57. John Kamm, "Things My Father Taught Me," University of Hong Lectures on Business and Culture, October 21, 1995.

58. Mancur Olson, "Dictatorship, Democracy, and Development," *American Political Science Review* (September 1993).

59. "Policies of Constructive Engagement Are a Failure," *Human Rights Watch Update*, September 1996.

60. Jacob Heilbrun, "The Sanctions Sellout," *New Republic*, May 25, 1998.

61. See "A Chinese Gold Rush? Don't Hold Your Breath," *New York Times*, September 14, 1994; and "In China, Art of the Raw Deal," *New York Times*, February 12, 1995.

62. Bruce Klatsky, quoted in *Business and Human Rights*, pp. 21, 31.

63. Ibid., p. 98.

64. Robert F. Dalzell Jr., "George Washington, Slaveholder," *New York Times*, February 20, 1999.

65. See Tommy Egan, "The Swoon of the Swoosh," *New York Times Magazine*, September 13, 1998. Labor activists remain far from convinced that Nike has reformed its ways. See public correspondence between Trim Bissell, et al., and Nike CEO Philip Knight, "Response to Nike's Claim to Have Reformed Its Practices," March 15, 2000.

66. Deborah L. Spar, "The Spotlight and the Bottom Line," *Foreign Affairs* (March/April 1998): 9.

67. The Hartman Group, "The Hartman Report, Food and the Environment: A Consumer's Perspective," 1996; and Paul H. Ray, *The Integral Culture Survey: A Study of the Emergence of Transformational Values in America* (Sausalito, Calif.: Institute of Noetic Sciences and Fetzer Institute, 1996).

68. Alan Cowell, "A Call to Put Social Issues on Corporate Agendas," *New York Times,* April 6, 2000.
69. U.S. Department of Labor, "20 Million Jobs: January, 1993–November, 1999," December 3, 1999.
70. Economic Policy Institute, "NAFTA'S Pain Deepens," November 1999.
71. Dana Rodrik, "Sense and Nonsense in the Globalization Debate," *Foreign Policy* (summer 1997): 20.
72. "The World as a Single Machine," *The Economist,* June 20, 1998.
73. Laurie Ann Mazur and Susan E. Sechler, *Global Interdependence and the Need for Social Stewardship* (New York: Rockefeller Brothers Fund), 1997.
74. U.S. Bureau of Labor Statistics, "483,000 U.S. Manufacturing Jobs Lost," March 10, 2000. See also Lawrence Mishel, Jared Bernstein, and John Schmitt, *The State of Working America, 1998–99* (Ithaca, N.Y.: Economic Policy Institute, 1999).
75. National Labor Committee, "Apparel Wages around the World," January 1998.
76. "NAFTA's Toll Minimal (Unless You Got Laid Off)," *Newsday,* November 26, 1997.
77. Rodrik, "Sense and Nonsense," p. 28.
78. "One America," *Wall Street Journal,* September 24, 1992.
79. "Testimony, Julia Esmeralda Pleites," National Labor Committee, November 17, 1998.
80. "Young Women in Free Trade Zones Injected with Depo-Provera," National Labor Committee, November 17, 1998.
81. *Business News,* August 21, 1996.
82. See Charles Kernaghan, "Behind the Label: 'Made in China,'" National Labor Committee, March 1998.
83. Ibid., p. 29.
84. Apo Leong, "Labour Rights in the Pearl River Delta," in Jennifer Porges, ed., *At What Price? Workers in China* (Hong Kong: Asia Monitor Resource Group, 1997).
85. "China Police Sell Farmers into Labour," Reuters News Service, December 8, 1999.
86. Charlene L. Fu, "Dissident Who Stayed for Chinese Rule Keeps up His Criticism," Associated Press, July 1, 1997.
87. U.S. Department of Commerce, "Monthly Trade Update," April 19, 2000; and U.S. Census Bureau, "U.S. Trade Balance with China," April 19, 2000.
88. Transcript of "Economic Policy Institute News Conference on the Impact of Trade on Jobs and Wages," Washington, D.C., October 20, 1997.
89. See Thomas Friedman, "Senseless in Seattle," *New York Times,* December 1, 1999.
90. "Why Russia Falls Short of IMF Criteria," *New York Times,* November 6, 1999.
91. "Trade Pacts Must Safeguard Workers, Union Chief Says," *New York Times,* November 20, 1999.
92. Quoted in Jonathan Mirsky, "Unmasking the Monster," *New York Review of Books,* November 17, 1994.

4. Forest and Ice

1. Thomas Nilsen, Igor Kudrik, and Alexander Nikitin, "The Russian Northern Fleet—Sources of Radioactive Contamination," *Bellona Report,* February 1996.

2. Igor Kudrik, "On the Brink of Nuclear Disaster," *Bellona Report*, July 24, 1997, describes the acknowledgment in July 1997 by the Russian ambassador to the United States at the premiere of an American movie about a 1986 Soviet submarine disaster off Bermuda that there had indeed been a serious danger that the explosion in one of the submarine's ballistic missile tubes could have prompted an attack on the United States.

3. Interview with Julia Tchernova by William F. Schulz, March 8, 2000.

4. "Wastes of War: Rotting Nuclear Subs Pose Threat," *Washington Post*, November 16, 1998.

5. Nilsen, Kudrik, and Nikitin, "Russian Northern Fleet," sec. 1.3.2.

6. Amnesty International, "Russian Federation: Grigory Pasko," Amnesty International Urgent Action Report, January 18, 1999. Russia's 1995 Federal Law on Information, Information Handling, and Protection of Information makes similar provisions.

7. Nikitin's report is the only publication "banned" in Russia at the moment, putting it in the distinguished company of the Bible and the works of Aleksandr Solzhenitsyn, among others, banned during the Soviet era.

8. Jon Gauslaa and Igor Kudrik, "The Nikitin Process," *Bellona Report*, September 24, 1998.

9. William Stoichevski, "A Day in the Life of Alexander Nikitin," *Bellona Report*, March 22, 1999.

10. Gauslaa and Kudrik, "Nitikin Process."

11. "Environmental Rights are Human Rights," Sierra Club (www.sierraclub.org).

12. According to the Nuclear Energy Organization, "the volatile radionuclides [from Chernobyl] . . . (iodine-131 and caesium-137) were detected in most countries of the Northern hemisphere. . . . During the first few weeks iodine-131 was the main contributor to the dose, via ingestion of milk. Infant thyroid doses . . . were about 0.1 mSv in North America. . . . Later on, caesium-134 and caesium-137 were responsible for most of the dose, through external and internal irradiation. The whole-body doses during the first year following the accident . . . [were] of the order of 0.001 mSv in North America." Nuclear Energy Organization (of the Organization for Economic Co-operation and Development), "Chernobyl: Ten Years of Radiological and Health Impact," November 1995.

13. Grigory Medvedev, *The Truth about Chernobyl* (New York: Basic Books, 1989) p. 20. Emphasis added.

14. See Alla Yaroshinskaya, *Chernobyl: The Forbidden Truth* (Lincoln: University of Nebraska Press, 1995).

15. Amnesty International, "Russian Federation: All Charges Should Be Dropped against Freed Prisoner of Conscience Grigory Pasko," Amnesty International News Service, July 20, 1999.

16. Grigory Pasko, "Before the Law," *Harper's*, October 1999.

17. "Russia Frees Journalist Who Exposed Nuclear Dumping," *New York Times*, July 21, 1999.

18. "Imprisoned Russian Writer Puts the Gulag on Line," *New York Times*, July 8, 1999.

19. Quoted in "Environmental Rights are Human Rights," Sierra Club (www.sierraclub.org).

20. Thomas Nilsen, "FSB Targets Academician," *Bellona Report,* July 14, 1999.
21. Thomas Nilsen and Nils Boehmer, "Dumping of Radioactive Waste," *Bellona Report,* January 1994.
22. Greg Neale, "Russia Faces 'New Chernobyl' Disaster," *Electronic Telegraph,* May 23, 1999.
23. Nilsen and Boehmer, "Dumping of Radioactive Waste," sec. 4.3.
24. Thomas Nilsen, "Naval Nuclear Waste Management in Northwest Russia," *Bellona Report,* October 1998.
25. Paul Johnston, et al., "Report on the World's Oceans," Greenpeace Research Laboratories, May 1998.
26. Tiffany M. Schauer, "The World's Hazardous Waste," *ENN Features,* July 8, 1998.
27. See "A Cooling Off Period," *The Economist,* November 29, 1997; and "Climate Changes," *Bellona Factsheet,* July 27, 1996.
28. Brian Fagan, "Forgettable Weather," *New York Times,* July 30, 1999.
29. Paul Rauber, "Heat Wave," and "Global Warming Impacts: Health Effects," Sierra Club (www.sierraclub.org); "Health Effects of Global Warming," Sierra Club, and "Scientists Link Changes in Rainfall Patterns to Global Warming," *Nature,* September 21, 1995. See also, for example, "Walruses 'Threatened by Climate Change,'" *BBC News,* November 9, 1998, and "Vanishing Wildlife and Habitats," Sierra Club (www.sierraclub.org).
30. "Rainforest Resources: Tropical Forests in Our Daily Lives," Rainforest Alliance (www.rainforestalliance.org).
31. See "Rainforest, Rights, and Rattan," *Rainforest Alliance,* January/February 1997; and "Indonesian Environmental Hero Acquitted in Landmark Case," Environmental Defense Fund, November 6, 1998.
32. Amnesty International, "Carlos Coc Rax: Indigenous Land Rights Activist Disappears," April 1999.
33. Mark Muro, "Mexico Courts Forest Disaster, Putting People and Plants in Danger," *Earth Times,* 1998.
34. See "Mexican Environmental Activists Arrested and Tortured," Sierra Club (www.sierraclub.org); and Amnesty International, "Rodolfo Montiel Flores and Teodoro Cabrera Garcia: Mexican Environmentalists Tortured," July 1999.
35. "Jailed Mexican Wins Environment Prize," *New York Times,* April 5, 2000. In the spring of 2000 Montiel, who has only a first-grade education, received the $125,000 Goldman Environmental Prize while still in prison. "The only award I've gotten from the government," he said, "is prison, so I don't know quite what to make about this prize from foreigners. Are you sure this doesn't involve some hidden punishment?"
36. Richard E. Benedick, "Environmental Diplomacy and the U.S. National Interest," in Dick Clark and Gordon Binder, eds., *The Convergence of U.S. National Security and the Global Environment* (Washington, D.C.: Aspen Institute, 2000), p. 25.
37. Quoted in Larry McMurty, "Broken Promises," *New York Review of Books,* October 23, 1997.
38. Elizabeth Economy, "Balancing Development and the Environment: China's Quixotic Quest," in Dick Clark, ed., *US-China Relations* (Washington, D.C.: Aspen Institute, 1998), p. 39.

39. Aaron Sachs, *Eco-Justice: Linking Human Rights and the Environment* (Washington, D.C.: Worldwatch Institute, 1995), pp. 44 ff.
40. Barbara Jancar, "Democracy and the Environment in Eastern Europe and the Soviet Union," *Harvard International Review* (summer 1990): 60.
41. Quoted in Lawrence Friedman, review of Edward Zuckerman, *The Day after World War III*, in *New York Times Book Review*, August 19, 1984.
42. William A. Nitze, U.S. Environmental Protection Agency, speech to the World Affairs Council, January 16, 1997.

5. Only a Plane Ride Away

1. U.N. Economic and Social Council, *Report of the Special Rapporteur on His Visit to the Russian Federation*, 1995.
2. A. Goldfarb and M. E. Kimerlin, *Russian TB Program: An Initiative of the International Center for Public Health* (New York: Public Health Research Institute), 1999.
3. Vivian Stern, *Sentenced to Die? The Problem of TB in Prisons in Eastern Europe and Central Asia* (London: International Centre for Prison Studies, 1999).
4. "Russia's TB Epidemic Creates a Global Threat," *USA Today*, March 25, 1999.
5. NBC Nightly News, October 4, 1999.
6. "Resisting Drugs, TB Spreads Fast in the West," *New York Times*, March 24, 2000.
7. Harvard Medical School/Open Society Institute, *The Global Impact of Drug-Resistant Tuberculosis* (New York: Open Society Institute, 1999).
8. ITA Tourism Industries Market Analysis, "Departures and Payments for U.S. Travelers Abroad (Outbound), 1997," December 1998.
9. "Russia's TB Epidemic."
10. Interview with Barry Kreisworth, June 5, 2000; and see Harvard Medical School/Open Society Institute, *Global Impact*, p. 63.
11. Institute of Medicine, *America's Vital Interest in Global Health* (Washington, D.C.: National Academy Press, 1997).
12. Harvard Medical School/Open Society Institute, *Global Impact*, p. 61.
13. Laurie Garrett, "The Return of Infectious Disease," *Foreign Affairs* (January/February 1996): 66–79.
14. "Mosquito Virus Exposes a Hole in the Safety Net," *New York Times*, October 4, 1999.
15. Jared Diamond, *Guns, Germs, and Steel: The Fates of Human Societies* (New York: W. W. Norton, 1997), pp. 206, 210.
16. Laurie Garrett, *The Coming Plague: Newly Emerging Diseases in a World out of Balance* (New York: Penguin, 1994), p. 257. The long-horned beetle, a threat to hardwood forests, probably arrived in the United States from Asia in the 1980s in wooden shipping pallets, and Zebra mussels brought from Eastern Europe in ships have caused $5 billion damage in the Great Lakes; see "Mosquito Virus."
17. Marshall Fisher and David E. Fisher, "Coming Soon: The Attack of the Killer Mosquitoes," *Los Angeles Times*, September 15, 1991.
18. See Richard Preston, "West Nile Mystery," *The New Yorker*, October 18 and 25, 1999.

19. "Global Microbial Threats in the 1990s," Report of the Committee on International Science, Engineering, and Technology Policy of the President's National Science and Technology Council, 1995.

20. World Health Organization, "Emerging and Re-emerging Infectious Diseases," Fact Sheet 97, August 1998.

21. "No. 1 Destination in 2020? Try China, Then France," *New York Times*, October 3, 1999.

22. Center for Disease Control, "Addressing Emerging Infectious Disease Threats," September 6, 1995.

23. William H. McNeill, *Plagues and People* (New York: Doubleday, 1977).

24. Sheldon Watts, *Epidemics and History: Disease, Power, and Imperialism* (New Haven, Conn.: Yale University Press, 1998).

25. Douglas Starr, *Blood* (New York: Alfred A. Knopf, 1999), pp. 231–49.

26. Cited in Jordan Kassalow, Council on Foreign Relations, Schulz e-mail correspondence, June 22, 2000.

27. U.N. International Covenant on Economic, Social, and Cultural Rights, Article 12.2.c.

28. Ibid., Article 11.1.

29. Garrett, *Coming Plague*, p. 256.

30. Centers for Disease Control, "Dengue Surveillance—United States, 1986–1992," July 1994.

31. "Jailed Cuban's Wife Pins Hope on Pope's Words," *New York Times*, January 30, 1998.

32. Amnesty International, "Cuba: New Cases of Prisoners of Conscience and Possible Prisoners of Conscience," January 1998.

33. Interview with Desi Mendoza Rivero by William F. Schulz, May 25, 2000.

34. Centers for Disease Control, "Imported Dengue—United States, 1996," July 10, 1998.

35. "Global Microbial Threats."

36. Garrett, "Return of Infectious Disease," p. 74.

37. A point made by the White House working group in "Global Microbial Threats."

38. Edward Hooper, *The River* (Boston: Little Brown, 1999).

39. Garret, *Coming Plague*, pp. 366–67.

40. Tony Barnett and Piers Blaikie, *AIDS in Africa* (New York: Guilford Press, 1992), pp. 69–70.

41. Garret, *Coming Plague*, p. 368.

42. Ibid., p. 211.

43. Jeffrey Goldberg, "Our Africa," *New York Times Magazine*, March 2, 1997.

44. Mirko Grmek, *History of AIDS* (Princeton, N.J.: Princeton University Press, 1990).

45. World Health Organization (WHO), "African Countries Urged to Declare HIV/AIDS a National Emergency," WHO Regional Office for Africa, Press Release, June 24, 1999.

46. Bradley Hersh, "Acquired Immunodeficiency Syndrome in Romania," *Lancet*, September 14, 1991.

47. A figure cited from the U.N. AIDS Programme in Geneva in Laurie Garrett, "Run-

away Diseases and the Human Hand behind Them," *Foreign Affairs* (January/February 1998): 141.

48. "AIDS Is Declared Threat to U.S. National Security," *Washington Post,* April 30, 2000, and National Intelligence Estimate, *The Global Infectious Disease Threat and Its Implications for the United States,* January 2000.

49. "Ancient Trade Route Brings Modern Virus to Remote China, Linxia," *AIDS Weekly Plus,* August 18, 1997.

50. See Chris Beyrer, "Burma and Cambodia: Human Rights, Social Disruption, and the Spread of HIV/AIDS," *Health and Human Rights* 2 (1998): 4; and "Continent Braces Itself for Upsurge in HIV Cases," *AIDS Weekly,* February 7, 1994.

51. Beyrer, "Burma and Cambodia," pp. 87–90; and Tezza O. Paret, Aurora Javate-de Dios, Cecelia Hofmann, and Charrie Calalang, "Coalition against Trafficking in Women and Prostitution in the Asia Pacific," (www.uri.edu/artsci/wms/hughes/catw).

52. Mam Bun Heng and P. J. Key, "Cambodian Health in Transition," *British Medical Journal,* August 12, 1995.

53. Beyrer, "Burma and Cambodia," pp. 90–92.

54. Ibid., p. 92.

55. Elizabeth Reid, "A Future, If One Is Still Alive," in Jonathan Moore, ed., *Hard Choices: Moral Dilemmas in Humanitarian Intervention* (Lanham, Md.: Rowman & Littlefield, 1998), p. 275.

56. Equality NOW, Women's Action 2.1, December 1996.

57. Jennifer Soriano, "Trafficking in Sex," (www.shewire.com), quoting the Planned Parenthood Global Partners Program, February 1, 2000. Brad Knickerbocker, "Prostitution's Pernicious Reach Grows in the U.S.," *Christian Science Monitor,* October 23, 1996. See also "Foreigners Misled into Forced Labor," *USA Today,* April 3, 2000; and "After the Fall, Traffic in Flesh, Not Dreams," *New York Times,* June 11, 2000.

58. Eoin O'Brien, M.D., "The Diplomatic Implications of Emerging Diseases," in Kevin M. Cahill, M.D., *Preventive Diplomacy* (New York, Basic Books, 1996), p. 259.

59. Chemical and Biological Arms Control Institute/Center for Strategic and International Studies, 2000, "Contagion and Conflict: Health as a Global Security Challenge," p. 36.

60. Jonathan B. Tucker, "The Eleventh Plague: The Politics of Biological and Chemical Weapons," reviewed in *Bulletin of Atomic Scientists,* March 13, 1997.

61. Brad Roberts, "1995 and the End of the Post–Cold War Era," *Washington Quarterly* (winter 1995).

6. Saving Money while Saving Lives

1. Committee to Protect Journalists (www.cpj.org), March 14, 2000.

2. In 1997 the national section of Amnesty International in Colombia was closed and its leaders evacuated to other countries because their lives were under threat.

3. In its 1994 report "Political Violence in Colombia: Myth and Reality," Amnesty In-

ternational estimated that between 1986 and 1993 "over 20,000 people died in political violence" (p. 16), and the number has risen each year since.

4. William F. Schulz, "United States Funded Human Rights Violators in Colombia," remarks at press conference, October 29, 1996. See also "American Drug Aid Goes South," *New York Times*, November 25, 1996.

5. "U.S. Aid Questioned in Colombia Battle," *Dallas Morning News*, August 16, 1999.

6. "Columbia Vows to End Abuses," *Washington Post*, July 22, 2000, p. A15; Human Rights Watch, "World Report 2000: Columbia," 2000; and "Columbia's Death Squads," *Mother Jones*, August 31, 2000.

7. General Accounting Office, "Drug Control: Narcotics Threat from Colombia Continues to Grow," June 1999.

8. "Driven by Fear, Colombians Leave in Droves," *New York Times*, March 5, 2000.

9. William F. Schulz, "Uncovering the Truth," *America*, November 13, 1999.

10. "Unearthed: Fatal Secrets," *Baltimore Sun*, June 11–18, 1995.

11. Remarks by President Clinton in Roundtable Discussion on Peace Efforts, March 10, 1999, Guatemala City, Guatemala. From the White House Press Office (www.pub.whitehouse.gov).

12. Schulz, "Uncovering the Truth." See also Andrew Reding, "Democracy and Human Rights in Guatemala," *World Policy Papers*, n.d., pp. 32–35; and Richard H. Immerman, *The CIA in Guatemala: The Foreign Policy of Intervention* (Austin: University of Texas Press, 1982).

13. "Archives Unearthed in Paraguay Expose U.S. Allies' Abuses," *New York Times*, August 11, 1999. Although the Clinton administration has released more documents on covert American involvement in Latin America than had previously been made public, much still remains hidden, including information regarding the possible U.S. role in Sister Dianna's abduction and torture, as well as crimes against at least Twenty-four other U.S. citizens caught in the maelstrom. See Schulz, "Uncovering the Truth."

14. "Senate Appropriations Committee, Foreign Operations, Export Financing and Related Programs Appropriations Bill 1995" 104th Congress.

15. "Pentagon Training Didn't Deter Rwandan Atrocities," *Washington Post*, July 28, 1997.

16. "End to Jakarta Military Aid Urged," *New York Times*, September 20, 1999; "How U.S. Trained Butchers of Timor," *London Observer*, September 19, 1999.

17. Demilitarization for Democracy, "Arms Un-control: A Record Year for U.S. Military Exports," April 1999. In 1995 the arms industry received $7.6 billion in federal subsidies (Oscar Arias, "Stopping America's Most Lethal Export," *New York Times*, June 23, 1999).

18. See Amnesty International, "China: The Use of Organs from Executed Prisoners," March 1995; "On the Harvesting of Organs from Executed Prisoners in the People's Republic of China," Statement by Amnesty International USA Before the Committee on Foreign Relations of the U.S. Senate, May 4, 1995; Amnesty International, "China: Death Penalty Log 1996, Parts I, II, and III," July 1997; and Amnesty International, "People's Republic of China: The Death Penalty in China: Breaking Records, Breaking Rules," August 1997.

19. Michael E. Brown and Richard N. Rosecrance, eds., *The Costs of Conflict: Prevention and Cure in the Global Arena* (Lanham, Md.: Rowman & Littlefield, 1999), pp. 25–52.
20. The figures Brown and Rosecrance cite are $1.3 billion to have prevented the crisis, as contrasted with $4.5 billion spent to deal with its consequences. Ibid., pp. 53–73.
21. "Documents Charge Iraqis Made Swap: U.S. Food for Arms," *New York Times*, April 27, 1992.
22. "Hunger Stalks Ethiopia Once Again," *Time*, December 21, 1987.
23. "Aid for Sudan's Hungry Keeps War Well Fed," *New York Times*, October 11, 1998.
24. Michael Maren, *The Road to Hell: The Ravaging Effects of Foreign Aid and International Charity* (New York: Free Press, 1997), p. 135.
25. "For Hurricane's Victims, No End to Disaster," *Washington Post*, August 1, 1999.
26. "Hurricane Mitch Wounds Still Raw," *Ideals World News*, November 6, 1999.
27. "Leaders in Bosnia Are Said to Steal up to $1 Billion," *New York Times*, August 17, 1999.
28. "For Foreign Aid That Works," *Christian Science Monitor*, August 25, 1999.
29. David Dollar and Lant Pritchett, *Assessing Aid: What Works, What Doesn't, and Why* (New York: World Bank/Oxford University Press, 1999). And a 1 percent increase in growth rate reduces poverty by 2 percent.
30. "The Real Cost of Aid," *Wall Street Journal*, August 18, 1999.
31. See, for example, Demetrios G. Papademetriou, "Migration," *Foreign Policy* (winter 1997–98): 18.
32. Amnesty International, "United States of America: Violation of the Rights of Foreign Nationals on Death Row," January 1998.
33. Amnesty International, "Pakistan: Violence against Women," p. 6.; Thom Shanker, "Sexual Violence" and Alexandra Stiglnayer, "Sexual Violence: Systematic Rape," in Roy Gutman and David Rieff, eds., *Crimes of War: What the Public Should Know* (New York: W. W. Norton & Co., 1999), pp. 323–27. Figures compiled by Christian Aid and posted January 19, 2000, on www.oneworld.org; and United Nations Population Fund, "Choices and Responsibilities: The State of World Population, 1994," p. 48.
34. UNICEF, *The State of the World's Children, 1995* (Oxford: Oxford University Press), p. 26.
35. Tahira Shahid Khan, "Chained to Custom," *The Review*, March 4–10, 1999, p. 9.
36. U.S. Agency for International Development, "Population InfoPack—Family Planning Protects the Environment and Our Global Future," USAID (www.usaid.gov), January 6, 2000.
37. "Women are the key to population," said Atef Khalifa, director of the U.N. Population Fund, in commenting on patriarchal conditions in the Middle East that contribute to lack of population controls. "An educated woman who has equal rights . . . will automatically choose a smaller family and better quality of life." "Equal Rights for Arab Women Called the Key to a Better Life," *New York Times*, November 19, 1999.
38. See, for example, U.N. Economic and Social Council, "World Survey on the Role of Women in Development," April 21, 1999; or Stephen Klasen, "Does Gender In-

equality Reduce Growth and Development? Evidence from Cross-Country Regressions," World Bank, November 1999.

39. Boutros Boutros-Ghali, "Sustainable Development and International Economic Cooperation: Advancement of Women," 1994 World Survey on the Role of Women in Development, Report of the Secretary General of the United Nations, Executive Summary, paragraph 9.

7. No Innocent Place

1. William F. Schulz, "Cruel and Unusual Punishment," *New York Review of Books,* April 24, 1997.
2. "Inmates Win $2 Million in Lawsuit over Abuse," *New York Times,* January 21, 2000.
3. "Inmates' Suits Target Wide Range of Officials," *St. Louis Post-Dispatch,* May 9, 1999.
4. Letter from Abraham Foxman to Pierre Sane, October 20, 1998.
5. "Notebook," *New Republic,* October 26, 1998. See also my reply in "Correspondence," *New Republic,* November 30, 1998.
6. Peter D. Hart Research Associates, Inc., "Report Card on Human Rights in the USA," December 1997.
7. Amnesty International, "USA: Police Brutality and Excessive Force in the New York City Police Department," June 1996.
8. Correspondence from Michael J. Farrell, deputy commissioner for policy and planning, New York City Police Department, to Pierre Sane, September 17, 1996.
9. "Benefit of the Doubt," *New York Times,* April 9, 1997.
10. William Bratton, *Turnaround: How America's Top Cop Reversed the Crime Epidemic* (New York: Random House, 1998), pp. 243 ff.
11. See U.S. Department of Justice, Bureau of Justice Statistics, "Police Use of Force: Collection of National Data," November 1997.
12. U.S. Department of Justice, Bureau of Justice Statistics, "National Data Collection on Police Use of Force," April 1996.
13. U.S. Department of Justice, Bureau of Justice Statistics, "Police Use of Force: Collection of National Data," revised January 6, 1998.
14. "One Third of Americans Believe Police Brutality Exists in Their Area," Gallup News Service, March 22, 1999.
15. "Report Says Many Officers Avoid Misconduct Penalties," *New York Times,* December 30, 1999. The New York Civilian Complaint Review Board itself complained in 1998 that in the first six months of that year, only 22 percent of the cases it had substantiated and sent to the department had been acted on ("Review Board Criticizes Police on Discipline," *New York Times,* September 5, 1998). The New York City Public Advocate put the number of charges dismissed by the department at 70 percent ("Public Complaints Are Played Down, Police Data Show," *New York Times,* September 15, 1999).
16. Amnesty International, "Police Brutality and International Human Rights in the United States: The Report on Hearings Held in Los Angeles, CA, Chicago, IL, and Pittsburgh, PA, fall, 1999," February 2000, p. 10.

17. Table.

Awards Paid in Police Misconduct Lawsuits

City	Dollar amount
Boston (1987–99)	$5,317,000
Chicago (1984–99)	$101,950,000
Detroit (1987–97)	$92,000,000
Los Angeles (1980–97)	$121,948,000
New York City (1994–96)	$70,000,000
Philadelphia (1993–96)	$32,600,000
San Francisco (1987–97)	$2,500,000
Washington, D.C. (1990–95)	$12,900,000
—Total	$439,215,000

Sources: American Civil Liberties Union, *American Prospect,* Amnesty International, *Boston Globe, Chicago Sun Times, Chicago Tribune; Detroit News,* Human Rights Watch, *The Nation, Newsday,* New York City Comptroller, *New York Daily News, San Francisco Examiner, Washington Post.*
Note: Because no readily accessible systematic records are kept by courts, comptrollers, police departments, or the Justice Department of settlements paid by U.S. municipalities in response to lawsuits related to police misconduct, this table should be regarded as representing *minimal* estimates for the years noted and hence is a significant understatement of the awards paid.

18. Human Rights Watch, "Shielded from Justice: Police Brutality and Accountability in the United States," June 1998, p. 78; and "How to Sue the Police (and Win)," *New York Times,* October 2, 1999.

19. "City Safer but Police Brutality a Concern, New Yorkers Say," Associated Press, June 17, 1999.

20. "One Third of Americans."

21. Amnesty International, "USA: Police Brutality." Between 1990 and 1998, 82 of the 115 police shootings of civilians in Chicago (or 71 percent) were African American, according to the *Chicago Reporter.* (Amnesty International, "Police Brutality and International Human Rights," p. 18.)

22. "Whitman Admits Police Used Race in Turnpike Stops," *New York Times,* April 21, 1999.

23. "Racial Bias Shown in Police Searches, State Report Asserts," *New York Times,* December 1, 1999.

24. David Cole, *No Equal Justice* (New York: New Press, 1999), pp. 40–41.

25. Ronald Hampton, "The Amnesty Hour," interviewed by William F. Schulz, KFNX-FM, Phoenix, November 23, 1998. See also "Police 'Culture' Breeds Brutality and Misconduct," *Chicago Citizen,* March 27, 1997.

26. Bob Herbert, "A Brewing Storm," *New York Times,* February 11, 1999.

27. Cole, *No Equal Justice,* p. 170.

28. See "Racial Disparities Seen as Pervasive in Juvenile Justice," *New York Times,* April 26, 2000; Human Rights Watch, "Statistics Show Race Disparities in Drug Incarceration," June 8, 2000, and *Report of the National Criminal Justice Commission: The Real War on Crime* (New York: HarperCollins, 1996).

29. Dinesh D'Souza, "Sometimes, Discrimination Can Make Sense," *USA Today,* June 2, 1999.

30. Cole, *No Equal Justice,* pp. 169–78.

31. "Police Corruption Inquiry Expands in Los Angeles," *New York Times,* February 11, 2000. "The Ramparts Litigation Could Bankrupt the City," *Los Angeles Times,* March 2, 2000.

32. "Jurors' Trust in Police Erodes in Light of Diallo and Louima," *New York Times,* March 9, 2000.

33. "Jurors Faulted Police Work in Murder Case of a Teacher," *New York Times,* February 13, 1999.

34. "Cities Reduce Crime and Conflict without New York–Style Hardball," *New York Times,* March 4, 2000.

35. Vera Institute of Justice, "Respectful and Effective Policing: Two Examples in the South Bronx," March 1999.

36. Harold Baer Jr., "The Mollen Commission Report: An Overview," *New York Law School Law Review* 40(1995): 73.

37. See Amnesty International, "Police Brutality and International Human Rights," pp. 28–36.

38. For a description of what can be done to reduce police brutality, see ibid. and a letter on the subject to President William J. Clinton, April 2, 1999, signed by twenty-two representatives of advocacy organizations, available from the Leadership Conference on Civil Rights, 1629 K St., N. W. Washington, D.C. 2000.

39. For details of Robin Lucas's story, see Amnesty International USA, "Not Part of My Sentence: Violations of the Human Rights of Women in Custody," March 1999.

40. Ibid.

41. Amnesty International, "Fact Sheet #3: Impact on Children of Women in Prison," March 1999.

42. "Perspectives," *Newsweek,* April 3, 2000.

43. "Report: Women in Prison Victims of Abuse," *USA Today,* March 4, 1999. Although some women prisoners do trade sex for favors from guards, such bargaining can hardly be regarded as consensual, given the coercive context in which the women find themselves, the almost total control guards exercise, the radically inequitable distribution of power, and institutionalized nature of the relationship.

44. "$8 Million Offered to End Attica Inmates' Suit," *New York Times,* January 5, 2000.

45. "Suing the Jailer," *Memphis Commercial Appeal,* November 25, 1998.

46. "$1.7 Million for Whistle-Blower," *Los Angeles Times,* June 11, 1999.

47. "Life after Prison: Lack of Services Has High Price," *Washington Post,* April 23, 2000.

48. Sasha Abramsky, "When They Get Out," *Atlantic Monthly,* June 1999.

49. U.S. Department of Justice, Bureau of Justice Statistics, "Prior Abuse Reported by Inmates and Probationers," April 1999.

50. "Much More AIDS in Prisons Than in General Population," *New York Times,* September 1, 1999.

51. See "Death, Neglect, and the Bottom Line," *St. Louis Post-Dispatch,* September 27, 1998; and Marc Mauer, *Race to Incarcerate* (New York: New Press, 1999), pp. 181; and "Much More AIDS."

52. "Fear of Crime Trumps the Fear of Lost Youth," *New York Times*, November 21, 1999.

53. "Legislator Seeks Execution Age of 11," *Dallas Morning News*, April 7, 1998.

54. Amnesty International, letter to Governor William Janklow, February 29, 2000.

55. Amnesty International, "Betraying the Young: Human Rights Violations against Children in the U.S. Justice System," November 1998. Estimates of the percentage of juveniles with mental health and substance abuse problems range from 20 percent ("Hard Time," *New York Times*, July 15, 1998) to 61 percent in a study conducted for the Georgia Department of Juvenile Justice cited in Amnesty International, "Betraying the Young," p. 34. Every year since 1989 five thousand to six thousand children have been sent to adult prisons ("Fear of Crime"), where they are far more likely to be abused and assaulted than in juvenile facilities (Jeffrey Fagan, et al., "Youth in Prisons and Training Schools," *Juvenile and Family Court Journal*, 1989; and Z. Eisikovitz and M. Baizerman, "Doin' Time: Violent Youth in a Juvenile Facility and an Adult Prison," *Journal of Offender Counseling, Services and Rehabilitation* 6, no. 3 (1983): 5–20.

56. The average prison sentence for juveniles convicted in criminal courts, according to the Bureau of Justice Statistics, September 1998 ("Juvenile Felony Defendants in Criminal Courts") was about nine years, which often would allow for release in less than that time.

57. "Juvenile Crime Study Gauges Impact of Drugs and Family," *New York Times*, September 18, 1988.

58. Donna M. Bishop, et al., "The Transfer of Juveniles to Criminal Court: Does It Make a Difference?" *Crime and Delinquency* 42, no. 2 (1996): 171–91.

59. Jeffrey Fagan, "The Comparative Advantages of Juvenile versus Criminal Court Sanctions on Recidivism among Adolescent Felony Offenders," unpublished manuscript, 1996.

60. "Arpaio Forgot What It's All About," *Arizona Republic*, April 4, 1998.

61. U.S. Attorney for the District of Arizona, "Agreement Reached Regarding Maricopa County Jails," Press release, October 31, 1997.

62. Roy Walmsley, "World Prison Population List," Research, Development, and Statistics Directorate, British Home Office, 1999.

63. "More Than 1M Nonviolent Prisoners," Associated Press, March 25, 1999.

64. Jackson, p. 99. From 1973 to 1995 the national murder rate was 9 per 100,000 while the state of Texas's rate was 13.4 per 100,000. "Death Sentences Being Overturned in 2 of 3 Appeals," *New York Times*, June 12, 2000.

65. They often needed that assistance because their original lawyers had been so entirely inadequate. See "Shoddy Defense by Lawyers Puts Innocents on Death Row," *New York Times*, February 5, 2000. The *Chicago Tribune* found that thirty-three people sentenced to die in Illinois had lawyers who were later disbarred or suspended, and many more had attorneys with no experience in capital cases ("The Death Penalty: When There's No Room for Error," *New York Times*, February 13, 2000).

66. "Police Refine Methods So Potent, Even Innocent Have Confessed," *New York Times*, March 30, 1998.

67. Alan Berlow, "The Wrong Man," *Atlantic Monthly*, November 1999.

68. "Death Sentences Being Overturned in 2 of 3 Appeals," *New York Times*, June 12, 2000. The Columbia University study cited in this story found that 37 percent of the errors in death penalty cases were the result of incompetent defense attorneys, 19 percent of misconduct by the police, 5 percent of bias by the judge or jury, 20 percent errors in instruction to the jury by the judge and the remainder miscellaneous. See also Barry Scheck, Peter Neufeld, and Jim Dwyer, *Actual Innocence* (New York: Doubleday, 2000).
69. Cole, *No Equal Justice*, pp. 133–34.
70. Paul Robinson, "Moral Credibility and Crime," *Atlantic Monthly*, March 1995, p. 76.
71. The *St. Petersburg Times* subsequently reported on January 25, 2000, that the adviser, Brad Thomas, had apologized.
72. Joan McCord, "Psychosocial Contributions to Violence and Psychopathy," paper delivered at the annual conference of the Queen Sofia Center for the Study of Violence, Valencia, Spain, November 1999.
73. Center on Juvenile and Criminal Justice, "How Have Homicide Rates Been Affected by California's Death Penalty?" April 1995.
74. According to the 1994 U.N. World Crime Survey, the homicide rate in the United States is 8.6 per 100,000, while in Canada it is 2.0 and in the United Kingdom, 1.4.
75. "Seeking Asylum, Some Immigrants Find a Fate Worse Than Criminal," *New York Times*, January 16, 2000. See also Amnesty International, "Lost in the Labyrinth," July 1999.

8. David Trimble's Tears

1. Adam Gopnik, "The Get-Ready Man," *The New Yorker*, June 19 and 26, 2000, p. 180.
2. William Finnegan, "A Slave in New York," *The New Yorker*, August 24, 2000, p. 52.
3. Quoted in Jonathan Spence, "In China's Gulag," *New York Review of Books*, August 10, 1995, p. 16.
4. Rickie Solinger, "Unsafe for Women," *New York Times Book Review*, March 20, 1994, p. 17.
5. Alexander Haig, Remarks for the Hudson Institute's James H. Doolittle Award Dinner, September 22, 1999.
6. Ronald Steel, *Temptations of a Superpower* (Cambridge: Harvard University Press, 1995), p. 125.
7. Richard N. Haass, *The Reluctant Sheriff: The United States after the Cold War* (New York: Council on Foreign Relations, 1997), p. 69.
8. Steven R. David, "Saving America from Coming Civil Wars," *Foreign Affairs* (January/February 1999): 105.
9. Haass, *Reluctant Sheriff*, p. 69. Emphasis added.
10. David, "Saving America," p. 105.
11. Robin Cook, "Foreign Policy and National Interest," British Information Services, January 28, 2000.
12. Winston Churchill quoted in Paul Wolfowitz, "Remembering the Future," *National Interest* (spring 2000): 41.

13. John F. Burns, "Methods of the Great Leader," *New York Times Book Review,* February 6, 2000.
14. Amartya Sen, *Development as Freedom* (New York: Knopf, 1999), pp. 227–48.
15. Robert Traer, *Faith in Human Rights* (Washington, D.C.: Georgetown University Press, 1991), p. 160.
16. Haass, *Reluctant Sheriff,* p. 51.
17. Sarah Anderson and John Cavanagh, "The Top 200: The Rise of Global Corporate Power," Institute of Policy Studies, September 25, 1996.
18. International Monetary Fund, "World Economic and Financial Survey," October 1999.
19. "For over a decade, Reebok has purchased products from your country," Paul Fireman wrote. "Today, in fact, Indonesia is the second largest supplier of Reebok footwear. . . . I respectfully suggest that as we embark upon a new year, now would be an auspicious moment for you to make a further gesture of Indonesia's steps toward greater democracy and transparency." Correspondence between Fireman and President B. J. Habibie, January 6, 1999.
20. In their recent study *The Sanctions Decade: Assessing U.N. Strategies in the 1990s* (Boulder, Colo.: Lynne Rienner, 2000), p. 209, authors David Cortright and George Lopez conclude that "the most important constant in the success of sanctions is not the type of measure applied but the degree to which sanctions are enforced. Compliance ultimately determines effectiveness."
21. Michael Hirsh, "At War with Ourselves," *Harper's,* July 1999.
22. Alan J. Kuperman, "Rwanda in Retrospect," *Foreign Affairs* (January/February 2000) and my reply, "The Path Not Taken," *Foreign Affairs* (March/April 2000): 94–118.
23. Michael Ignatieff, "The Next President's Duty to Intervene," *New York Times,* February 13, 2000.
24. Samuel P. Huntington, "Robust Nationalism," *National Interest* (winter 1999–2000): 37.
25. John Bolton, "The U.N. Steps out of Line," *Washington Times,* May 31, 1998.
26. Josef Joffe, "The Worst of Times," *New York Times,* November 21, 1999.
27. Robert Kaplan, "The Return of Ancient Times," *Atlantic Monthly,* June 2000, p. 14–18.
28. For details of this story, including the court-martial of Col. Yehuda Meir and Yitzhak Rabin's retraction, see John Conroy, *Unspeakable Acts, Ordinary People: The Dynamics of Torture* (New York: Knopf, 2000).
29. "Women's Global Views Examined by Survey," *New York Times,* June 7, 2000.
30. Jared Diamond, "The Greening of Corporate America," *New York Times,* January 8, 2000.
31. Loung Ung, *First They Killed My Father* (New York: HarperCollins, 2000), pp. 105–6.

Acknowledgments

Amnesty International USA (AIUSA) keeps me pretty busy. I'm on the road for the organization about 70 percent of the time, or at least it feels like 70 percent of the time. So when I had the opportunity, thanks to the generosity of the AIUSA board of directors, to take a five-month sabbatical to write this book in the fall/winter of 1999–2000, I was thrilled. I'll take sitting at home in front of a word processor any day to dealing with another canceled flight out of La Guardia Airport, and my literary agent, Chris Calhoun, had kindly seen that I had an excuse to sit there.

My absence from regular work, however, meant that Curt Goering, AIUSA's senior deputy director, and our senior manager colleagues had to take on added responsibilities, and so it is they whom I first need to thank for making this book possible. They make me proud to serve with them.

Once I had carved out the time to write, I needed a top-notch research team to help supply facts and figures, readings and references. Once again Amnesty came to the rescue in the form of Christine Doyle, our superb coordinator of research, and her crackerjack team, including Trine Christensen, Julie Leonard, Stuart Palatnick, Nicole Purin, and Sushil Raj. Other Amnesty staff people and volunteers joined in at various points to clarify an issue, help me think through a point, or critique a section of the manuscript. For all that help I am very grateful to Vienna Colucci, Sheila Dauer, Brian Evans, Scott Harrison, Michael Heflin, Barbara Joe, Michael O'Reilly, Paul Paz y Mino, Steve Rickard, Carlos Salinas, and Liz Torpey.

Of course the book comes alive in good measure because of the human rights defenders I describe in it. I am exceptionally fortunate to know or to have come to know people like Hina Jilali, Natasa Kandic, Robin Lucas, Dianna Ortiz, Dita Sari, and Alexander Nikitin's daughter, Julia Tchernova, most of whom I interviewed especially for this project.

Many other people were also extraordinarily generous with their assistance. Allen Weinstein read the chapter on democracy and security and Elliot Schrage, then of Columbia University, the chapter on economics. Carl Czjackowski of Brookhaven Laboratories, Thomas Nilsen of the Bellona Foundation in Norway, and Matthew Ryan of Purdue University helped with various parts of the environment chapter. The chapter on health was strengthened by the assistance of Jordan Kassalow of the Council on Foreign Relations, Barry Kreiswirth of the Public Health Research Institute, Srdjan Matic of the Open Society Institute, and Carol Mitnick of Harvard's Program on Infectious Disease and Social Change.

There are a few people who deserve special mention for going well above and beyond the customary call of employment or friendship. Mort Winston of the philosophy department of the College of New Jersey read and critiqued three of the chapters with particular attention to chapter 1. Curt Goering, Michael Posner, the widely respected "dean" of the human rights community and for twenty-three years executive director of the Lawyers Committee for Human Rights, and Helene Atwan, my exemplary editor as well as the director of Beacon Press, all read the entire manuscript and offered invaluable counsel. I would like to be able to blame each of them for any failings in the book, any oversights, misinformation, or just plain bad calls, but I am going to have to be adult about this and take responsibility myself for what is published under my name. Besides, I didn't take all the advice they tendered, though I surely appreciated it all.

Finally I want to sing the praises of two people without whom the book would literally never have come into existence. My assistant, Rachel Ward, spent hours researching aspects of almost every chapter and, no doubt far more laboriously, took major responsibility for the physical preparation of the manuscript. And Cassandra Ryan, AIUSA's media coordinator, took overall responsibility for the entire project, from conception to completion: coordinating researchers, researching topics herself, running down stray facts and notations, scheduling appointments for me with many of those referenced above, and doing anything else that needed doing to see the manuscript finished successfully. This book is every bit as much these two remarkable women's as it is mine and I will be forever in their debt.

—WILLIAM F. SCHULZ
November 2000

Index

Abacha, Sani, 68
Abdelaziz, Talal bin, 14
Abiola, Mashood, 77
Adams, Samuel, 31
Adidas, 96
Africa, 5, 59, 130. *See also names of individual countries*
AIDS (acquired immunodeficiency syndrome), 129, 130–133, 166
Albright, Madeleine, 11
Algeria, 139
Alien Tort Statute of 1789, 93
Alinsky, Saul, 59
All China Federation of Trade Unions (ACFTU), 99
American Civil Liberties Union, 6, 117
Amin, Idi, 53, 129–131
Amnesty International, 1, 10, 15, 31, 136, 150–151, 188, 195
Anti-Defamation League of B'nai B'rith, 150
Aquinas, Thomas, 28
Arbour, Louise, 6
Arendt, Hannah, 25
Aris, Michael, 40
Arpaio, Joe, 168
Asahi Shimbun, 110
Asia, 131–133. *See also names of individual countries*
Asian Pacific Economic Cooperation (APEC), 73

Atlantic Monthly, 192
Atlas Shrugged (Rand), 66
autocracies, 62

Baltimore Sun, 138
Barry, Robert, 73
Barshefsky, Charlene, 71
Beijing Jeep, 90
Bellona Foundation, 106–107
BellSouth, 86
Bentley College, 42
Bergsten, Fred, 73
biological weapons, 134
Birnbaum, David, 92
Boise Cascade Company, 116
Bolton, John, 32–33, 190
Book of Laughter and Forgetting, The (Kundera), 39
"boomerang, the," 127
Bosnia, 53, 140–141
"Bosnia: One Big Yawn," 9
Botswana, 79
Boutros-Ghali, Boutros, 145
Boyevaya Vaktha (Battle Watch), 109–110
Bratton, William, 154
Brazil, 87
Brown, Michael E., 140
Buber, Martin, 179
Buchanan, Milly, 42–43
Burma, 1, 38, 40, 43, 71, 92, 93, 132, 133

business, 66–104; China and, 84–86; contracts, 85–86; corporate liability and,
92–94; corporate reputations and, 91–
92; corporations and politics, 68–69;
delinking trade and human rights,
69–70; economic crises, 79–81; economic incentives and political reform,
71–72; economic sanctions, 101; free
press and, 87–88; globalization and,
101–104; Hong Kong and, 72–73; Indonesia and, 73–77; international investments, 67–68; new markets and, 88–
89; political instability, 77–81; Shell
Oil and, 68; Singapore and, 70; transparent regulations for, 84–85. *See also*
commercialist argument; corruption;
workers' rights
Business News, 98
Business Week, 85–86

Cabrera Garcia, Teodoro, 116–117
Cahn, Doug, 90
Callahan, David, 64–65
Cambodia, 132
Camus, Albert, 5
Capitalism and Freedom (Friedman), 66
Capitol Corrections Resources, 149
Carter, Jimmy, 11, 52–53, 57
Castaño, Carlos, 135
Ceausescu, Nicolae, 57–58, 131
Cedras, Raoul, 57
Centers for Disease Control (CDC), 124,
126
chemical weapons, 134
Chernobyl nuclear power plant, 108–109
Chevron, 79
Chicago Council on Foreign Relations, 8,
11
Chile, 5, 54, 56
China: business practices of, 84–86;
contracts in, 86; corruption and, 82;
democracy and, 47–48; economics
and, 69, 71, 72, 79, 80; environment
and, 118; international law and, 35;
Internet users in, 101–102; new mar-
kets and, 88–89; public health, 124;

safety-licensing standards of, 84; Tia-
nanmen Square in, 39–40; trade with,
185, 186; workers' rights in, 90, 98–99
China Labour Bulletin, 99
Christians, 19
Christopher Commission, 155
Christopher, Warren, 118
Churchill, Sir Winston, 182
Cioran, E. M., 179
Civilian Complaint Review Board
(CCRB), 153
civil rights movement, 2
Clifton, Doug, 9
Clinton, Bill, 10, 13, 63, 69, 81, 138–139
CNN effect, 6
Coc Rax, Carlos, 116
Cole, David, 159–160
Colombia, 87, 135–137
Coming Plague, The (Garrett), 128
commercialist argument, 65, 67, 69, 72
communitarianism, 21
compassion fatigue, 6
Confucius, 183
Connolly, Cyril, 188
conservative vs. liberal, on human rights
issues, 11
Constant, Emmanuel, 175
constitutionalism, 50, 51
constitutional liberalism, 49
Consuello Murillo, Ines, 138
Convention on the Rights of the Child,
35, 167
Cook, Robin, 32, 182
corporations, 68–69, 91–92, 92–94, 186–
187. *See also* business; *names of individual corporations*
corruption, 60–61, 81–83, 87–88, 103,
142–143, 160–161
*Costs of Conflict: Prevention and Cure in
the Global Arena, The* (Brown and
Rosecrance), 140–141
Council on Foreign Relations, 15
crimes, human rights, 53–57
criminal justice, 162–169; health of prisoners and, 166; incarceration rate, 169;
juvenile offenders and, 166–167;

prison abuse and, 162–165; recidivism rates and, 167–168. *See also* death penalty

Critique of Pure Reason (Kant), 28

cruelty, 23, 24, 25–26

Cuba, 101, 126–128

customary law, 6

Czechoslovakia, 39

Daley, Richard, 152

Dallaire, Romeo, 141

David, Steven R., 181, 182

death penalty, 169–175. *See also* criminal justice

Declaration of Independence, 19, 20

democracy, 38–65; champions of, 40–41, 45; China and, 40, 47–48; economics and, 66–71, 79; ethnic conflict and, 59–60; European growth and, 89; free election in, 41–42; illiberal, 49–50; Kandic and, 43–45; Mansfield on, 50–51; Mao on, 61–62; number of countries with, 49; politics in, 48; promotion of, 46, 50, 51; Snyder on, 50–51; Taylor and, 42–43; United States and nondemocratic countries and, 62–63; war and, 45–49, 50; Zakaria on, 49–50

dengue fever, 126–128

Diallo, Amadou, 154

Dinescu, Mircea, 58

Dinesen, Isak, 21

Dingit, Loir Botor, 115–116

Doctors Without Borders, 121

D'Souza, Dinesh, 159

Duvalier, Baby Doc, 53

economics. *See* business

Economist, The, 14, 65

Edison Mission Energy Company, 83

Egypt, 23, 49, 64, 128

electroshock weapons, 147–149, 168

El Salvador, 23, 96–97

empathy, 24–26

environment, 105–119; China and, 118; concept of "environmental security" and, 118–119; forests and, 114–117, 119,

195; global warming and, 114, 123; greenhouse gases and, 113–116; ocean radioactive waste dumping, 112–113; Russia and, 105–111

environmental movement, 10, 195–196

Ethiopia, 141–142

ethnic conflict, 59–60

exports, 67–68

Extra-Dangerous Zone, 109–110

Fagan, Brian, 114

Fair Labor Association, 91

Far Eastern Economic Review, 88

Fay, Michael, 183

Federal Security Service (FSB), 106, 111

Fireman, Paul, 187

Fisher, Richard, 73

Flanagan, Ronnie, 161

Foreign Affairs, 49, 50

Foreign Assistance Act, 195

Foreign Corrupt Practices Act, 82–83

forests, 114–117, 119, 195

Formosa Textiles factory, 96–97

Foxman, Abraham, 150, 176

Freedom House, 60

Friedman, Milton, 66

Friedman, Thomas, 86, 103

Fujimori, Alberto, 49

Gandhi, Mohandas, 180

Gao Feng, 90

Garrett, Laurie, 128

Garzon, Jaime, 135–137

GE Capital, 83

Gifford, Kathie Lee, 91–92, 97–98

Giuliani, Rudy, 154

globalization, 14, 67, 101–104, 124

global warming, 114, 123

God, as source of rights, 19–20

God That Failed, The (Crossman, ed.), 35

Goldberg, Jeffrey, 130

Goldman Environmental Prize, 115

Goldstone, Richard, 56

Gordon, Irwin, 98

Gottwald, Klement, 39

Greece, 5, 63

greenhouse gases, 113–116
Greenspan, Alan, 71–72
Guatemala, 80, 137–139
Guatemalan Historical Clarification
Commission, 139

Haass, Richard N., 181, 182, 184
Habibie, B. J., 81
Haig, Alexander, 180–181
Haiti, 53, 118–119
Hamill, Robert, 177–178
Hammurabi's Codes, 3
Hampton, Ronald, 157
Han Dongfang, 98–99
Harper's, 9
Harrison, Aden, Jr., 171
Hart, Peter D., 151
Havel, Vaclav, 5, 40, 182
Hayek, Friedrich A., 66–67
health. *See* public health
Helms, Jesse, 11–12, 35
Henninger, Daniel, 88
Hepburn, John, 168
Herbert, Bob, 158
heroes, human rights, 5, 40, 41
Herzberg, Abel, 31
Hewitt, Don, 31
Hiebert, Murray, 88
Hirsh, Michael, 188
HIV (human immunodeficiency virus).
See AIDS (acquired immunodefi-
ciency syndrome)
Hobsbawn, Eric, 191
Holocaust, 4, 5
Hong Kong, 72–73, 82, 99
Houston Chronicle, 68
Humanitarian Law Center in Belgrade,
44
Hume, David, 20
Huntington, Samuel P., 71, 190
Hussein, Saddam, 141, 182

Ibrahim, Anwar, 61, 80
Ignatieff, Michael, 189
immigration, 122–123, 143–144
India, 59

Indian Law Resource Center, 117
Indonesia, 54, 73–77, 83, 115, 116, 139, 187
International Covenant on Civil and
Political Rights, 35
International Criminal Court, 54, 54–56,
195
international forces (IFOR), 55
international investments, 67–68
International Labour Organization, 98
International Monetary Fund (IMF), 83,
103, 141
International Red Cross, 125
International War Crimes Tribunals, 6,
44, 53–54
Internet, 101–102, 103
Iran, 62
Ireland, Northern. *See* Northern Ireland
Islam, xvi
Israel, 32, 49, 192

Jackson, Stonewall, 34
Jancar, Barbara, 118
Jefferson, Thomas, 62
Jilani, Hina, xiv-xvii
Jilani, Malik Ghulam, xiv
Joaquin Chamorro, Pedro, 125
Jordan, 49

Kagan, Robert, 11
Kamm, John, 89, 187
Kandic, Natasa, 43–45
Kant, Immanuel, 27–28, 45–46
Kaplan, Robert, 192
Karadzic, Radovan, 55
Kaufman, Denny, 147–149
Kennan, George, 13
Kenya, 139, 116
Khan, Mohammad Ayub, xiv
Khan, Tahira Shahid, 145
Khmer Rouge, 132
Kim Dae-jung, 71
Kissinger, Henry, 11
Klatsky, Bruce, 80, 90
Kmart, 84–85
Kony, Joseph, 29
Kosovo, 33, 44, 48, 50, 54, 55, 63, 188

Kovalyov, Nikolai, 111
Kreisworth, Barry, 122
Kristol, William, 11
Kundera, Milan, 31, 39
Kuperman, Alan J., 189
Kyoto Climate Change Conference in
    1997, 114

Lake, Anthony, 10
La Prensa, 125
Latin America, 135–139. *See also names of
    individual countries;* South America
law, 34–36. *See also* rule of law
Leahy, Patrick, 195
Lee Kuan Yew, 183
Lee Teng-hui, 47–48
Lenin, Vladimir Ilich, 62
Levin, Gerald M., 87–88
Levin, Jonathan, 160
Leviticus, 23
lex talionis, 172–173
Liang Shi Handbag Factory (China), 97
Libby, Willard, 119
liberal vs. conservative, on human rights
    issues, 11
Liberia, 21–22, 42, 43
London Convention of 1993, 112
Louima, Abner, 154, 156
Lucas, Robin, 162–164
Lu Guizhu, 89
Lukashenka, Alyaksandr, 49

Maathai, Wangari, 116
Malaysia, 79
Mandela, Nelson, 40, 182
Mansfield, Edward D., 50, 51
Mao Tse-tung, 61–62
Marx, Karl, 70
Mayorets, Anatoly Ivanovich, 109
McCord, Joan, 173–174
McDonald's, 85
McKinley, William, 49
media, 8, 87–88, 109, 127
Medvedev, Grigory, 108–109
Mendes, Chico, 116
Mendoza Rivero, Desi, 126–128

Menem, Carlos, 49
Mengistu Haile Mariam, 141–142
Merchant of Venice, The (Shakespeare),
    24
Merleau-Ponty, Maurice, 28
Mexico, 8, 116–117
Miami Herald, 9
Middle East, 63
military intervention, 188–190
Miller, Robert Lee, Jr., 170–171
Milosovic, Slobodan, 44, 45, 54
Milosz, Czeslaw, 92
Mladic, Ratko, 55
Mobil Oil, 92
Mohamad, Mahathir, 61, 79–80
Moi, Daniel Arap, 83
Montanists, 19
Montiel Flores, Rodolfo, 116–117
morality, 6–7, 13, 18, 20, 27–34, 36, 179
"Moral Necessity of Metaphor, The"
    (Ozick), 23
Morgenthau, Hans, 31
Myanmar. *See* Burma

NAFTA (North American Free Trade
    Agreement), 94, 95
National Commission for Truth and Rec-
    onciliation (Chile), 56
natural law, as source of rights, 20–21
Neier, Aryeh, 5
Neporozhny, P. S., 108
new realism, 13, 36, 180, 193–194
New Republic, 151
Newsday, 95
New York City, 153–154, 160–161
New York Times, 63, 158
NHK (television station in Japan), 109
Niebuhr, Reinhold, 34
Nietzsche, Friedrich Wilhelm, 24–25
Nigeria, 77
Nike, 91, 96, 97
Nikitin, Alexander, 105–108
Nitze, William A., 119
No Equal Justice (Cole), 159–160
norms, 26
Northern Ireland, 161, 177–179, 185

Nuremberg trials, 5
Nye, Joseph S., Jr., 32
Nyerere, Julius, 81

Ogata, Sadako, 143
Olson, Mancur, 89
open societies, 59
Operation Condor, 139
Organization of Ecologists of the Sierra
    de Petatlan, 116
Ortiz, Dianna, 137–139
Ozick, Cynthia, 23

Paiton Energy Corporation, 83
Pakistan, xiii–xvii
Pasko, Grigory, 109–111
Peng, Jimmy, 72–73
People's Daily, The, 88
People's Liberation Army (PLA), 85
Perception of Corruption index, 60
Perpetual Peace (Kant), 45–46
Pinochet, Augusto, 11, 54, 56, 139
Pleites, Julia Esmeralda, 96–97
police misconduct, 152–162; corruption
    and, 160–161; extent of, 154–155; liabil-
    ity claims, 155–156; in New York City,
    153–154, 160–161; police testimony and,
    160; race and, 156–160; "Ramparts"
    scandal in Los Angeles and, 160; solu-
    tion to, 162
Politically Incorrect, 168
political stability index, 80
Pol Pot, 53
population control, 144–145
postmodernism, 21
pragmatism, as source of rights, 21
Prasad, Binda, 59
"Precarious Triumph of Human Rights,
    The" (Rieff), 10
public health, 120–134; amplifiers of dis-
    ease and, 124–125; biological/chemical
    weapons and, 133–134; China and, 124;
    climate change and, 123–124; connec-
    tion between health and human
    rights, 125; epidemics, defense against,

128–129; global trade and, 123; immi-
    gration policy and, 122–123; migration
    and, 133; relationship between poverty
    and disease, 125; tuberculosis and, 121–
    122; war and, 124–125
Public Health Research Institute, 121
pungli, 83
Putin, Vladimir, 110

Rabin, Yitzhak, 192
Radio Free Asia, 99
"Ramparts" scandal (Los Angeles), 160
Rand, Ayn, 66–67
Reagan, Ronald, 194
realists, 13, 15, 33, 180, 183, 186; democracy
    and, 64–65; exceptionalism and, 190;
    military intervention and, 188; moral-
    ity and, 31, 32, 179; war and, 47. *See also*
    new realism
Red Cloud, Chief, 117
Redstone, Sumner, 87, 88
Reebok, 187
refugees, 175
religious persecution, 144
Revolutionary Armed Forces of Colum-
    bia (FARC), 135
Rieff, David, 10
rights: discussion about, 17–19; sources
    of, 19–21; statements of, 3–4
"Rise of Illiberal Democracy, The," 49
Road to Serfdom, The (Hayek), 66
Roberts, Brad, 134
Robinson, Mary, 54
Robinson, Paul, 172
Rodley, Nigel, 120–121
Rodriguez, Pinon, 127
Rodrik, Dani, 78, 96
Romania, 57–59
Roosevelt, Eleanor, 4
Rorty, Richard, 30
Rosecrance, Richard, 140
Rubin, Robert, 87
rule of law, 61, 78, 80, 81, 82, 84, 143, 182.
    See also law
Russia, 103, 105–111, 112–113, 120–121
Russian Federal Law on State Secrets, 107

Rwanda, 6, 10–11, 41, 53, 133, 139, 140–141, 189

Safir, Howard, 153
Sakharov, Andrei, 5, 40
Sari, Dita, 74-77
Saro-Wiwa, Ken, 68
Sarwar, Samia, xiii-xiv, xvi-xvii, 144
Saudi Arabia, 49, 64
Schulz, William F., 33, 42–43
Sen, Amartya, 41, 82, 84, 96, 183
sexual orientation, 144, 175–176
Shakespeare, William, 24
Shalamov, Varlam, 5
Sharansky, Anatoly, 5
Shell Oil, 68
Sierra Club, 111
Singapore, 60, 70
60 Minutes, 31
SLORC (State Law and Order Restoration Council), 93
Smith, T. V., 48
Snyder, Jack, 50, 51
socially responsible investing, 91
Solzhenitsyn, Aleksandr, 5
Somoza, Anastasio, 125
Sophal, Thong, 4–5
Soros, George, 59
South America, 87. See also Latin America; names of individual countries
South Korea, 79, 88
Soviet Union. See Russia
Soyfer, Vladimir, 111
Spender, Stephen, 34–35
Stalin, Joseph, 31
St. Clair Commission, 155
Steel, Ronald, 181
Stiglitz, Joseph, 86
Stith, Charles, 81, 82
St. Louis Post-Dispatch, 166
Stolz, Richard, 138
Straits Times, 70
stun technology. See electroshock weapons
Sudan, 142
Suharto, 73–74

Sukarnoputri, Megawati, 76
Suu Kyi, Aung San, 40, 41, 51
sweatshops, 91, 97
Szilard, Leo, 119

Taiwan, 47–48
Taliban, 22–23
Talisman Energy, 92
Tanzania, 81, 82
Taylor, Charles, 42
Tchernova, Julia, 106
Thailand, 88, 133
Thatcher, Margaret, 54
Timmerman, Jacobo, 5
Tokes, Laszlo, 58
Tokyo trials, 5
Tonelson, Alan, 13
Transparency International (TI), 60, 81, 82
travel, 144, 185
Trimble, David, 177–179
Truth about Chernobyl, The (Medvedev), 108–109
tuberculosis, 121–122, 166
Tu Fu, 103
Turkey, 63, 139

Uganda, 29–30, 53, 129–130
United Nations, 4, 142
United Nations Human Rights Commission, 4, 195
United States: charitable giving in, 7; corruption and, 82–83; democracy and, 62–63; electroshock weapons in, 147–149; foreign policy goals of, 8, 11; human rights violations in, 150–152; influence on other countries, 64; International Criminal Court and, 55–56; in Latin America, 135–139; law and human rights, 35; military assistance to other countries, 139–140, 141; presidents on human rights, 12–13; promotion of, 46–48; promotion of democracy, 50, 51; public health in, 124; refugees, 175; trade deficit of, 100; world role for, 8–9. See also criminal

justice; death penalty; police misconduct
United States Chamber of Commerce, 72
United States Federal Bureau of Prisons, 148
United States National Security Council, 131
Universal Declaration of Human Rights, 4–6, 19, 20, 21, 26–27, 94, 184, 190
UNOCAL, 93

Vietnam War, 2
virtue, 31
Volpe, Justin, 154, 156

Wall Street Journal, 70, 77
Wal-Mart, 97, 98
Washington, George, 90–91
Washington Post, 11
Wei Jingsheng, 40

Wigglesworth, Sir Vincent, 46–47
Women's Action Forum, xv-xvi
women's movement, 10
women's rights, xv-xvi, 75–76, 144–146
workers' rights, 74–77, 89–91, 94–100
World Bank, 77, 83, 85, 87, 141, 143
World Bank Development Report, 90
World Court, 35
World Health Organization, 121
World Trade Organization, 84

Xi Jang, 72–73

Yeats, William Butler, 4
Yegerov, Nikolay, 112
Yugoslavia, 6, 43–45, 50

Zakaria, Fareed, 49, 50, 51
Zhou Enlai, 62
Zonis, Marvin, 80